100 THINGS
MARINERS FANS
SHOULD KNOW & DO
BEFORE THEY DIE

100 THINGS
MARINERS FANS
SHOULD KNOW & DO
BEFORE THEY DIE

Michael Emmerich

TRIUMPH
BOOKS

Library of Congress Cataloging-in-Publication Data

Emmerich, Michael, 1959–
  100 things Mariners fans should know & do before they die / Michael Emmerich.
     pages cm
  ISBN 978-1-62937-070-5
  1. Seattle Mariners (Baseball team)—History. 2. Seattle Mariners (Baseball team)—Miscellanea. I. Title. II. Title: One hundred things Mariners fans should know and do before they die.
  GV875.S42E55 2015
  796.357'6409797772—dc23
                                        2014040624

This book is available in quantity at special discounts for your group or organization. For further information, contact:
  Triumph Books LLC
  814 North Franklin Street
  Chicago, Illinois 60610
  (312) 337-0747
  www.triumphbooks.com

Printed in U.S.A.
ISBN: 978-1-62937-070-5
Design by Patricia Frey
Photos courtesy of AP Images unless otherwise indicated

To my daughter, Hannah

Contents

Introduction

To paraphrase Kermit the Frog, "It's not always easy being a Mariners fan." Every other fan base in professional baseball except the Nationals has experienced at least one trip for their favorite team to the World Series. (Even the downtrodden Cubs have treated at least a portion of their fan base to an appearance in the Fall Classic.) Seattle, however, is still waiting for its first taste of baseball's penultimate.

That doesn't mean M's history is devoid of the truly spectacular. Few franchises can point to anything quite as spellbinding and transformative as the 1995 Mariners. And other than Cubs fans of 1906 (all surviving members please raise your hand), only Mariners fans have cheered for a club that won 116 regular season games.

M's fans have also been fortunate to follow a handful of some of the game's all-time greats, many of whom are destined for the Baseball Hall of Fame. Numerous more established franchises have gone decades without the pleasure of watching on a daily basis Cooperstown-worthy talent.

So it's certainly not all gray skies for Mariners fans. If you are a fan of recent vintage, this book will help you understand that. It will also introduce you to all the ups and downs of the Mariners over these last four-plus decades. If you are a longtime fan, it will stir memories of all those things that provoked your emotions over the years—both the good and not so good. And for fans of all ages and years of service, there are some helpful tips and ideas on enriching your experience as someone who avidly follows the Mariners.

A quick word about the stats employed in this book. I use a mix of old school and advanced statistics in the book, depending on the period and relevancy. I tried to avoid using any of the truly arcane new statistics, however. Wins Above Replacement (WAR) is one exception.

1 1995 Regular Season

The Mariners were reborn in 1995 as a source of civic pride, an institution of public good, and a guidepost in the lives of its citizens. Stadium politics, strike fallout, and fan apathy all crumbled as the Mariners bulldozed over past demons.

The baseball strike of 1994 dragged into '95. Major league owners threatened to begin the year with replacement players. Fans' disgust with baseball peaked as a result. Finally, the two sides settled and camps opened weeks late. In Peoria, Arizona, site of Mariners spring training, John Ellis, the mouthpiece of Mariners ownership, told the entire team the M's, losing money by the fistful, needed a new stadium and that winning the division would help the cause immeasurably. Without a publically financed new park, he warned, the owners would sell, likely spelling the end of baseball in Seattle. A ballot initiative for a new stadium was introduced the same month. Polls showed it losing by 30 points. "Do you know what kind of pressure that is," Jay Buhner said in 1996, "that the future of the franchise is on your shoulders? Man, that's pressure."

At first, ownership cut the M's budget. Other teams quickly inquired about the Mariners stars. Manager Lou Piniella and general manager Woody Woodward pleaded for an expanded budget, arguing now was not the time to pinch pennies. Ellis and the board eventually agreed. Then a slow start to the season became a crisis on May 26 when superstar Ken Griffey Jr., while making a highlight reel catch against the center-field wall of the Kingdome, broke his left wrist. "Just a disaster," said team president Chuck Armstrong. A few weeks later, Chicago White Sox pitcher Wilson Alvarez sized up the Mariners sans Griffey and sneered: "Who do they have in the lineup? Edgar Martinez is the only guy who does any real damage."

Martinez, for sure, but then later Mike Blowers kept the Mariners afloat during Griffey's absence. Randy Johnson also rolled. Yet, on August 2 Seattle trailed the California Angels by 13 games. Only two teams in history had ever rallied from a greater deficit. The M's familiar fate prompted Piniella to joke that managing the Mariners was like going to the dentist.

The playoffs, however, actually remained a possibility because of the wild-card, just added, auspiciously, in 1995. The Mariners trailed the Texas Rangers by just two games. That emboldened Woodward to add instead of dump in July and August. Leadoff man Vince Coleman; reliever Norm Charlton, a former Mariner; and starting pitcher Andy Benes arrived via waivers or trade, the first time in history the Mariners made midsummer moves designed to upgrade the current roster. "There's no doubt about it," Woodward said a year later. "If there is no wild-card...[we] move some salaries and get young."

Griffey returned on August 15 to find the Mariners 11½ game behind California but within sight of Texas. A deflating loss that night to the Minnesota Twins, who scored five unearned runs in the ninth inning to win 7–6, pierced hopes that Junior would spark an immediate surge. The Mariners won the next night in Coleman's debut with the speedster collecting two hits and stealing a base to ignite a 6–4 comeback win. The Mariners failed to build on the victory, though, and by August 24 they'd lost four of five games and trailed the Angels by 11 and Texas by four.

Same old Mariners.

After a players-only meeting, the M's fell behind the New York Yankees and trailed 7–6 heading into the bottom of the ninth inning at home. Not once in 1995 had the M's triumphed when losing after eight innings. On John Wetteland's first pitch, Griffey, still with a four-inch metal plate and seven screws in his wrist, turned on a 96 mph fastball and punished it. The upper-deck shot sent a charge throughout the Kingdome. "We looked around," recalled Blowers in 2005. "If this guy is healthy and ready to go, we had a chance...We all smiled and said, 'Here we go.'"

Boosted by the return of vintage Griffey, the Mariners won six of eight games. On August 31, Johnson couldn't make his start in Fenway Park due to a sore shoulder. Rookie Bob Wolcott, 21 years old and with two career major league appearances, started instead and held the American League East-leading Boston Red Sox to two runs in six innings. The M's blasted the Bosox 11–2.

Definitely not the same old Mariners.

Meanwhile, the Angels started to wilt, setting up six weeks likely unequaled in MLB history for its far-reaching effects on a franchise. Down seven-and-a-half games to the Angels on September 1, the Mariners first zoomed past Kansas City, Texas, and finally the Yankees to seize the wild-card lead. As the M's stampeded over the wild-card contenders, management decided to put up flags tracking the wild-card race. After all, the Mariners still trailed the Angels by six games with 16 to play. Buhner objected: "Take that [bleeping] banner down...Let's not settle for second best."

Buhner's bravado failed to awaken the Angels, whose slide deepened with nine straight losses in mid-September. "It was the nastiest funk I've ever seen in baseball," recalled Halo infielder Rex Hudler. "We needed our manager to step up, and [Marcel Lachemann] couldn't do it. He went into a shell."

On September 20, the M's wiped out the Angels' lead entirely. Like their crawl from deep in the standings, the Mariners kept clawing back in game after game. "Nonstop comebacks," recalled reliever Jeff Nelson. Twelve times in September the M's fell behind and still won. Four times they cracked game-tying or winning homers in the eighth or ninth inning.

Improbable heroes emerged almost nightly. Journeyman Doug Strange hit a ninth-inning pinch-hit three-run homer to tie a game,

Losing Rights

"Refuse to Lose" was not original to the Mariners. The University of Massachusetts basketball team, among others, had adopted it first. By 1995 it had been trademarked by someone in South Carolina and then, unbeknownst to the Mariners, sold to John Calipari, the coach at UMass at the time. When the M's, who thought they had all rights cleared, started using the slogan on shirts and banners, Calipari sued the Mariners for $500,000. According to M's president Chuck Armstrong in a speech at the University of Washington, Seattle never paid Calipari a dime, but Major League Baseball settled with him for $6,000.

later won by a Griffey single. Coleman shocked three nights later with his first career grand slam to lead another comeback. Backup outfielder Alex Diaz added a three-run pinch-hit homer in the same game. Then on September 24, after the Angels had won to shave the Mariners lead to one-and-a-half games, Tino Martinez rescued the M's with a two-run homer in the ninth off Oakland A's closer supreme Dennis Eckersley. "I don't care who we played…we knew we were going to beat them, because we were so confident, and had such good chemistry," said M's shortstop Luis Sojo.

Mariners fans, unaccustomed to pennant races, responded slowly. On the day the M's moved into a first-place tie with the Angels, attendance was less than 26,000. Radio ratings had started to climb earlier as the Angels' lead shrunk. But reaching the summit of the AL West standings seemed to win over the final skeptics. The next night attendance exploded and never slipped below 46,700 the rest of season. "The fans would not let us quit," said bench coach John McLaren. "They absolutely supported us, pushed us to the hilt." Meanwhile, signs reading "Refuse to Lose" started sprouting up everywhere, filling the Kingdome like boats on Lake Union for the Fourth of July. The Mariners—and entire city—adopted it as a motto.

Something else happened. Folks across the Pacific Northwest found baseball dictating their lives and schedules. Work ended sharply at 5:00, dinner was at 6:00. Appointments could wait. So could laundry or yard work. The hypnotic daily effect of pennant race baseball put the region in a trance—for the first time ever.

Winning also had the effect Ellis had hoped. King County voters cast their ballots on the new stadium initiative on September 19. Buhner and other Mariners had actively campaigned on behalf of the measure—in the heat of the pennant race—and polls revealed quickly escalating support. The morning of the 20th, the day the Mariners caught the Angels, it appeared the M's resurrection had swung voter sentiment in favor of the measure. But then absentee ballots started to arrive, and the initiative ultimately failed by 1,082 votes. In the thrall of Mariner Mania, community leaders vowed to continue the fight. Refuse to Lose had passed into politics.

During the final weekend of the season, the Mariners, which closed on a 25–11 run, took two of four from the Rangers. The Angels, facing a depleted—and the Mariners complained disinterested—Oakland pitching staff, swept the A's. That meant the madcap AL West race would require an extra game to decide.

Ken Griffey Jr.: The Beginning

As absurd—and unsettling—as it may seem today, the Mariners almost passed on Ken Griffey Jr. in the 1987 amateur draft, a year they owned the No. 1 pick. Their always meddlesome owner, George Argyros, objected to picking Griffey because the M's had been burned the year before by selecting a high school shortstop, Patrick Lennon, who had off-the-field issues. Argyros wanted a college pitcher. Moreover, Griffey didn't play baseball his senior year in high school because of grades. That raised concerns about his work ethic. Junior also stumbled on the mental aptitude test the Mariners gave him.

But Roger Jongewaard, the Mariners scouting director, remained steadfast in his desire to select Griffey. He talked to Griffey's high school coach at Moeller High in Cincinnati who assured Jongewaard that Griffey was an intelligent kid merely bored by school. Studying and academics ranked well behind Griffey's real passion: baseball. And so did the battery of tests major league teams shoved in his face. Jongewaard eventually persuaded the skeptics in the M's organization, including Argyros, that the Mariners had to pick Griffey. "George, we can't afford not to take this guy," Jongewaard told his owner. "He is that special."

While playing together on the Mariners, Ken Griffey Sr. (left) helped his son, Ken Griffey Jr., adjust to life in the big leagues. (Getty Images)

Argyros relented—with two conditions. Jongewaard would pay, probably with his job, if Griffey failed. And Junior needed to be signed before the M's drafted him. After a few tense days of negotiations with Griffey, who initially demanded perks such as a Porsche, he agreed to sign with the M's for $175,000, the most the M's had ever paid a draft pick. The Mariners persuaded Griffey to sign before the draft by selling him on the prestige of being the No. 1 pick. Seattle selected Griffey over a handful of other prospects, only two of whom ever reached the majors—pitcher Willie Banks, who compiled a 33–39 record in the majors, and pitcher Mike Harkey, Argyros' preference, who appeared in 131 games.

"He has the most ability of anyone we've seen," said Jongewaard after selecting Griffey, the son of major league star Ken Griffey Sr. "He is ahead of many of his peers because he knows the game on and off the field." He also predicted Junior would move fast through the minors because of natural ability and high comfort in a major league baseball environment. "The one thing about him, which was different than other prospects, is that he never felt the pressure that other kids do to perform with scouts in the stands," said Mariners scout Tom Mooney to Boston.com years later. "He was a kid who really cared about the game and he wanted to be great. And at the time there was no better player in the country."

Three days after the draft, Griffey worked out for the Mariners in the Kingdome. The national media scrambled to book flights to Seattle, a heretofore mostly forgotten baseball outpost. *Sports Illustrated*, *The Sporting News*, ESPN, and dozens of local TV crews recorded the session. Griffey, using his father's bats, drove a number of pitches into the right-field seats. He displayed lightening-quick bat speed and a left-handed swing as sweet and golden as fresh Washington corn. "I was born with it," Griffey used to say. Mariners coaches and players watched in wonder. "Wow," said Mariner third-base coach Ozzie Virgil, "Let's play him tonight."

Griffey made his professional debut on June 16, 1987, in Bellingham, Washington, in the Rookie League. A standing room only crowd of 2,516 gave him a boisterous ovation as he trotted to his position. "I wasn't expecting all of that," he told the local paper afterward. It proved to be the highlight of the day. Griffey, starting in center field, failed to get the ball out of the infield, grounding out three times, striking out once, and taking a walk. He shrugged off the stale performance, telling reporters after the game he just needed to make adjustments. Those came the next day when Griffey collected his first hit, a three-run homer.

Two weeks into the season, however, he became homesick and almost quit. Jongewaard thought Griffey, only 17, actually suffered from boredom in a league he came to dominate, a league for mostly college baseball veterans. The homesickness pangs eventually disappeared and, as predicted, Griffey blazed through the minors, hitting above .300 and showing off his diverse skills. "I'm not saying he's Willie Mays yet," said Don Reynolds (Harold Reynolds' brother), who the Mariners assigned to monitor Griffey. "But if he keeps it together, he can get there."

A loud spring in 1989 forced the M's to reconsider their plans to start Griffey in Triple A Calgary. On April 3 Junior made his major league debut in Oakland, along with rookies Omar Vizquel at short, Edgar Martinez at third, and Greg Briley in left. On the second pitch he saw, Griffey laced a double into center. Two fly outs reached the warning track, the second after Junior fouled off five two-strike pitches in an eye-opening at-bat against A's pitcher and original Mariner, Rick Honeycutt. "I threw him two sliders for strikes," Honeycutt recalled, "and then a fastball that he somehow got the bat on. Then it was slider, slider, slider, and he kept hanging in. He made some very good adjustments on me. He seems to know what he's doing." Griffey's manager, Jim Lefebvre, watched spellbound. "The kid just has God-given talent. We saw the debut of a great player tonight."

Seven days later, Griffey made his Kingdome debut, a 6–5 win against the Chicago White Sox. In his first at-bat, he flicked a home run to the opposite field. "He's an easy out for me," said Chicago pitcher Eric King defiantly after the game. "The only thing he hit off me was a mistake."

"Whatever floats his boat," Griffey responded tartly. For the next 10 years as a Mariners player, Griffey capsized the boat of many opposing pitchers, who learned "the Kid" could hit just about anything.

3 Junior: His Career and Legacy

Name a cliché intended to describe the matchless contributions a player makes to a franchise, and Junior's legacy to the Mariners would apply. Safeco Field is the House that Griffey Built. He's front and center on the Mariners' Mount Rushmore. M's history is measured in units of B.G. and A.G. (before Griffey and after Griffey). And he was, quite literally, a franchise savior.

From his first major league at-bat as a poised 19-year-old Griffey bewitched not just Seattle but all of Major League Baseball. That he could draw heavy attention in Seattle, a baseball purgatory at the time, was a testament to his exalted talent. "As far as I'm concerned," said M's catcher Dave Valle during a Griffey hot streak in 1993, "he's the best thing that's happened to the game in a long time. If he were in any other city, he would be the Michael Jordan of baseball."

Comparisons to five-tool Hall of Famer Willie Mays cropped up immediately: the power, the arm, the speed, the moxie. He hit long, majestic home runs. A crushed dinger in Anaheim in May of

1997, for instance, disappeared far over the fence and was never found. He hit them often. In back-to-back seasons, 1997–1998, he bashed 56 home runs each and he topped the 40-homer mark six times in a Mariners uniform. And he was money in pressure-packed situations, none bigger than his walk-off homer on August 24, 1995, that beat the New York Yankees and ignited the M's blistering late-season run. Griffey, as he often reminded reporters, was more than just a home-run hitter. Four times he finished in the top 10 in batting average and he amassed double-digit stolen-base totals 10 times.

Junior also beat opponents with his glove, treating outfield fences as Playscapes and advancing runners as clay pigeons. Perhaps the most memorable of his "Spiderman catches" came against the Yankees on April 26, 1990. Jesse Barfield launched a soaring fly ball toward the gap in left-center field that screamed home run. As soon as Barfield connected, Griffey broke back on the ball and raced to the fence, where he timed his leap perfectly to reach over the wall and grab the ball just before it landed for a home run—400 feet away from home plate. Griffey beamed as he descended to the ground holding the ball up for everyone to see. "Just reminding everyone that I was in town," he said with a sly grin after the game. In the first month of his major league career, he mimicked Mays to make a breathtaking over-the-shoulder catch 400 feet from home plate to rob Toronto's Fred McGriff of extra bases. Then he outran a Pat Borders blast one batter later. For good measure, Junior went 4-for-4, including the game-winning home run against the Blue Jays. Said McGriff after the game: "I was pretty sure coming in that Griffey was for real. He is. He is no fluke." Watching from third base was his teammate, Edgar Martinez. "From the beginning, you could tell right away he was a five-tool player," said Martinez in a 2010 interview. "They don't come around very often. He was a guy that had a lot of confidence, even as a young player, just the way he carried himself."

Junior's at-bats almost instantly turned into can't-miss TV in Seattle. Griffey feats in the field became water cooler conversations. And his youth and exuberance inflamed the interest of tens of thousands of young fans in the region and nationally. In postgame interviews Griffey wore his cap backward. In response, playgrounds and schools became populated with kids doing the same, and many of them donning No. 24 Griffey jerseys.

In May of 1990, Griffey appeared on the cover of *Sports Illustrated* and later *GQ,* and with each monster home run and scintillating defensive play, his fame spread wider than his range in center field. Fox, which broadcast major league games on Saturday and the postseason, researched the most recognizable name in baseball and discovered Griffey won in a landslide over Cal Ripken, Jr. According to Slate magazine, Junior's Upper Deck rookie collecting card became the most popular in baseball history. He even threatened the hegemony of NBA star Michael Jordan as most marketable athlete nationally. Griffey had his own chocolate bar—which he couldn't eat because of allergies—Nike ad campaign, and Wheaties box.

In part through Nike's prominent advertising campaigns, Ken Griffey Jr. became the Pacific Northwest's first true superstar athlete.
(David Eskenazi)

The fame came with a price. Considerably more complex than his infectious smile and charming public persona suggested, Griffey chafed at his loss of privacy and almost committed suicide, ingesting hundreds of aspirin, during January of 1988. He could be sullen and stubborn, occasionally threatening to leave Seattle and squawking about disrespect. He clashed sporadically with some of the M's other stars, most notably Alex Rodriguez. But for the most part, and especially for a star of his magnitude, Griffey retained a one-of-the-guys quality. His best friend on the team was Jay Buhner. They drove each other to improve and served as a soundboard during difficult times. They horsed around together, needling one another and hatching practical jokes. Outside the locker room, they hung out as well. One favorite activity was riding ATVs in the mountains, where Griffey, according to Buhner, handled the machine the way he does everything else: effortlessly. "Junior is my brother from a different mother," Buhner often joked.

After 11 seasons with the Mariners, Griffey grew tired of living so far from his family in Florida. He also viewed the M's new open-air home as of July 1999, Safeco Field, with skepticism. The large dimensions of the outfield and the heavy air of the Puget Sound concerned him. As a result, the Mariners traded Griffey during the '99 offseason to the Cincinnati Reds. Beset by injuries and yielding to advancing age, Junior, 30 at the time of the trade, failed to duplicate the sheer brilliance of his years in Seattle. Some blamed Griffey's rash of injuries on his disinclination to stretch and lift weights. Others cited it as a reason no one ever implicated Griffey for steroid use.

In 2009 Griffey returned to the M's, a young team looking for veteran leadership and some pop. Junior delivered one last time, hitting 19 home runs while helping the Mariners win 85 games, an improvement of 24 games from the prior season. On the final day of the schedule, his teammates carried him off the field. Griffey came back the next season but struggled. Finally, he retired in June, quietly slipping away with no press conference or fanfare. His retirement came 75 years to the day after Babe Ruth called it quits and 23 years to the day the Mariners drafted him No. 1.

Like one of his no-doubter home runs, Griffey's final career tallies make him a surefire Hall of Famer: 630 home runs, sixth all time; 10 Gold Gloves; one MVP plus four top five finishes; and 13 All-Star appearances, including an MVP. "There were times he played in a whole different league, a whole different level, from the rest of us," Buhner recalled with wonder.

4 1995 Postseason

The 1995 best-of-five American League Division Championship Series lined up like this for the Mariners. Game 1 would be their third game in three days in three different time zones. Their pitcher from out of this world was out until at least Game 3 and would probably only pitch once in the series. The franchise had never appeared in a postseason. If that wasn't daunting enough, fabled Yankee Stadium was the site of the first two games. Many past greats and great teams had melted from the heat of competing in the most intimidating postseason venue in Major League Baseball.

That's what the Mariners faced heading into their first ALDS in major league history.

They also faced a Yankees team that had reignited New York's zeal for baseball. The Bronx Bombers were making their first trip to the postseason since 1981, ending the franchise's longest post-season drought since 1920.

New York was primed, and the Yankees didn't disappoint in the first two games. They battered starter Chris Bosio and the Mariners pen for a 9–6 win in Game 1. "Yankee Stadium was the loudest I've ever heard," said Yankees manager Buck Showalter. Ken Griffey Jr. rose to his pedigree though, blasting two homers in the losing cause.

Game 2 launched a volley of twists and turns in the series that elevated the '95 ALDS to legendary status. Journeyman Yankee catcher Jim Leyritz ended Game 2 with a two-run home run in the bottom of the 15th inning—in a driving rain. It came after Griffey had squeezed the noise out of Yankee Stadium with a solo shot in the 12th inning only to have the Mariners bullpen surrender a run in the bottom half.

The 7–5 win put the Yanks up 2–0 in the series and dumped the Mariners into another do-or-die situation. "I knew we were in trouble," Edgar Martinez said. "But I felt that if we could just win that first game at home, we had a great chance to win the series."

In front of 57,944 Kingdome fans doing their best Yankees fan impersonation, Randy Johnson made his postseason debut. He tamed the Bronx Bombers bats with 10 strikeouts and help from closer Norm Charlton to give the Mariners their first ever postseason win, 7–4.

In Game 4, facing elimination again, Bosio allowed five early runs. As an uneasy silence gripped the Kingdome, the M's summoned another comeback, tying the game with help from a three-run jack by Edgar and then jumping ahead on Griffey's fourth homer of the series. Unbowed, the Yankees tied it in the eighth. Edgar unwrapped the tie with a grand slam that nearly blew the roof off the Kingdome to put the Mariners up 10–6 en route to an 11–8 series evener.

With the entire region riveted to its radios and TVs for the deciding fifth game, the Mariners once again dug a hole. Seattle starter Andy Benes allowed four runs while David Cone of the Yankees limited the M's to two through seven innings. In the bottom of the eighth, Griffey edged the M's closer with a solo homer. Three more Mariners reached in the inning to load the bases. As the noise in the Kingdome threatened eardrums, Piniella sent up pinch-hitter ace Doug Strange. On Cone's 147th pitch of the game, Strange drew a game-tying walk. "I remember stepping out of the batter's box and saying, 'I can't believe how loud it is,'" he said.

In the top of the ninth, the first two Yankees got on base. The Mariners bullpen stirred. Then out popped an unlikely savior, Randy Johnson. The crowd went bananas. The Big Unit snuffed out the rally and struck out the side in the 10th. "Randy comes in and blew three fastballs by Wade Boggs. I couldn't even see [the pitches]. He was so pumped," Strange said. Meanwhile, the Mariners threatened in the ninth, but Showalter brought in Game 3 Starter Jack McDowell, and he smothered the rally. In the 11th the Yanks pulled ahead on a single by Randy Velarde.

The "Refuse to Lose" mantra would need to be roused once more.

Joey Cora led off against McDowell and laid down a perfect drag bunt single. "That's the play that stands out to me," said Yankees first baseman Don Mattingly. Griffey followed with a single that sent Cora to third. Edgar Martinez, 11-for-20 in the series, stepped to the plate. "Right now, the Mariners are looking to tie," said Dave Niehaus urgently on the Mariners radio broadcast. "They would take a fly ball; they would love a base hit into the gap." On an 0–1 pitch, Martinez rifled a double down the left-field line. Cora scored, and Griffey sprinted toward third. He never stopped. M's third base coach Sam Perlozzo defied baseball convention (which says don't send a runner from third with no outs) by waving Griffey home, where he beat the throw. "The gamble of all gambles," said Mariners bench coach Lee Elia. "I just remember looking up and seeing a hand waving," recalled Griffey. In the broadcast booth Neihaus delivered the call of his career, one spiced with the mother of all "My oh mys."

The Mariners raced out of the dugout like schoolchildren on the last day. Then they buried Griffey under a pile, which became the most famous photo in Mariners history. The rivets holding together the Kingdome nearly popped from the vibrating noise. "I was in the hallway [hitting off a tee]. I came running out, jumping and screaming," Jay Buhner said. "I couldn't get by [pitcher Bob Wolcott]; he was 10 feet in the air. Just awesome."

"M's Do It," blared the *Seattle Post-Intelligencer* the next day in the paper's largest type since WWII. Seattle, consumed by Mariners hysteria, started making plans for the promised land. "Believe me, Cleveland doesn't know what it's getting itself into," shouted Piniella during a rally before the American League Championship Series.

Alas, the M's couldn't complete the dream journey, falling to the Indians 4–2 in the ALCS. The pitching never lined up well, and the bats dozed for long stretches. Highlights included rookie Wolcott's sterling effort in Game 1 when he stymied the thunderous Tribe 3–2, and Buhner's three-run homer in the top of the 11th of Game 3. Facing elimination, Johnson pitched Game 6 but faded late. "It wasn't until I was watching the World Series on TV that I realized how mentally and physically drained I was," Johnson said. The same applied to his teammates, who had spent the past 10 breathless weeks fighting off elimination at every turn.

After the final out, following a pause to ponder the end, the Kingdome crowd cheered. They cheered as the Mariners headed to the dugout. They cheered as Elia and then Piniella addressed the team in the tunnel. Fifteen minutes after the end of the game, the crowd continuing cheering. "Fellas, there's one more thing I want you to do," Piniella told his team. Without saying another word, the players started to re-dress and head back toward the field. Hardly any of the 58,000 fans had left. They roared even louder at the sight of the ballplayers responsible for their loving embrace of a franchise mostly derided or ignored before now. The appreciative M's threw hats and gloves to the fans as souvenirs. "I have never in my life seen a city respond quite the way Seattle did," said Piniella, who wept, along with many of his players. Johnson said: "It was like they wanted an encore. They were waiting for another song. But the lights came on, and the show was over."

During the final week of the season, the Washington state legislature passed a bill granting public funding for a new stadium. Thus ended an amazing run unlike anything Seattle or baseball had ever seen.

5 The Birth of the Mariners

There's no sugarcoating it. Major League Baseball did not give birth to the Mariners. A lawsuit did.

When the Pilots skipped town after a lone season, Seattle felt gamed by owners, who were neither sufficiently capitalized nor ready for the big time, and by conniving Major League Baseball officials, who looked the other way as a slick car salesman from Milwaukee hijacked the Pilots.

A group of city and state leaders, led by state's attorney general Slade Gorton and King County Executive John Spellman, decided that Seattle would fire back. To that end, in the fall of 1970, they filed a lawsuit against the American League on behalf of Washington citizens calling for a new team in Seattle and $7 million in damages.

The lead attorney for the plaintiffs was Bill Dwyer, who had argued unsuccessfully during the Pilots' bankruptcy trial proceedings that Seattle deserved more than a year to prove it could support Major League Baseball.

A man of eclectic taste, Dwyer wrote books, acted, climbed mountains, owned an oyster house, collected art, enjoyed history, and quoted Shakespeare. He was also on the winning end of numerous high-profile trials, none more notable than a 1964 libel case involving Washington state legislator and alleged communist John Goldmark. Later as a federal judge he ruled in favor of environmental groups in the famed spotted owl case, which dramatically changed how the U.S. Forest Service managed its land.

In the prime of his career, Dwyer proved a worthy foe for MLB. He argued that an implied contract had existed between the American League and the state, county, and city (the People of Washington) that granted a permanent major league franchise to Seattle. In return the state, county, and city agreed to refurbish the minor league ballpark the Pilots would use initially and to support a $40 million bond issue to fund a domed stadium, which the Pilots would eventually occupy. The people had held up their end of the bargain, Dwyer argued. The minor league park, Sicks Stadium, had been upgraded, and voters had passed the bond issue. By allowing the Pilots to move despite two different local offers to buy the team, the American League had failed to live up to the terms of this agreement and were thus in breach.

The case dragged on for six years before finally going to trial in 1976. Judges hoped a settlement could be reached, but the AL insisted Seattle drop the lawsuit before discussing a settlement and putting a new team in the city. Dwyer trusted the American League as much as a hen trusts a fox so he ignored their overtures. Then MLB dangled the possibility of moving an existing franchise to Seattle—either Oakland or San Diego. But Dwyer refused to take the bait until both sides agreed to a binding contract putting a team in Seattle. Baseball wouldn't do that.

Once the trial started, which was held in Snohomish County and with only two jurors who ever saw the Pilots play in person, Dwyer eviscerated the defense. He exposed gaping holes in their arguments and revealed a series of duplicitous moves taken by the league. Some of the highlights:

- The AL argued that Seattle couldn't support a major league team. Dwyer countered that the Pilots actually had outdrawn four other franchises, including three teams around since 1901 (Indians, Phillies, and White Sox).
- When the AL complained that Sicks Stadium was unsuitable for Major League Baseball, Dwyer produced photos from old ballparks currently in use by major league teams, such as Detroit and Cleveland, to prove that Sicks was superior in many respects to these parks. "Some of them," Dwyer said, "you couldn't sit down without getting a splinter, and the plumbing was nothing to write home about."
- Dwyer produced evidence that secret negotiations took place between the Pilots owners (Max and Dewey Soriano and William Daley) and Bud Selig, a wealthy car dealer and eventual buyer of the Pilots, in August of 1969. And that the two parties came to a handshake agreement to sell the team during the 1969 World Series. All of this happened while Seattle actively sought to find local buyers and six months before a judge ruled that the Pilots were insolvent, and the American League could thus sell the team to whomever it wanted.

The plaintiffs also proved persuasively that the American League never took seriously either of the two local groups interested in buying the Pilots. Dwyer illustrated the reason dramatically:

Milwaukee had in place an agreement with an influential concessionaire company (Sportservice) that was blocked from doing business in Seattle due to local competitive bidding laws. Even more damaging, Seattle's attorneys demonstrated that not only did Sportservice have a prior agreement with Selig to serve as Milwaukee's exclusive concessionaire, but that the company in October of 1969 also entered into a loan agreement with Selig to help the car dealer buy the Pilots. That, contended the plaintiffs, was a conspiracy to sell the team.

Over and over, Dwyer tied up American League witnesses in knots. Washington Senators owner Bob Short, Oakland A's owner Charlie Finley, and American League president Joe Cronin all stumbled through damaging testimony. When Cronin finished testifying, the *Seattle Post-Intelligencer*'s Fred Brack was slack-jawed: "At the end of his testimony, when he was dismissed, he rose in front of the jury from the witness stand, climbed down, walked across the courtroom, and stuck out his hand and shook Bill Dwyer's hand in front of the jury after making a fool of himself, frankly, in his testimony."

With its case crumbling, the American League capitulated, agreeing to grant Seattle a new franchise and to pay damages—well short of the $7 million the plaintiffs demanded in the lawsuit. After six years of legal tangles, Seattle had its baseball team back and made history in the process. No major league team had ever been secured through litigation.

The man who made it all possible, Dwyer, lived long enough to see the M's flourish, passing away a few months after the Mariners set an American League record with 116 wins.

6 Edgar Martinez

Mariano Rivera, the future Hall of Fame Yankees closer, treated major league hitters like a whale does krill, effortlessly gobbling them up by the thousands. But there was one hitter whom Rivera just couldn't entrap. "I couldn't get him out," Rivera said of Edgar Martinez. "He had my breakfast, lunch, and dinner." And that as much as anything speaks to the hitting prowess of Martinez, the rare ballplayer who ate Rivera for lunch.

Martinez signed with the Mariners in 1982 as a free agent out of Puerto Rico, where he lived with his grandparents following his parents' divorce and his subsequent move from New York. When he turned 11, his parents reconciled, but Martinez chose to stay with his grandparents, who operated a cash-strapped transport business in Dorado, Puerto Rico. "I felt my grandparents needed me," he said in a 2001 interview with *The Seattle Times*. "I remember all the work they needed to do."

Initially, the Mariners didn't realize the gem they had. Other nuggets in the system always glistened more at least in the eyes of management. First Jim Presley. Then Darnell Coles. Martinez started his professional career late at the age of 20. In his minor league debut in 1983, he hit a flyspeck .173. Even though Martinez followed that up with a strong season at the plate (.303 batting average, .414 on-base percentage, and 15 homers), the Mariners pegged him as a defense-first third baseman. He possessed soft hands and made few errors. Said M's director of player development Bill Haywood: "His glove is his strength. Hitting over .300 is a pleasant surprise."

By 1990 Martinez, despite three years in the upper minors hitting .329, .363, and .345, was still viewed as a backup at best by the organization. But one by one, the Mariners third-base hope-fuls failed. With their options narrowing, the M's finally turned to Martinez. He went nuts from the opening bell, hitting .321 in April and .350 in May. A slight tapering for the remainder of the season failed to dim spirits. At 27 Martinez had finally earned a full-time job in the major leagues. "We made a mistake with him," Jim Lefebvre said. "We thought we needed a power guy at third base. But we switched to Edgar...and he started hitting and never stopped."

American League pitchers should have sent the M's chocolates for keeping this hitting machine under wraps. For the next 14 years, Martinez pounded them senseless, as if he were trying to make up for those years lost. He won batting titles in 1992 and 1995, the first two-time right-handed winner in the AL since Luke Appling in the 1930s and 1940s. Three times he led the AL in on-base percentage, twice in doubles, and once in RBIs. Displaying more round-tripper power than ever imagined by the M's, Martinez clubbed at least 24 homers six straight seasons and he made seven All-Star appearances. Martinez hit bad pitching. He hit good pitch-ing. He hit indoors. He hit outdoors. And he drilled line drive after line drive. Good thing. Martinez collected 2,247 hits on a set of wheels better suited for plowing through the snow than beating out infield singles. "He's the best right-handed hitter I've ever seen," said then-San Francisco Giants manager Dusty Baker in 2001.

Legends are forged by responding when it matters most. Nail-biting pennant races and the postseason summoned some of Martinez's best. He hit .398 (after a .402 June) and slugged .786 in August 1995, a pivotal month that set up the drama to come. He followed that with an .892 on-base plus slugging percentage (OPS) in September. Martinez slammed seven home runs in 17 career American League Division Series games, and his two-out double to drive in Joey Cora and Ken Griffey Jr. with the winning runs in Game 5 of the 1995 ALDS is the most celebrated and high-stakes moment in Mariners history. "That will probably be my greatest memory," Martinez said.

Moreover, Game 5 doesn't happen without Martinez's seven RBIs (a playoff record at the time) in Game 4, which forced a fifth game. Four of those came benefit of a grand slam, a ball Martinez smoked that whistled just a few feet above second base and kept rising until it nearly tore through the center-field backdrop. If the double was his greatest memory, the grand slam, as he told Kirby Arnold in *Tales from the Seattle Mariners Dugout*, was the biggest hit of his career.

No word describes Martinez more accurately than *steady*. Regardless of the circumstance, he usually remained calm and composed. Under pressure he was as cool as a cucumber. This consistency is reflected on his bubble gum card. For nine seasons from 1995–2003, his OPS never dropped below .888, and his batting average fell beneath .300 only twice. Churning out All-Star-caliber seasons year after year can give the impression hitting comes easy. But Martinez worked relentlessly to maintain his excellence. Said former teammate Stan Javier about the work ethic Gar learned from his grandfather: "I've never seen anybody—maybe Don Mattingly—work as hard as Edgar Martinez. I'm talking eyes, hands, feet. He spends hours and hours in the batting cage."

In 2004 Martinez retired—with Hall of Fame offensive numbers (.312 batting average, 309 home runs, .418 on-base percentage). Advanced statistics strongly support his admission. But he has fallen well short of the 75 percent necessary for induction. Three reasons stand out as to why. First, Martinez, who the M's discovered lacked range in the field, spent most of his career as a designated hitter. Biases against the position still run deep in the Baseball Writers Association. Martinez's presumptive status as the greatest designated hitter in history actually counts against him in the eyes of many voters. The second reason was just bad luck.

By the time his career started in earnest, most Hall of Famers had already accumulated 1,000 or more at-bats. As a result Martinez lacks the eye-grabbing numbers—like 3,000 hits or 600 home runs—that guarantee a stamp into the Hall.

The final reason, a lesser one, is also in part why a street bears his name in the shadow of where he came to work for 18 years. Martinez was not a publicity seeker or a self-promoter. He merely showed up every day and quietly performed his job. "It's the way he comes to the ballpark and is the same every day," former teammate Norm Charlton explained to *The Seattle Times* in 2004. "He comes in and does his work before the game, then he goes out on the field and he produces, then comes back and does the rest of his work after the game, then he goes home and goes to bed and comes back and does the same thing the next day."

Equally important, as the M's other stars left for greener pastures, Martinez stayed in Seattle. Loyal to the Mariners until the very end, he was the ultimate company man. A little more me-first pizzazz may have enhanced his Hall of Fame chances at the expense—one presumes—of his local adoration. "He isn't your typical superstar," said teammate Bret Boone in 2001. "In today's game once you get to a certain level it's like you're expected to act differently. Edgar doesn't follow that."

"Not much happened until Edgar arrived on the scene," Mariners club president Chuck Armstrong said the day Martinez announced his retirement. "If you visualize any significant moment in Mariners history, Edgar is there. He is the one constant."

7 2001: Chasing History

Alex Rodriguez, in a coldly calculated move, bolted before the 2001 season for Texas riches. A year prior, Ken Griffey Jr. had forced a trade to Cincinnati. Two-and-a-half years earlier, Randy Johnson departed under messy circumstances. Over a span of three years, the Mariners had lost three Hall of Fame-caliber players. Moreover, star Jay Buhner missed most of the 2001 season with an injury. And yet the M's didn't sink. Instead, they won so much they challenged records set during the Teddy Roosevelt administration.

A central reason was Ichiro Suzuki, who was signed out of Japan during the offseason to play right field. Ichiro, as everyone called him in Japan, featured a style more in step with the baseball of Teddy's time: slap hitting, speed, defense. Improbably, this throwback to the Honus Wagner era enraptured baseball and sparked the Mariners to one of the greatest regular seasons of all time.

The 2001 Mariners were about more than just Ichiro—even if his breathless play dominated most of the conversation. As an F5 tornado requires just the right mix of colliding jet streams, wildly successful baseball teams are the result of a confluence of perfectly blended factors. Ichiro added an essential component. So did newcomer and former Mariner Bret Boone. Signed to play second base, he arrived bulkier and wielding Thor's hammer for a bat, clubbing a career high and desperately needed 37 homers. Previous talent, some acquired to replace the departing future Hall of Famers, flourished and added wonderfully married seasoning as well. That included John Olerud, Japanese reliever Kazuhiro Sasaki, Arthur Rhodes, Mark McLemore, Carlos Guillen, Freddy Garcia, Jamie Moyer, Jeff Nelson, Stan Javier, and Norm Charlton. And bedrock Edgar Martinez was, significantly, vintage Edgar Martinez.

Preseason the Mariners appeared strong but hardly capable of threatening decades-old records. "It wasn't a great, great team on paper," said the *Seattle Post-Intelligencer*'s Jim Street. "If you look at the '95 Mariners, they had a lot more talent in its lineup. But it was like all the stars were aligned, every free agent clicked." Mike Sweeney, who later played for the Mariners but starred for the Kansas City Royals, said at the time: "I think when they had [Ken] Griffey, A-Rod, and Randy Johnson, they had three superstars, but that [didn't] necessarily make them a good team. Once they left, the Mariners really jelled as a team. They don't have three head guys; they have 25 equal guys, and I think that's what makes them a great team."

The M's won a major league record 20 games in April, which included a series sweep in Oakland, something no Mariners team in history had ever done. On May 17th they beat the Chicago White Sox 5–1 to go 31–9. "If we went 31–9 in our next 40 games, we'd have the greatest record in the history of the game," said Boone in jest. "We all know that's not going to happen."

It didn't happen, though just barely. But it sure seemed as though every Mariners ball put in play found a hole. Or that the M's allowed runs as often as rain falls in Death Valley. Or that deficits evaporated more quickly than politician promises. With two outs, the Mariners really prospered. *Two outs, so what?* became a rallying cry around Safeco Field, which was packed to capacity daily. "Enjoy the ride," said announcer Dave Niehaus during midseason. "You may never see anything like it again."

In late May and early June, Seattle won 15 consecutive games. After the Mariners dug out of a 6–0 hole against Oakland to win 12–10, the A's John Jaha acknowledged the obvious. "This team [the M's] right now is as good as any I've seen."

At the All-Star break, the Mariners were 63–24 and no longer chasing just a division title. They started eyeing the all-time record for wins in a season of 116, set by the Chicago Cubs in 1906. In August, they won 20 games again, which put them on the cusp of 100 wins. On September 5 the Mariners reached that lofty total to become the second fastest team in major league history to collect 100 victories. "It means more than I thought it would," said manager Lou Piniella on winning 100. "I didn't think I'd get this emotional."

Five days later, the M's stood 104–40 with a magic number of two. Through the first 144 games, they had suffered no losing streaks of more than two. They had established a major league record with 29 consecutive non-losing road series. On offense, the M's thrived at situational hitting. "We don't have any big egos in this offense," Boone said. "We just go out and hit." On defense, they constructed, in the words of Cameron, "the Great Wall of China. You can't get anything through." And both the starting rotation and bullpen sprang very few leaks. So solid in every respect, the Mariners needed few late-inning dramatics or ridiculously loony comebacks to pad their record. "It's frustrating to play against them," said Minnesota Twins first baseman Doug Mientkiewicz. "But on the other hand, it's pretty fun to watch."

As the Mariners slept in during a three-game series against Anaheim on September 11, chaos and tragedy erupted on the East Coast. Terrorists hijacked four commercial planes. Two of them rammed into the Twin Towers in New York, one into the Pentagon in Washington, D.C., and the fourth crashed in a field in Pennsylvania. Suddenly, baseball and magic numbers and records seemed a trifle matter. The Mariners watched the day's nightmarish events unfold on TV. By midday MLB commissioner Bud Selig announced all games were canceled until September 18. Three days later, on September 14, the Mariners caught a flight home on the first day airspace reopened. Tensions across the country remained high, but the Mariners had to quickly refocus on baseball.

The M's pursuit of history had begun to create distractions and added pressure even before 9/11. "It started two months out with the media [presence] so big in our clubhouse, asking 'Are you guys going to break the record,'" said Boone in *Sweet Lou*. "It was like postseason media coverage."

When the season resumed, the M's goals remained the same: wrap up the division and make history. That meant few rests for the regulars, who lobbied Piniella to keep them in the lineup. The M's clinched the division on September 19 after two straight wins at home. They reacted with a toned-down, champagne-free celebration: a moment of silence, a prayer, patriotic songs, and waving of the American flag by the players and fans. Emotion overwhelmed many. Thousands of fans sobbed. Javier broke down in tears. "It was the best way we could show our love for the Seattle fans and people of America," Cameron said. *Seattle Post-Intelligencer* columnist Art Thiel wrote the next day: "They found a way to honor their achievements, fans, and country without histrionics, triteness, or bad taste. A season of greatness found a seminal expression apart from the game."

The M's followed with a four-game losing streak, the first real letdown of the season. But they rallied to win 10 of 11 and in the process topped the Yankees' American League record of 114 wins set in 1998. On October 6, the second to last day of the season, the Mariners won 1–0 on a Boone homer to tie the Cubs' 116 wins. "If you assembled an All-Star team and put them in our division, they couldn't win 116 games," Boone said postgame. On the final day of the season, the Mariners stumbled 4–3 to the Texas Rangers. They would have to share the record with the 1906 Cubs and hope they had something left for the playoffs. "The night we won 116, everyone just went 'Whew,'" said Boone. "Then it was like, 'Wait a minute, we have to go to the playoffs now.'"

8 Tiebreaker Playoff

Whew. The Mariners' long, implausible, ridiculously dramatic regular season charge to overtake the Angels ultimately ended in a tie, which meant a one-game playoff to determine the winner of the American League West in 1995. Though rare, tiebreaking games had produced some of baseball's most treasured moments, including Bucky Dent's blast over the Green Monster in 1978, which Lou Piniella witnessed live in a New York Yankees uniform. It seemed fitting then that this pennant race for the ages should end with something rare.

On September 18, the day the Mariners drew within two games of the Angels, Seattle had won a coin flip granting them the home field for any tiebreaker. The home-field advantage and Randy Johnson taking the hill dulled the sting from the two games they'd just lost in Texas to surrender the lead. "We had that trump card," said Jay Buhner, remembering the confidence spiking through the Mariners as they headed home. In games started by Johnson, the M's were 27–3 in 1995. In all other games, they were 52–63. For their part the Angels, on life support just two days ago, felt lady luck had finally re-embraced them. Plus, they had pounded Johnson, who would be pitching on three days rest, in early August. "It was a crazy situation," recalled Angels infielder Eduardo Perez in *Tales from the Seattle Mariners Dugout*. "But we thought we couldn't lose."

In Seattle, fans waited in line for two hours to purchase tickets on Sunday night. Rain fell the entire time, but the fans kept coming. By 1:00 PM on Monday, the Kingdome parking lot was packed. By 1:30 the sellout crowd of 52,000 throbbed in anticipation of the first pitch. Across Seattle, schoolchildren played hooky,

*Randy Johnson
raises his arms
in triumph
after defeating
the California
Angels 9–1 in a
one-game playoff
to capture the
American League
West division.*
(Getty Images)

line workers at Boeing came down with Mariner flu, and a rash of "appointments" erupted in downtown offices.

In a season rife with the improbable, a strange twist of fate awaited the Mariners. Mark Langston, former Mariners All-Star and the player traded for Johnson, would take the hill for the Angels. The good news for Seattle: the Mariners had scored nine runs off Langston in two starts during the season. Said a fan to a reporter from *The Seattle Times* before the game: "I remember

Langston when he played for us. He never had heart, and Randy always has heart."

Langston showed plenty of heart early, keeping the Mariners bats in check through four innings. Johnson, meanwhile, opened the game retiring the first 17 batters he faced. The offenses may have been quiet, but the Kingdome fans hung on every pitch, rose to their feet on two-strike counts, and roared like the engine of a 727 after each Angels out. Finally, in the bottom of the fifth inning, Langston flinched. With two on and one down, Vince Coleman drove in Dan Wilson with a single to give the Mariners a 1–0 lead. Behind a run and with Johnson dealing, the Angels' pregame optimism started to sink. "Randy was throwing pellets," said Angels infielder Rex Hudler. "You could barely see the ball."

As the game crept along at 1–0, tensions rose. "Every pitch, every out was very intense, nerve-packed," recalled Buhner 10 years later. The score remained 1–0 heading into the bottom of the seventh inning. To this point Johnson had allowed only a single. Chants of "Ran-dee! Ran-dee!" intensified with each out. But even the seemingly invincible Big Unit could get touched for a run or two. The Kingdome pined for insurance runs.

On cue, Seattle loaded the bases with one down. Coleman then lined out to short right but not deep enough to score a run. That brought up shortstop Luis Sojo, the journeymen infielder from Venezuela enjoying a career year at the plate. *Put the ball in play*, Sojo thought. *This is your moment. Concentrate on what you're doing.* On the first pitch, he swung. His bat shattered in the direction of Langston, who at first was relieved to see what appeared to be a weak dribbler to sure-handed Angel first baseman J.T. Snow. But the ball came off the bat funny, and it squeezed just passed Snow's glove and then rolled all the way into the Angels bullpen. *We're done*, Langston thought immediately. *We're in big trouble.*

Indeed, all three runs scored as Angels right fielder Tim Salmon struggled to retrieve the ball, which allowed Sojo to take third. Then the stubby shortstop chugged home when Langston's relay throw sailed past catcher Andy Allanson. "Everybody scores!" screeched Rick Rizzs over the Mariners Radio Network as the M's took a 5–0 lead. The crowd, naturally, went berserk. "I've never heard a place as loud as the Kingdome after that play," Sojo said. "We weren't able to talk for the next 20 minutes." As the Mariners celebrated, Langston picked up a piece of Sojo's splintered bat and slammed it down. "I'll always remember Langston lying there in the dirt across home plate, looking up at the ceiling with that look on his face," said Mariners president Chuck Armstrong.

The Angels knew they were done. The Mariners knew it. And so did the fans. As an exclamation point, the M's added four more runs in the eighth. Johnson allowed a home run in the ninth and then closed out the game with a strikeout of Salmon. After strike three Johnson raised his arms triumphantly, adopting a pose as majestic and iconic as the Space Needle. Then the fans poured onto the field, the players escaped into the locker room, and everyone in the Kingdome let out a huge exhale, which expelled 19 years of losing and frustration. "This is a dream come true to this organization, this city, this town," Buhner told reporters. "People are going crazy, and yet bigger and better things are yet to come. Who knows what's next? We've just got to keep riding the magic carpet."

When the champagne stopped flowing, the Mariners boarded a bus for their flight to New York, where the Yankees waited in the American League Division Series. The street was lined with screaming fans and honking horns, a testament to Seattle's arrival—finally—as a Major League Baseball town.

9 Randy Johnson

Every great team needs a stopper. That one starting pitcher who can douse losing streaks before they erupt into brushfires. Randy Johnson played that role for the Mariners splendidly.

Few would have used that word to describe Johnson the day he arrived in Seattle in May of 1989. The Mariners gave up All-Star pitcher Mark Langston for three unproven hurlers from the Montreal Expos, including Johnson. Mariners infielder Jim Presley called the deal the saddest day in M's history. For sure, no one expected Johnson, a wiry, 6'10" lefty who threw 100 mph gas that sprayed in all directions, to emerge as the jewel of the trade. Pitchers as tall as Johnson, the tallest major leaguer in history, struggled with mechanics (an ability to repeat an optimal delivery). That was the prevailing wisdom, and through the first 26 years of Johnson's life, conventional wisdom was winning. His intimidating presence on the mound, sonic express fastball, and developing slider helped him rack up huge strikeout numbers in the minors. As expected, though, Johnson's large frame and herky-jerky three-quarters delivery subverted his mechanics. In a nutshell he had little control, leading the league in walks and hit batsmen.

The Expos drafted Johnson with the second overall pick in the 1985 draft. The high pick surprised other scouts and organizations because Johnson walked 104 hitters in 118 innings as a junior at USC. Self-conscious about his height in high school, Johnson, a Northern California native, savored campus life, majoring in fine arts and working as a photographer for the school newspaper and rock music magazine. On the pitching mound, however, Johnson struggled not only with his control, but also his emotions. Bad calls by umpires and misplays by teammates easily derailed him.

He wanted to return for his senior year to work out the kinks and improve his demeanor on the mound. Montreal persuaded him to sign instead.

The day he became a Mariner, Johnson still battled the twin demons of walks and emotional maturity. It was the reason his name came up third when pundits discussed the blockbuster trade. His first three years in a Mariners uniform represented more of the same. When on, he terrified hitters. When off, he frightened them even more. Johnson's triple-digit fastball, described by teammate Bill Krueger as authentic Nolan Ryan 100-mph grade, jumped on the hitter in a blur. Often they swung and missed. Just as often they watched the ball sail wide or high or to the screen. Or, in their worse nightmare, they froze as an errant fastball bruised their flesh. From 1990 to 1992, Johnson led the league in walks. In '92 and '93, he led the league in hit batsmen while posting ERAs in the threes. The M's remained patient, though, and glimpses of the fantasy Johnson, the one harnessing all of his pitches, occasionally emerged. The most spectacular of these came in 1990 when he threw a no-hitter, albeit one with six walks.

Something clicked after the All-Star break in 1992. In his final 11 starts of the season, Johnson went 5–2 with a 2.65 ERA and averaged 10 strikeouts a game. Many credit a lengthy talk Johnson had with Nolan Ryan in June of that year for the turn-around. A 15-minute courtesy chat before a game in Texas turned into a 60-minute professor-to-student exchange. Ryan shared his routines and dissected Johnson's mechanics. "Randy started doing all that stuff they talked about, and all of sudden he just took off," said M's trainer Rick Griffin in *Tales from the Seattle Mariners Dugout*.

Walks remained a problem the rest of the season, but in 1993 Johnson started slowly chipping away at the number of free passes he issued each year. Meanwhile, his strikeouts zoomed, aided by improving command and a slider with the bite of a Lou Piniella tirade. In 1993 he won 19 games and whiffed 308 batters—and cut his walks per nine innings almost in half. Henceforth, Johnson became the man of the Mariners' dreams. Ending losing streaks. Extending winning streaks. Messing with the psychology and the strategy of the opponent. "Randy changed the game before the first pitch because the other team would take all of its left-handed hitters out of the lineup," recalled his former battery mate, Dan Wilson. (The two won 72 percent of all starts they made together.)

Although Johnson learned to channel his emotions in a positive direction when on the mound, he remained fiery and intense while pitching. He waved his arms in every direction after big strikeouts. He pounded his chest and uncorked loud and untamed screams as he thundered into the dugout after pivotal third outs. Many great athletes carry a chip on their shoulder, one that provides a source of motivation and fires the soul. Johnson, told he'd never make it because of his height, pitched with a perpetual grudge, a quality that carried over into the dugout and resulted in sporadic friction with a few teammates. "If I'd been a nicer guy, I wouldn't have been as good a pitcher," Johnson told *The News Tribune* in 2012. Once he got into a shoving match over music volume in the locker room with teammate David Segui, who sprained his wrist in the altercation. Segui didn't mince words when reporters asked him about the injury. "I hurt it on a 6'10" piece of sh--," he said. On days of scheduled starts, especially, he hunkered down and swatted away even the most benign overtures to engage him.

The M's weren't paying Johnson to play nice with his team-mates, though most coexisted fine with him. They paid Johnson for times like 1995. Big Unit, as he became known, scorched down the stretch of the M's franchise-saving romp through September. In his last ten starts of that season, Johnson went 7–0 in 74-plus innings, allowing only 12 runs and 44 hits while striking out 99 batters. These numbers amaze under any circumstance, but consider the context: the pressure of pennant race baseball and the dramatic cycling up of offense that started the prior year. Then he capped off the run by suffocating the Angels for a complete-game shutout in the M's winner-take-all playoff victory. "There's nobody…in baseball as dominating as Randy," said his teammate Andy Benes. Johnson finished 18–2 and led the league in ERA (2.48) and strikeouts. He also won the Cy Young, the first Mariner in history to win the award (or any major award).

Johnson missed the brunt of the 1996 season because of back surgery, which set the stage for the unfortunate events of 1998. He recovered from the surgery and menaced his way through the 1997 season with a 20–4 record and two 19-strikeout performances. "That was the best pitching I've ever seen," said Chicago White Sox broadcaster Ken Harrelson after witnessing the second one. But during the offseason the Mariners refused to offer him a contract extension. They questioned the wisdom of giving a 34-year-old pitcher big money, especially one a season removed from serious back surgery. That upset the sensitive Johnson, who also had never fully recovered from an awkward exchange he had with M's president Chuck Armstrong days after Johnson's father died unexpectedly of a brain aneurysm in December of 1992. Armstrong, unaware Johnson's father had died, asked him on a visit to the M's offices how his holidays had been.

Johnson started slowly in 1998, which heated up rumors, fanned by many in the press, that he was deliberately tanking to force the M's to trade him at the deadline. Johnson pitched poorly by any standards, though he was victimized by poor run support, an unreliable bullpen, and a spate of bad luck. But no obvious pattern emerged to suggest he wasn't trying. The most likely explanation, corroborated by later reports and testimony from teammates, is that the weight of uncertainty dragged down his performance. In any event the M's traded Johnson to Houston, where he subsequently went on a tear, going 10–1 with a 1.28 ERA (which reignited speculation about his effort in Seattle).

The Big Unit won 130 games in a Seattle uniform. He started his post-Mariners career at age 35 and remarkably won more games in other uniforms. Indeed, like red wine, scotch whiskey, and the Seven Wonders of the World, Johnson actually got better with age. When he retired at the age of 46, he had accumulated 303 victories, five Cy Youngs, 4,875 strikeouts, and a game in which he whiffed 20 batters. Awkward in interviews, surly at times, private, introspective, and always unforgivably intimidating on the mound, Johnson was also the greatest pitcher in Mariners history—and one of the greatest of all time. In 2012, he was elected into the Mariners Hall of Fame. In January of 2015, he was elected to Baseball's Hall of Fame in Cooperstown, New York.

10 Safeco Field

The Mariners' slick new home, which opened in 1999, is a testament to the talent, will, and grit of the 25 men who rallied the Mariners to their first playoff berth ever in 1995. If that team had followed the path of previous M's squads, Safeco Field would probably be a parking lot today, providing pricey parking for members of the 12th Man. Major League Baseball fans in Seattle would probably be relegated to adopting teams in other cities and mounting the occasional effort to bring the sport back to the city.

That's not to say the new park, which cost more than half a billion dollars to build, came without controversy. After King County voters narrowly rejected a tax to fund the new stadium, the state legislature, intoxicated over the Mariners' miraculous division title and deep run in the playoffs, pulled one over on voters and authorized a new tax nonetheless. Most voters celebrated—but not all.

Today the heated politics and debate that surrounded the birth of Safeco Field are a faint memory. The park is generally considered one of the game's jewels. Its retractable roof, arresting views of Puget Sound, strong sight lines, and multiple activities to occupy the time before, during, and after games make it a bucket list item for many baseball fans.

Ground broke on the new park on March 8, 1997, and Ken Griffey Jr. was one of those given the honor of shoveling the first dirt. On July 15, 1999, Safeco Field debuted to a starry-eyed sellout crowd of 44,607, many of whom were watching their first major league game on real grass. The game ended with a blown save, something Mariners fans at the time had seen in weary abundance. Within two years Safeco would host an All-Star Game and bear witness to one of the greatest regular seasons in Major League Baseball history. But it's still waiting to host a World Series game.

Dimensions
Left Field: 331 feet
Center Field: 401 feet
Right Field: 326 feet

The Skinny on Seats
Diamond Club or All-Star Club Suites
High rollers have two options for watching the Mariners in luxury and comfort. The Diamond Club provides a bounty of food and all drinks included in the $175-300-plus price per ticket. Food can be delivered to your seats, which are right behind home plate, but if you choose to sit at a table to eat or drink, you can only watch the game on TV. A less lavish but still hearty food spread is offered in the All-Star Suites, which are located in the Suite Level just above the Terrace Level. Food is included but not alcohol. The cost is just a shade below $200, but you can see the action on the field from anywhere in the suite.

Lower Box (Sections 119–141)
They provide the best views in the ballpark and are considerably cheaper than the Club Level seats and are a good value compared to the major league parks.

Terrace Level
These seats ring the park just above the lower level and provide a heated indoor area where you can buy food and sit at tables while watching the game on TV. The average price is around $47.

Best Value Seat
The Lower Outfield Reserved Seats (sections 102–109, 151, and 152) provide a great view of the action at a reasonable price.

Bleacher Seats
The center-field bleachers offer a better view than the left-field bleachers, which also provide no protection from the elements.

View Reserved vs. View Box Seats
Both of these upper-deck seats offer fantastic views not only of the action on the field, but also of Puget Sound and downtown Seattle. The best value is the View Reserved Seats just a few rows behind the View Box Seats.

Attractions
Moose Den and Kids Clubhouse
Located in center field, this area provides a playground for children and a room where fans can pose with the Mariner Moose for a photo. You need to reserve a spot in the playground ahead of time. There are no reservations for meeting the Mariner Moose, though he's usually only in his den during the middle innings.

Beer Garden (outside the center-field fence)
This is a playground for singles and adults.

Bullpen Market (behind left-field fence)
This area offers interactive games and activities.

Home Plate Gate
The main entrance is designed to resemble Ebbets Field.

Safeco Field Art
Scattered through the park is baseball artwork ranging from Dale Chihuly's Glass Bat Sculpture, which hangs down from the ceiling at the southwest entrance, to "The Defining Moment," a mural representing Edgar Martinez's 1995 game winner against the Yankees in the 1995 American League Division Series. (South Atlantic Street also was named after Martinez in 2004.)

Other features include the *Dave Niehaus statue*, the *Baseball Museum of the Pacific Northwest* (located on main concourse level), *Mariner Hall of Fame* (located inside the Baseball Museum), *Outdoor Fireplace* (behind center field), and *Famous Baseball Quotations* (found on the gates to the park).

Safeco Field Tour
Tours of the park are available most days. They leave from First Avenue on the south side of the park. You'll see, among other things: locker rooms, dugouts, the press box, and the control room for the retractable roof, one of only three in Major League Baseball.

Food
Besides the standard baseball fare of hot dogs, sausages, pizza, pretzels, and popcorn, Safeco offers an eclectic mix of food: fish and chips and fish dogs (from Ivar's), garlic fries, Ich-roll (sushi),

Parisian crepes, tortillas, gourmet food from renowned local chefs like Ethan Stowell, and, of course, multiple different microbrews. Hit It Here Café is a full-service restaurant located in right field. Only a few tables, however, offer good views of the game. You can also order food from your iPhone and have it delivered directly to your seat, no matter where you're seated.

11 Ichiro

For years, stars of the Japanese major leagues had migrated to the United States. Before 2000 all of them had been pitchers. When outfielder Ichiro Suzuki, a star of supernova quality in Japan, expressed interest in testing his ability in the United States, skeptics howled. Major league pitchers, they warned, will overpower the 5'9", credit card-thin Ichiro. A month into his first season, the howling turned to surprise and then awe.

Ichiro, which means *firstborn* in Japan, was the second-born son of a factory manager in Aichi, Japan. His father recognized his son's baseball ability early on. For three to four hours a day, 360 days a year, Ichiro honed his skills under the supervision of his demanding father. He would later say he practiced so much he only had five or six hours a year to play with his friends.

At 18 Ichiro debuted in Japan's Pacific League. At 20 he broke the league record for hits. For the next seven years, Ichiro won every batting title and earned seven gold gloves. His popularity in Japan skyrocketed to rock star levels just as his father, who saved his childhood things for a museum he hoped to open, had planned. Meanwhile, the Mariners, set to move into a brand new stadium and wanting to add more star power, invited Ichiro to tour Seattle in 1998 and work out with the Mariners in spring training.

After the 2000 season, Ichiro yearned for a new challenge—and to escape the bubble his life had become in Japan. The Mariners, owned by Japan's Nintendo, made their move intrigued not only by Suzuki's skills, but also by his potential appeal to the large Pacific Northwest Asian American community. After beating out the usual big-market teams with a $13 million posting fee to Orix, Ichiro's club in Japan, the Mariners signed Suzuki for $14 million over three years.

Early on, Mariners manager Lou Piniella wondered if Ichiro was more a public relations move than a sound baseball decision. After watching Suzuki repeatedly hit weak grounders to the left side of the infield at the beginning of spring training, Piniella's suspicions rose. Wrote Larry Stone in *The Seattle Times*: "[Piniella] honestly thought this guy was not any good. He said, 'I've got to see you pull the ball. Show me you can pull the ball.' And Ichiro proceeded to pull the ball five times in a row. I think that's when Lou began to see what the guy could really do."

Driven by an increase in walks and a startling spike in power, waves of runs represented baseball in the new millennium. Ichiro neither walked nor hit for much power. Yet he was fantastically successful—by rarely striking out and rescuing the simple single from scorn and oblivion. Although he hit home runs in batting practice, Ichiro, hitting from the left side, poked and chopped and flung at the ball with his bat. "He doesn't hit," Piniella said. "He serves like a tennis player." Those serves usually bounced the baseball over the head of infielders, blooped it over their gloves, or squeezed it past them. Those times when an infielder could make a play, Ichiro, who jerked toward first base as he swung, exited the batter's box quicker than a sneeze, which put tremendous pressure on the defense to hurry a throw. He set a league record with 192 singles in 2001, a staggering number of them infield hits.

In his first month as a Mariner in 2001, he hit .336. The next month he hit .379. Subsequent months offered more of the same. At the end of his rookie season, a year in which the Mariners won an American League-record 116 games, Ichiro claimed the batting title with a .350 average. Pitchers desperately searched for holes in his swing but discovered the lefty's plate coverage almost limitless. "I just have a wider strike zone," he said after a 6-for-9 stretch against a baffled Boston Red Sox staff. "There is no secret to getting him out," said Boston manager Grady Little. "All you can do is concentrate on getting the other eight guys." Suzuki also led the league in stolen bases with 56, making him just the second player ever (Jackie Robinson was the first) to win both the batting and stolen-base title in the same year. He also hit .445 with runners in scoring position.

The Oakland A's and everyone else learned early that Ichiro brought more than a buffet of singles and stolen bases. On April 11 he gunned down Oakland's Terrence Long at third base after Long attempted to go from first to third on a single. "I'll tell you what, you could hang a lot of clothes on that throw," Piniella said. Long was equally impressed, saying: "It was going to take a perfect throw to get me—and that's what he did." What became known as "the Throw" served strong notice to the rest of MLB. "We won't be running on Ichiro," said a scout from the AL West. The league also quickly realized that Suzuki brought the complete package in the field: laser strong arm, good speed, and preternatural instincts that helped him to track down most fly balls in his zone—and some outside of it. Safeco fans dubbed right field "Area 51," a tribute to Ichiro's splendid play in right and his jersey number.

For his efforts, both at the plate and in the field, the 27-year-old won the Rookie of the Year Award and the AL MVP Award. In the 2001 American League Division Series, he hit .600 against the Cleveland Indians and slugged .650. "What he did to us in the playoffs, he shouldn't have done," said Indians GM John Hart. "I mean, that's unfair."

Ichiro's early success made him an instant hit in Seattle—and the U.S. He appeared on the cover of *Sports Illustrated* two months into his Mariners career. He led all major leaguers in All-Star votes, collecting 3.4 million. Fans clamored for Ichiro No. 51 jerseys—Randy Johnson's old number—and other merchandise, which moved quicker than chocolate bunnies at Easter time. For instance, Ichiro Bobblehead Day generated lines that formed overnight—a Mariners first. And Levi's limited edition Ichiro jeans sold out in six minutes.

Moreover, his popularity in Japan, already at stratospheric levels before, shot to the moon as he became a sensation in America. More than 100 members of the Japanese media chronicled his first spring training in 2001. Many stayed in the U.S. to cover his every move thereafter. So many fans from Japan flooded into Safeco Field that the Mariners added signs throughout the ballpark in Japanese. For those who couldn't see Ichiro live, Japanese TV eventually broadcast every Mariners game. "The Mariner games are shown on TV in the mornings in Japan," said Masa Niwa in 2001, a reporter for the Japanese magazine *Number* who had lived in Seattle since 1995. "The children are at school. The first question they ask when they get home is, 'Mom, how did Ichiro do today?'" Suzuki even enchanted Japan's prime minister, who declared that, "Ichiro made him proud to be Japanese." Alas, for Japan, Ichiro's success in the U.S. had a bittersweet element to it. MLB started raiding Japanese baseball of many of its stars.

Contributing to the public's fascination was Ichiro's enigmatic personality.

Though over the years he picked up some English (and spoke it with his teammates), Suzuki only interacted with the press through an interpreter. And he often gave meta-spiritual, opaque, or—especially later—downright goofy answers to media questions. He also learned some Spanish, often surprising Latin players by dropping Spanish slang on them in the heat of the battle. He once said: "No corro casi" (roughly "I don't have my legs today") to Detroit Tigers shortstop and former Mariners teammate Ramon Santiago before stealing third base.

Ichiro also engaged in a cavalcade of odd rituals and quirks. In the on-deck circle, he squatted and turned side to side. At the plate he'd raise his bat high and then point it at the pitcher before tugging at his sleeve, a ritual he repeated before every pitch. On the bench he performed acupressure on himself, rubbing a small wooden stick on his feet. "If your feet are healthy, you're healthy," he explained. He also wore sunglasses while watching TV at home to keep his eyes sharp.

In subsequent years Ichiromania cooled. His parade of 200-hit seasons, however, continued unbroken, as he shattered Wee Willie Keeler's record of eight consecutive seasons with at least 200 hits. As a Mariners player, Ichiro won two batting titles, broke George Sisler's record for hits in the season, earned 10 Gold Gloves, and played in 10 All-Star Games.

It wasn't all mountains silhouetted against a brilliant sunset. Over time some fans tired of his no-power act. And occasionally tensions rose between Ichiro and a handful of his teammates, which were no doubt exacerbated by the procession of losing seasons in his final years. With his contract up at the end of 2012, he asked the Mariners to trade him. They obliged by sending Ichiro to the Yankees in July of that year. "Simply put, Ichiro changed Major League Baseball and the game at the international level," said Mariners president Howard Lincoln. "I'll miss watching the most exciting all-around player I've ever seen in my lifetime."

"When I imagine[d] taking off a Mariners uniform, I was overcome with sadness," said an emotional Ichiro at his sayonara press conference.

12 Dave Niehaus

Dave Niehaus called Mariners games on radio and TV from the franchise's inception until he died unexpectedly from a heart attack in 2010 at age 75. For many, he *was* the Seattle Mariners, a constant and stirring presence whose grace, honesty, and exuberance played well in both good times and bad. That's why a life-size statue of him sits inside of Safeco Field.

At first, however, Seattle didn't know what to make of Niehaus, an import from California hired away from the Angels. In one of his first public appearances, he was introduced as "Dave Neusse." Then when he finally took to the airwaves, Pacific Northwest baseball fans sniffed in disapproval. "All we heard about was Leo Lassen," said Ken Wilson, Niehaus' 1977 broadcast partner. Lassen had called Seattle Rainier games for three decades from the 1930s and set the standard for baseball play-by-play in the Puget Sound. "It was, essentially, that you guys will never be as good as Leo Lassen."

Born in Indiana, Niehaus attended the state's flagship university, where he planned to study dentistry. Those plans changed when he wandered into the renowned IU radio and television department and discovered a passion for broadcasting. Upon graduation in 1957, Niehaus landed a job covering the Los Angeles Dodgers for Armed Forces Radio. A few years later, he provided broadcasts of the New York Yankees and New York Rangers before heading back to Los Angeles to handle the major L.A. teams. He moved permanently into baseball in 1969 when the Angels hired him to team with Dick Enberg, a college classmate, and Don Drysdale to call games on radio station KMPC.

In 1976 the Mariners approached Niehaus about the play-by-play job. Minority owner and actor Danny Kaye, a Hollywood resident, had listened to Niehaus do Angels games and liked his work. Although Niehaus was comfortable in Southern California, the lure of being the No. 1 guy, after sharing a booth with two others, proved tempting. So, he flew to Seattle for an interview with Mariners president and general manager Dick Vertlieb. "I'll never forget walking into his office on First Avenue," Niehaus told *The Seattle Times* in 2008. "He had one chair, a barber's chair, the kind you pump up. I sat in the barber's chair, and he's over here, interviewing you. I spent all day interviewing with Dick." At the end of the day, Niehaus told Vertlieb his salary demands, an amount that exceeded the GM's salary. Vertlieb responded tersely that Niehaus wasn't going to make more money than him. "Dick, I don't care how much you make," Niehaus said bluntly. "This is what it's going to take to move my family and three kids."

The Mariners, of course, met his salary demands, and Niehaus eventually became the Leo Lassen of his generation, even bringing a piece of Rainiers history with him. He used to ring a bell from Sicks Stadium for each Mariner run scored.

For 34 seasons Niehaus' deep, expressive voice crackled from homes, offices, and cars throughout the Pacific Northwest. Armed with a curator's knowledge of baseball history, an unreserved zeal for his subject, an adept facility with words, a keen sense of timing, and aptly deployed candor ("you've got to tell the truth," he often said), Niehaus offered everything a baseball fan could desire in a broadcaster.

Signature calls? He had a chest full of them. *Swung on and belted*; *that ball will fly away*; *Get out the rye bread and mustard, Grandma, it's grand salami time*; *It's loooooowww and outside*; and *My oh my*! "Fly away" was Niehaus' home run call. He deployed it at varying lengths and decibels, depending on the type of round tripper and the circumstance. Homers in question during flight received the "Stairway to Heaven" treatment, building slowly in intensity. On no-doubters Niehaus paused. Then he ripped out a call that shook the booth. Then he fell into silence again as the ballplayer rounded the bases. "A home run call is certainly part of an announcer's signature," Niehaus said in a 1993 interview. "In 1978 I heard a music group on the radio, and they were singing something about 'fly away.' I knew it was good."

His ability to translate into words what he was seeing on the field? "He's like Red Barber or Mel Allen," said Tony Ventrella, a KING-TV sportscaster in the 1980s and early '90s. "He paint[ed] the picture for you as well as anyone has ever done. He [gave] you a sense of the drama and most important a sense of history and perspective." Ken Levine, Niehaus' broadcast partner in 1992, recalled a game against the Orioles that underscored Ventrella's praise. "I remember we were in Baltimore, and there was a routine fly to left field. Dave described it as a white dot against the black night. You just sit there and say, 'Wow.'"

Perhaps Niehaus' greatest strength was his ability to excel regardless of the circumstances. Lousy years and games never flattened his enthusiasm or professionalism. Without hyperbole or falseness, he could turn the routine into something worth appreciating. But when the occasion demanded the grandiose, like 1995, he also met the challenge. No Mariners fan will ever forget Niehaus' call of the winning runs in Game 5 of the American League Division Series. In a year bursting with memorable moments, Niehaus kept nailing it with spine-tingling calls and descriptions. "To this day…[I] still get goose bumps talking about 1995 because Dave made us feel it," said longtime broadcast partner Rick Rizzs. "Not too many announcers have the ability to make you not only see it and hear it, but feel it."

In 2008 Niehaus received baseball broadcasting's highest honor, the Ford Frick Award, and with it Baseball Hall of Fame recognition. "Radio plays with the mind," he said during his induction speech. "It gives you a mental workout and delusions of grandeur."

13 2000 Regular Season

As promised, the Mariners sunk a portion of the increased revenues from Safeco Field into the 2000 salary budget. They needed to. At Ken Griffey Jr.'s adamant behest, the Mariners traded their superstar during the winter. The return was intriguing but no sure thing.

The M's expanded budget, however, enabled astute new general manager Pat Gillick, who had built Seattle's expansion mate Toronto Blue Jays into a powerhouse during the early 1990s, to fill numerous holes, starting with the bullpen.

Lefty Arthur Rhodes and closer Kaz Sasaki arrived via free agency to finally solve the M's stubborn bullpen problems. Former All-Star first baseman John Olerud, super utility man Mark McLemore, and starting pitcher Aaron Sele also came on board. Center fielder Mike Cameron and Griffey swapped places in the trade. "Look at our club, and it's gotten a heck of a lot more solid in a hurry," effused manager Lou Piniella during the offseason. None of the acquisitions were a whiff, including Rickey Henderson, whom the M's added in May. The 41-year-old future Hall of Famer hit only .238, but his .362 on-base percentage and 31 steals served as a catalyst for the offense.

The newcomers helped the mainstays—Alex Rodriguez, Edgar Martinez, Jay Buhner, and Jamie Moyer—lead the Mariners to another franchise record in wins with 91. And another postseason appearance. In contrast to past M's playoff teams, this one prospered with pitching and defense. The Mariners finished second in the American League in both. The Kingdome-Safeco Field switcheroo doubtlessly played a part.

The Mariners peaked in June and July. The dog days of August stole their mojo before they recovered to duke it out with the

Oakland A's in a tight pennant race that whipped the emotions like a flag in a hurricane.

On August 11 the M's grew their lead to seven games over the A's, which Oakland chain sawed down to one-and-a-half two weeks later after the Mariners lost eight straight to the Cleveland

Edgar Martinez belts his 25th home run during the Mariners' 91-win season in 2000.

Indians and Detroit Tigers. Seattle's heretofore reliable pitching hit a slump, as the M's allowed nine runs or more in seven straight games—a streak of infamy duplicated only once in major league history, back in 1901.

The Mariners maintained a gossamer thin lead for the next month until the A's barreled into a frenzied Safeco Field. Oakland dazed the M's by taking the first three games to move one percentage point ahead. "We've been doing it with smoke and mirrors for 155 games," said Piniella, referring primarily to the offense, which during the series and for parts of the season hibernated. "We'll do it with smoke and mirrors for seven more." The Mariners salvaged the fourth game 3–2, putting on display their team's greatest assets. "It's not the same team in the past where you have guys hitting home runs" Martinez said. "The key is pitching and defense." The Mariners led the division by a game. They led the Indians by two games for the wild-card.

Oakland closed out the season like Secretariat, winning six of their last seven to move into first place. The Mariners finished strong as well, taking four of their last six and going 18–10 in September. But they needed to win their final two games in Anaheim to ensure a playoff spot. "We are out of mulligans," Piniella said after the Angels hammered the Mariners 9–3 on Friday night to knock them out of first place. On Saturday, the M's pulled out their driver and hit a 300-yard tee shot straight down the fairway. They clubbed the Angels 21–9.

That set up a tension-soaked Sunday. The Indians won early in the day. So did the Athletics to clinch the American League West. If the M's lost, Seattle would be forced into a playoff game against the Indians. The Mariners, who had lost seven of nine to Cleveland in the regular season, enjoyed playing the Indians as much as sailors enjoy bad weather.

Sele allowed two runs early. Single runs by the M's in the fourth and fifth inning tied the score. With the game still tied in

Walk-Up Music

The Mariners were one of the first clubs to regularly greet each home player at-bat with a song. The tradition began in 1993. Four notable songs: Ken Griffey Jr.'s "Hip, Hop Hooray" by Naughty by Nature, which triggered a wave of dancing in the Kingdome stands for each Griffey at-bat; Jay Buhner's "Bad to the Bone," which played off his nickname; Luis Sojo's "Macarena," which he adopted before it became an insanely popular global one-hit wonder and later dance; backup catcher Joe Oliver's and later Alex Rodriguez's "Who Let the Dogs Out," which an M's employee discovered and started playing before Oliver's at-bats. The heretofore-obscure song, which had claimed numerous different artists, became a staple at Safeco Field at the turn of the century.

the seventh, third baseman David Bell, known more for his glove than his bat, drilled a solo homer. Raul Ibanez, fighting through a second difficult season after seven years in the minors, added a two-run double. Sele held the Angels in check into the sixth inning. The big-game effort deep-sixed the reputation Sele had earned as a Texas Rangers pitcher of crumbling under pressure. The bullpen closed it out with three-and-a-third flawless innings. "We've been tense for half a year," Martinez said above the din in the joyous locker room, "This celebration is taking all that pressure out and having fun."

"We may have had bigger names in other years," said Piniella, who silenced the critics from the previous year. "But I told the players...this is the club I've probably enjoyed managing the most. They played with tremendous character, they played hard, they played to win."

14 Felix Hernandez

Signed out of Venezuela at the age of 16, Hernandez weighed 260 pounds. His youthfully chubby torso and puffy face were topped by a thick, bushy head of hair. "Fat Felix" is how Hernandez describes himself at that age. He would soon be known by an infinitely more flattering nickname.

With a fastball that touched 100, Hernandez turned heads almost immediately. Mariners scout Pat Rice breathlessly wrote that the young Venezuelan, who was 16 years old and a high school sophomore, had Hall of Fame talent. As he zoomed through the minors, toying with hitters in some cases years older, word spread quickly that something special was brewing down on the farm. In 2005 the Mariners promoted the 19-year-old to the big leagues. The day he took the mound, August 5 against the Detroit Tigers, everyone had already dubbed him King Felix, and anticipation for his debut roused a slumbering fan base.

Hernandez pitched five innings and struck out four while allowing two runs, only one earned. The Mariners lost 3–1, but King Felix's debut didn't disappoint. "He was a young fireballer that came up and was supposed to be the second coming," said his then-teammate Willie Bloomquist. The "second coming" finished out the year in a fashion that failed to dim everyone's soaring expectations. He went 4–4 with a 2.67 ERA.

Baseball isn't supposed to be this easy even for the supremely talented. The next season King Felix learned the game gets the best of everyone when he slumped to 12–14 while posting a puffy soufflé of an ERA at 4.52. Staggered by his first real baseball struggle, Hernandez dedicated himself to losing weight by changing his diet and working out more intensely. Thirty pounds lighter he went 14–7 with a 3.92 ERA in 2007. The next year he stumbled to 9–11 despite a solid 3.45 ERA. However, in his only at-bat of the 2008 season, he hit a grand slam. The blow, on June 23, 2008, remains the only grand slam by an American League pitcher in the era of the designated hitter.

He bounced back in 2009, winning 19 games and earning an All-Star berth, and hasn't looked back since, though Hernandez's velocity dropped a few years into his career, which initially spawned a cottage industry of concerned fans and pundits. It turned out that Hernandez was merely evolving as a pitcher. Early in his career, King Felix wanted to overpower hitters with his fastball. "I was just a young guy who threw hard," he told *Mariner Magazine* in 2014. "I realized that I didn't have to throw hard to get an out. If I hit the corners and messed with hitters by throwing breaking balls, I could be good." In the prime of his career right now, Hernandez works the corners, mixes in a stew of wickedly spiced breaking balls highlighted by a change-up, and features a 93 to 95 mph fastball that, in the words of Mariners catcher Mike Zunino, "moves four to five inches every time."

Since 2009 when Hernandez reined in the fastball and became a "pitcher," he has strung together a run of seasons remarkable for their consistent excellence. His ERA has yet to rise above 3.47 during that time. He regularly pitches late into games—and not just to eat innings. Since 2005 no pitcher has recorded more games with eight innings pitched while allowing fewer than one run than Hernandez. He also has the most quality starts during the same time period. In 2014 King Felix set a major league record by going at least seven innings while allowing two runs or fewer in 16 consecutive starts. "There are two pitchers I've been around in the last 10 years who I don't think you can separate in how consistent they've been from start to start," said M's pitching coach Rick Waits in *Mariners Magazine*, "and they're Pedro Martinez and Felix Hernandez."

Mariners fans adore Hernandez not just for his stellar work, which has included a perfect game and a Cy Young Award, but because he has shunned opportunities to leave Seattle. Twice he signed extensions to stay in the Pacific Northwest unlike so many past Mariner greats. After agreeing to a seven-year $175 million deal, Hernandez became emotional, breaking down when he encountered Mariners employees cheering him on his way to a press conference announcing the agreement. "It was unbelievable," he told *The Seattle Times.* "He engages people on a personal level," said Randy Martinez, Mariners vice president of marketing.

Hernandez, just one of the guys in the clubhouse and accessible outside of it, embraces his status as the face of the franchise. That's another reason fans adore him. They show up in droves to sit in King's Court for each of his starts at home, regardless of how well the team is doing. Hernandez's time as a Mariner has coincided with the franchise's crushing difficulty to score runs, which has dramatically depressed his win totals and perhaps cost him even more Cy Young Awards. "It's baseball," Hernandez says. "It happens."

15 2001 Postseason

In the playoff era, which began in 1969, six teams had won at least 105 games. Only the 1998 Braves had failed to reach the World Series. The mood around Seattle and in the M's clubhouse before the 2001 playoffs was World Series or bust. "Everybody in here wants to win the World Series title," said Mark McLemore. "Everybody. That's what it's all about."

But days before the end of the magical regular season, the Mariners suffered a scare that hung over the clubhouse the rest of the year. Carlos Guillen was diagnosed with tuberculosis and put on the disabled list through at least the American League Division Series. All of his teammates had to be tested for the airborne spread disease. Nine tested positive, though none showed symptoms. They were put on preventative medication for nine months.

In Game 1 of the ALDS against the Cleveland Indians, the Mariners appeared drained and distracted. Indians starter Bartolo Colon stopped them cold, shutting the M's out on six hits in eight innings. The heart of the Mariners order went one for 19. Safeco Field, rocking before the first pitch, fell into uneasy silence as the game ended.

Safeco reawakened the next day, when Moyer, who had bewildered Cleveland twice during the regular season, turned the tables on the Indians. He blanked the Tribe through six-plus innings. The bullpen allowed a harmless run as the Mariners evened the series with a 5–1 victory. Mike Cameron and Edgar Martinez paced the offense with homers. "Moyer dominated us," said Indians general manager John Hart. "The only other pitcher who can dominate us four games a season is Pedro Martinez."

The series moved to Cleveland. One of the few—perhaps only—embarrassing 2001 regular season moments experienced by the M's occurred at the hands of the Indians. In August the Tribe wiped out a 12-run deficit to beat and humble the Mariners. In Game 3 Cleveland struck again, embarrassing Seattle with a 17–2 thrashing. The Indians celebrated intemperately, as if they'd wrapped up the series. "It may have been 17 runs, but it was one game," warned an annoyed Cameron.

Jacobs Field hummed the next day as the Tribe went in for the kill. For six innings it appeared the previous day's shellacking had stunned the Mariners into a state of paralysis. The Tribe's ace, Bartolo Colon, held the M's without a run, which extended his scoreless ALDS streak to 14 innings. Luckily, Freddy Garcia mowed down the Indians as well, though he'd been nicked for a single run in the second inning.

After 116 wins…we couldn't lose 1–0, Mariners reliever Jeff Nelson remembers thinking. "But we hadn't done anything for six innings. You're thinking, *Oh my God.*" Then the best situational hitting team in baseball scraped together a run on a walk, a hit-and-run, and a sacrifice fly. That brought up Ichiro, the only Mariner in the series with a hot bat. The right fielder took a 97-mph waist-high fastball and squirted it into right field to score the go-ahead run. Tom Lampkin laughed on the bench, saying: "How does he do it? I don't even know if he's aware that guys are on base. His ability to stay on an even keel is amazing." The Mariners never relinquished the lead and won 6–2 to even the series.

Game 5, back home in nervous Seattle, remained tight throughout. The Mariners scored two runs in the second on a single by Mark McLemore. Jamie Moyer continued to mystify the Tribe, yielding just one run. In the fourth, he struck out the side, ringing up the meat of the Indians order, Juan Gonzalez, Ellis Burks, and Jim Thome with called third strikes. It was the only time all season Moyer struck out the side. "He's the Greg Maddux of the American League," said Indians shortstop Omar Vizquel after Moyer wiggled out of a bases-loaded, one-out jam with a double play off the bat of Roberto Alomar, who had hit .424 during the regular season with runners in scoring position. "You know what he is going to throw, but somehow he gets you."

Moyer departed in the seventh. The M's added a run in the bottom of the seventh, and the bullpen slammed the door for a 3–1 win. The Mariners and Seattle breathed a sigh of relief equal to that of a motorist who walks away unscathed from a rollover accident. The World Series dream, which hung by a thread at times during the ALDS, remained alive.

The Yankees, in the unfamiliar role of sentimental favorite due to the city's devastation on 9/11, quashed the Mariners' dreams in the American League Championship Series. Edgar Martinez suffered from a pulled groin and scuffled, and the rest of the M's bats, mostly quiet against Cleveland, remained stuck in neutral. Seattle lost the first two games at home. Piniella publically vowed the Series would return to Safeco Field. But after winning Game 3 in New York 14–3, the Mariners blew a late lead and lost on a walk-off homer in Game 4. The season ended with a thud the next day as the Yankees snuffed out the Mariners' World Series hopes with a 12–3 thumping. Yankees fans and media skewered Piniella for his prediction. Privately, the M's manager admitted, "he felt good for [New York]," considering the suffering the city had been through.

"It wasn't supposed to be like this," said a disconsolate Bret Boone afterward. "It wasn't supposed to end here." Even though it ended unceremoniously, the 2001 season had been beyond remarkable. "I think 116 wins will stand for a long time," reflected Mariners president Chuck Armstrong.

16 Mariners Artifacts in Baseball's Hall of Fame

A visit to Baseball's Hall of Fame in Cooperstown, New York, is a bucket list item for every baseball fan. Naturally, Mariners fans who make the trek will want to browse the memorabilia pertinent to their favorite team. Here's what you'll find:

- Tickets from the first game in the Kingdome, vs. California, *April 6, 1977*
- Ball from the first game in the Kingdome, vs. California, *April 6, 1977*
- Glove and jersey worn by Gaylord Perry when he won his 300th game, *May 6, 1982*

- Ball used and cap worn by Randy Johnson when he threw a no-hitter, *June 2, 1990*
- Ball used and cap worn by Chris Bosio when he threw a no-hitter, *April 22, 1993*
- Bat used by Ken Griffey Jr. to record his eighth consecutive game with a home run, *July 20–28, 1993*
- Signed ball from Randy Johnson's 19-strikeout game, *June 24, 1997*
- Ball used by Randy Johnson during his 19-strikeout game against Chicago, *August 8, 1997*
- Cap worn by Ken Griffey Jr. when he hit three homers to set a major league record for most home runs in April, *1997*
- Bat used by Ken Griffey Jr. to hit 53rd home run, *September 17, 1998*
- Bat used by John Olerud to collect the first hit at Detroit's Comerica Park, *April 11, 2000*
- Spikes worn by Kazuhiro Sasaki when he was AL Rookie of the Year, *2000*
- Lineup cards from a game in which Shigetoshi Hasegawa faced Ichiro Suzuki, *April 13, 2001*
- Bat used by Bret Boone when he hit 33rd homer of season, breaking Joe Gordon's AL mark for most homers by a second baseman, *September 4, 2001*
- Ichiro bat from the ALCS after he won AL Rookie of the Year and MVP, *2001*
- Bat used by Mike Cameron when he hit four home runs against the Chicago White Sox, *May 3, 2002*
- Bat used by Bret Boone when he and Cameron twice hit back-to-back homers, *May 3, 2002*
- Ball from Jamie Moyer's 21st win, marking fifth time a team had used all five starters for entire season, *September 28, 2003*
- Ichiro bat used to collect his 262nd hit of the season, *2004*
- Ichiro bat used to collect his 200th hit of the season, *2004*

- Spikes, batting gloves, wristbands, sunglasses, and elbow guard worn by Ichiro Suzuki when he collected his 261st and 262nd hits, *2004*
- Ticket stubs from games in which Ichiro added to his hit record, *October 2–3, 2004*
- Game jersey worn by Edgar Martinez in the final contest of his career, *October 3, 2004*

17 2000 Postseason

Barely able to catch their breath, Seattle squared off against the Chicago White Sox in the American League Division Series.

The matchup was a contrast in styles. The Mariners won by asphyxiating offenses. The White Sox, who won 95 games and clinched the American League Central comfortably, napalmed pitchers with the best offense in the AL. Chicago's pitching, however, was in tatters, frayed by a rash of injuries primarily to their starting rotation. Only Game 1 starter Jim Parque, a 13-game winner, was completely healthy. "Gideon's Army," moaned Sox manager Jerry Manuel when asked about his staff on the eve of the playoffs.

The series opened in Chicago. In Game 1 the M's fall behind 4–3. Then in the fourth, starter Freddy Garcia found further trouble by loading the bases with one out. Brett Tomko relieved him. He repelled the Sox rally and pitched a total of two and two-third scoreless innings. The Mariners tied the game in the seventh on Mike Cameron's single then won it 7–4 in the 10th on back-to-back homers by Edgar Martinez and John Olerud.

Before Martinez's homer, Piniella called timeout to chat with Mike Cameron, who had singled and was trying to steal second base. No one had ever seen a manager call timeout to deliver instructions to a runner. Piniella told Cameron the exact pitch to run on. "He said if the catcher sets up outside, it would be a pitch I could run on," said Mike Cameron in *Tales from the Seattle Mariners Dugout*. "The guy calls a timeout and tells me how to steal a base. Unbelievable." Asked what he said to Cameron, Piniella joked: "I told him the NASDAQ was down 113 points today. And Cisco was a hell of a buy."

In Game 2 Jay Buhner launched a 399-foot homer off Mike Sirotka, a member of Manuel's Gideon's Army due to a tender elbow, and Paul Abbott gave the Mariners a strong five and two-third innings to pace a 5–2 win. Two road games. Two wins. And little to complain about. "We need the rest," said Buhner in reference to a possible sweep. "We've had a month of tough games."

Returning to Safeco Field in front of 48,010 delirious fans for the park's first postseason ever, the Mariners and ChiSox wrestled to a stalemate over eight innings. Entering the bottom of the ninth, the score stood 1–1, and John Olerud led off with an infield single and advanced to second on an error. Rickey Henderson pinch ran and moved to third base on a bunt by Stan Javier and to third on an error. With no outs Piniella called for a squeeze. He told pinch-hitter Carlos Guillen to bunt toward first because Frank Thomas "can't throw a lick." But Guillen, in his lone at-bat in the series, swung at the first pitch and fouled it off. Piniella steamed on the bench. On the next pitch, though, Guillen laid down a perfect drag bunt toward Thomas to easily score Henderson. The Mariners swept the series, and Buhner got his wish. "Imagine winning a series on a dang squeeze," said a relieved Buhner.

The bedrocks of pitching and defense led the way with squirts of small ball and power. "Pitching and defense are the constants of the game," Piniella said. "Our defense kept making plays, [and] our bullpen did a fantastic, fantastic job." Piniella had a spectacular series as well. "It was exciting to watch him manage," Buhner said.

"He usually had three different scenarios going at once. He was way ahead of everybody else." Manuel even conceded he'd been "outmanaged" in the series.

Up next: the Yankees. New York had lost 15 of 18 down the stretch in September and won only 87 games. A shell of their recent juggernauts, they nonetheless rallied to take down the favored Oakland A's in the ALDS.

Before the Yankees series, Jamie Moyer, a Yankee Killer during the regular season, was injured on the final pitch of a simulated game. A batted ball fractured his left kneecap. Moyer missed the series, and the M's lost in six games. "I believe if we'd had a healthy Jamie Moyer...we would have beaten [New York]," said Piniella a year later.

The Mariners won the first game 2–0 behind a masterful effort from Garcia. The next day, the Yanks blew open a close game in the eighth, scoring seven runs off Arthur Rhodes and Jose Mesa to win 7–1. Back home the M's took only one of three, salvaging the last game when John Olerud and Edgar Martinez clubbed consecutive homers in a 6–2 Seattle win. That sent the series back to New York for a sixth game, where the M's blew a 4–0 lead. Left-handed power hitter David Justice delivered the key blow, a three-run homer to give the Yankees a 6–4 lead. The Yankees tacked on three more, which made the three runs the M's scored off the usually untouchable Mariano Rivera superfluous in the 9–7 loss. "What hurts is knowing that it only comes this close so often...Still it was a great ride," said Buhner.

Alex Rodriguez, in what turned out to be his final game as a Mariner, went 4-for-5. Facing an uncertain winter, as A-Rod's free agency loomed and Piniella was without a contract, the manager reflected on the franchise's certainties: "With the new park, new revenues, the good fans, and good players, [Seattle] is one of the top 10 organizations in baseball."

18 Lou Piniella

Some say baseball managers don't matter much. Talk to anyone around the Mariners from 1993–2002 and you'd hear a list stretching longer than Randy Johnson's wingspan why that's bunk. They'd tell you Lou Piniella, the M's skipper during this time, mattered—a lot.

No one expected Piniella, a former Rookie of the Year, All-Star, and World Series champion manager, to seriously consider the Mariners job in 1992. The Mariners were looking for their 11th manager in 16 seasons, a fact that underscored the dreariness of the franchise's early years and dead-end nature of the job. Moreover, Piniella was an East Coast guy. His family lived in Florida, 6,000 miles away. Plus, he was in the midst of untangling a few business deals from his playing days that had gone sour, leaving him $350,000 in debt. But he was out of a job after willingly leaving the Cincinnati Reds and cheap, eccentric owner Marge Schott.

Mariners general manager Woody Woodward had tried to hire Piniella in 1988, but the effort died on the vine. This time around the Mariners were in a better state, and Woodward thought he could offer a winning argument. As a courtesy, Piniella agreed to meet in Seattle with the new owners. But he wasn't seriously thinking of taking the job. Several of the owners dined with Piniella and his wife. Woodward and John Ellis, the public face of the M's ownership group, left the dinner horrified. The other owners asked pointed, sometimes insulting questions. One wanted Piniella to explain why the Mariners should even consider hiring someone "just let go" by the Reds. "They were numbers guys and technical supermen interested in statistics," said Ellis in *Sweet Lou*. "And I thought, *My gosh, they're going to turn this guy off.*"

The opposite happened. Piniella felt challenged. Days later when Ellis asked Piniella if his heart would really be in the job and whether he could succeed where so many had failed, Piniella's competitive nature kicked into overdrive. After persuading his skeptical wife, he accepted the job, receiving a three-year deal for $800,000.

During his career Piniella played baseball with passion and fire. It made him a favorite of fans, especially in the Bronx, who appreciated his pedal-to-the-metal approach. He managed the same way. The Mariners knew of Piniella. They'd seen his animated arguments with umpires in New York and Cincinnati. They'd heard how he brawled with relief pitcher and All-Star Rob Dibble in the Reds dugout. They certainly expected a little different clubhouse from the one run by the placid Bill Plummer, Piniella's predecessor.

Days into spring training, they found out just how different. After the Mariners blew an 8–2 lead to the Chicago Cubs on a grand slam in the ninth, Piniella saw a park across the street where kids were playing catch. He barked at the bus driver as they were pulling out of the Cubs complex to "stop the f...ing bus." Piniella stood up and then snidely said: "Why don't some of you pitchers get off and see if you can get some of these kids out because you sure as hell can't get big leaguers out." Piniella then sat down, and the bus continued on in mostly silence.

Later that spring Piniella drove home another message when he locked the snack room at the M's Peoria, Arizona, Cactus League training facility for "discipline and sacrifice." Said M's pitcher Chris Bosio in *Sweet Lou:* "He's like, 'Apple Jacks? Cheerios? Sandwiches with freaking toothpicks? Flavored coffees? What the hell are we running here? This ain't no freaking country club.'" It would be the first of hundreds of clubhouse tirades over the next 10 years.

The most important and consistent message Piniella delivered from the start was that winning mattered the way breathing mattered. "Before [Piniella] got to Seattle, our goal was to finish above .500," Jay Buhner said. "Well screw .500...When I was traded from the Yankees, we were winning on every level. It was an organization where the mentality was imprinted on you that it's not how you would win but that you will win. If you didn't, we just ran out of outs today. Lou brought that mentality. And after a while, you're damn right people buy into it."

Losses of any kind tore Piniella up. Spring training, April, playing out the string, whatever. Lose two games in a row, and he'd stop shaving. Lose more, and he'd drop other daily routines, like buttoning his shirts. "I've never seen anybody so consumed with winning and what it takes to win as Lou," said assistant coach and future M's manager John McLaren in *Tales from the Seattle Mariners Dugout*. "That's all he's about. There are no false pretenses whatsoever."

Not surprisingly then, Piniella considered stats and personal glory for losers. Moving a runner over was valued over hitting a double—unless the two-bagger occurred in service to the former. Initially, M's superstar Ken Griffey Jr. distrusted Piniella. Part of it stemmed from discord between Lou and Griffey Sr. triggered by Piniella's decision to release Senior from the Reds in 1990. In short time, though, Griffey came around. "What you had to like most about Lou was that he let you go out and play," he said after Piniella's first season with the Mariners. "If he liked something, he told you. If he didn't, he told you, too…Guys respond to being treated right, treated honestly. He gave us everything we needed."

Everything included excellent dugout managerial skills. He picked up clues and tells from the opposition and regularly outmaneuvered the opposing skipper. Piniella owned New York Yankees manager Buck Showalter during the 1995 American League Division Series. "I always felt we had an advantage because Lou was in our dugout," said Mike Blowers in *Tales from the Seattle Mariners Dugout*. "He knew the other teams hitters and he knew their pitchers."

The Piniella advantage also included the skipper's sharp insights on hitting and his ability to pass along his knowledge lucidly. Said Edgar Martinez in *Sweet Lou*: "He knows hitting very well; he knows the swing. He loved it. He loved talking about mechanics, how to read pitches. He'd have other players indicate when they'd get a certain pitch, and Lou would give us ideas on how to get an advantage. He gave us a lot of ideas to help us in certain situations."

He also had lots of ideas on how to break out of bad habits or slumps and took an active role in searching for solutions to problems. Said pitching coach Bryan Price in *Sweet Lou*: "Lou would never be satisfied just watching a team go out and repeat the same performance. He's not going to watch the team struggle without doing anything about it." During hitting slumps, for instance, he would order even the highly paid middle of his lineup to hit-and-run and squeeze bunt.

One knock against Piniella was that he preferred veterans. It would be more accurate to say he preferred players thoroughly vetted. Every young ballplayer needed to pass a few tests before earning Piniella's trust. If he rode you hard, he liked your potential. If you stood your ground and barked back, he really liked you. It told him you wouldn't buckle under pressure. Said Bret Boone, a rookie Piniella's first year in Seattle, in *Sweet Lou*: "I always told the players, 'You need to go into his office, stand up to him, and you need to talk to him if you want to get his respect because if he doesn't respect you, he'll never accept you. It's important not to be afraid, to voice your opinion, to speak one-on-one." Catcher Dan Wilson, quiet and mild-mannered by nature, initially struggled to cope with Piniella's harsh tactics. But he weathered the storm and became one of Piniella's all-time favorites.

The Mariners struggled to find enough pitching during Piniella's first few years. The Kingdome, which was catnip to hitters, didn't help. But Piniella had a well-deserved reputation for disliking pitchers. He locked horns with Randy Johnson on a number of occasions, but to his credit, he knew when to back off. Piniella left most pitching duties to his coaches, who served as buffer between the manager and the staff.

Many who knew Piniella before Seattle thought he mellowed after coming to the Mariners. Ken Griffey Sr., who made amends with the skipper and joined him as a coach in Seattle, agreed. "More patient," he said when asked to explain the difference. Yes, he still raged against bad calls, hurled bases, destroyed water coolers, started fires in the clubhouse after tirades (once he kicked down the food table, which dropped lit sterno cans on the carpets underneath), terrified rookies with a knifing glare, and demanded excellence. "Now I look at the whole picture," Piniella said in a 1998 interview. "I want to win the war, and if I have to lose a skirmish or two along the way, who cares?" He also seemed to really enjoy his time in Seattle, revealing more emotion and a greater willingness to laugh.

When Piniella finally stepped down as Mariners manager after a 10-year run, he held every M's managerial record, including most wins, best winning percentage, and years managed. At the end Piniella decided to move on for a number of reasons. He feuded with new CEO Howard Lincoln over a comment he made to a Houston writer about the 1998 Randy Johnson trade, and then his father's health began deteriorating. In October of 2002, the Mariners released Piniella from his contract and, in an unusual move, traded him to Tampa Bay for a player. Piniella was elected to the Mariners Hall of Fame in 2014. Ceremonies included a luncheon attended by most of the big names he managed in Seattle.

19 Perfect Game

In the year of the perfect game, Mariners ace Felix Hernandez threw the *perfect* perfect game on August 15, 2012. No drama, until the end. No close calls. No hard contact.

In Major League Baseball history, only 22 perfect games (27 up, 27 down) had been thrown before Hernandez took the mound that day. Oddly, two of them had occurred earlier in 2012. More oddly, one came against the Mariners at Safeco Field, which inspired Felix. "I've got to throw one," he said to himself after watching Chicago White Sox pitcher Philip Humber throw a perfecto against his Mariners. Triple oddly, the Mariners had already racked up a no-hitter of their own two months ago when six M's pitchers combined to blank the Los Angeles Dodgers in Seattle.

Even though King Felix rolled into his Wednesday afternoon start against the Tampa Bay Rays on fire (three shutouts since June 28 and 4–0 with a 1.64 ERA in his previous seven starts), no one expected perfection. No sane baseball fan ever would. Add in the odds against a third perfect game in the same season (1,294–1) and, well, let's just say it seemed more than a long shot.

But warming up in the bullpen before the game, Hernandez discovered he had all four of his pitches—fastball, curveball, slider, and change-up—working exceptionally well. By the third inning, he knew this was no ordinary day. *Something's going on right now*, he said to himself. His teammates started noticing as well. "When you see [Rays All-Star Evan] Longoria swinging at balls in the dirt," said second baseman Dustin Ackley, "you know something has to be going on."

Tampa Bay's approach in the past against Hernandez had been to swing at fastballs early in the count. Hernandez crossed them up by going to his off-speed pitches early and often. Catcher John Jaso was a former Ray and knew the hitting tendencies of much of the Rays' lineup, which only enhanced Hernandez's repertoire. "He was able to just make pitches in any count," Longoria said after the

After pitching a perfect game against the Tampa Bay Rays in 2012, Felix Hernandez celebrates his historic achievement.

game. "The stuff was on par with anything I've seen." Added teammate B.J. Upton: "He was electric. That's just the bottom line."

After Hernandez struck out the side in the sixth, the crowd, especially the rabid King Felix section, started to sense something big was happening. There had been only two moments of danger—and they were mild. Outfielder Eric Thames tracked down Sam Fuld's first inning leadoff fly ball at the warning track. "I saw it hit, got on my horse, and went off and caught it," he said. Later, shortstop Brendan Ryan made a nice throw from the hole to edge the speedy Upton at first.

In the seventh, Matt Joyce worked Hernandez, who on the day only went to three three-ball counts, for eight pitches before grounding out. That same inning Rays manager Joe Maddon blew a gasket over what he deemed was umpire Rob Drake's overly generous strike zone. Drake ejected Maddon, whose old-school strategy to disrupt and rattle Hernandez in a tight 1–0 game failed. "I was yelling at Joe to get out of there," said Mariners manager Eric Wedge as Safeco Field lustily booed Maddon while he protested.

Hernandez gained strength as the game dragged on. In the eighth inning, he struck out the side. While King Felix barely broke a sweat, his teammates became increasingly anxious. "I don't know if Felix was nervous, but I was," said outfielder Franklin Gutierrez. "I was shaking and looking around." Echoed first baseman Justin Smoak: "That's the most nervous I've ever been in my life on a baseball field."

After retiring the first two batters in the ninth, Hernandez paused and took a walk around the mound to catch his breath. Then he fell behind 2–0 to Sean Rodriguez before rallying to even the count. The crowd, on its feet since the beginning of the ninth, screamed in anticipation. *Throw it over the plate. Throw it over the plate*, Hernandez said to himself. Jaso called for a change-up, and Hernandez delivered a beauty. It froze Rodriguez, who had been expecting a fastball. "Strike," barked the home-plate umpire.

Hernandez immediately pointed to the sky, contorting his body into the shape of a crooked V, a pose captured on film that's entered Mariners lore. The 21,889 Mariners fans, beaten down by years of losing, erupted in joy.

Though it was the third perfect game thrown against Tampa Bay since 2009, it was the first perfect game in Mariners history. "I can't believe that just happened," Jaso said to himself after Rodriguez fanned to end the game. "[Hernandez] never did struggle. He kept making good pitches the whole way through."

Hernandez struck out 12 batters in the 1–0 victory, just two short of Sandy Koufax's record for whiffs in a perfect game. He generated a remarkable 26 swing and misses and fanned five of the last six batters, one on a 96 mph fastball. "I don't have words to explain this," Hernandez said after the game. "[Mariners fans] deserve it. And I deserve it, too. It's unbelievable."

20 Jay Buhner

Like UPS, Jay Buhner delivered everywhere. He delivered at the plate and in the field. He delivered as a teammate and in the clubhouse. He even delivered as the rare modern professional athlete who didn't always shrink from the attention of fans outside the ballpark. Of all the glory year stars, Buhner was the most accessible, and his contributions traveled far beyond the white lines.

The Texas-raised outfielder arrived in crunchy Seattle via a July 1988 trade with the New York Yankees. He showed up wearing a cowboy hat, Wrangler jeans, and a brushpopper shirt. He also came with a nickname, "Bone," shortened from Bonehead. He earned it in high school when a fly ball lost in the lights landed on his head.

Buhner shook off the blow without injury, which prompted his coach to crack: "It's a good thing you've got a bony head."

Buried on the Yankees depth chart, Bone relished the chance to escape New York, even if Seattle represented the polar opposite in both baseball terms and personal style. But getting a chance to play every day—as the M's promised after giving up hometown veteran Ken Phelps in the trade—trumped everything. Mariners outfielder Henry Cotto had played with Buhner in the minor leagues. "You better believe Buhner can play," Cotto told a reporter. "He's big, strong, but he can run and throw and catch the ball." The M's immediately plugged him into the lineup, and he made his first delivery as a Mariner, hitting 10 home runs and walking 25 times in just 192 at-bats. And he displayed a bazooka arm with the accuracy of Google Maps. The only comedowns could be found in his batting average (.224) and excessive strikeout totals. Nonetheless, it appeared the M's had found a long-term answer in right field.

Jim Lefebvre arrived the next season and begged to differ. He sent a chapped Buhner down to the minors to start the 1989 season, even though Bone had led the M's during the spring in home runs and RBI. Lefebvre detested Buhner's high strikeout totals. Eventually, Bone forced his way back into Lefebvre's plans and the M's lineup. On June 5 Buhner hit a ninth-inning game-tying home run and as he crossed the plate he touched the bill of his helmet with his middle finger, staring down Lefebvre in the process. Buhner, who struggled to control his temper early in his career, sparred with Lefebvre during the manager's entire tenure with the Mariners. Their feud reached its apex in the middle of the 1990 season when Lefebvre pulled Buhner for a pinch-hitter. Bone went berserk. "Jay took a bat and went [into the tunnel] behind the dugout and started smashing the wall just in back of where Lefebvre was sitting," catcher Dave Valle said. "So Jimmy gets up and goes around the corner to confront him, but Jay is just in a fit of rage.

He had the craziest look in his eye, and we were afraid what he might do." His teammates eventually dragged him all the way into the locker room before things could escalate.

Buhner outlasted Lefebvre and really developed as a ballplayer and person under Lou Piniella, the Yankees manager, ironically, at the time of his trade to Seattle. He had his best year to date under Sweet Lou in 1993, and then as the Mariners fortunes improved so did his production. The latter was obviously a big reason for the former. Over a three-year period starting in 1995, Buhner hit 40, 44, and 40 home runs respectively. He walked a bunch, drove in more than 100 runs each season, and set career highs in slugging (.566 in '95) and on-base plus slugging percentage (.926 in '96). He also struck out 454 times. "You might as well pencil in 150 strikeouts for me," he once said. "But I'm not going to worry about it."

Neither did anyone else. Every at-bat seemed to end in drama—a home run, a knock, a violent hack at nothing but air. Nobody was hotter for the M's in the unforgettable September/October ride of 1995. Batting behind Ken Griffey Jr. and Edgar Martinez, Buhner swatted 14 home runs. None was more timely and pulsating than his bomb against Minnesota on September 13. That's when Buhner, who had hit homers in the four previous games, stunned the Twins with a three-run jack late to cap a 7–4 come-from-behind win. Only 16,000 Kingdome fans witnessed it, but Buhner's blast and the rally victory seized the city like a sun-drenched day, and crowds increased posthaste. "Where would we be without Jay?" Randy Johnson wondered as the Mariners wrapped up an epochal September.

Bone's bat did much of his talking. But few outfielders in the '90s featured a better arm. Second in outfield assists in 1991 and '92 (and first among right fielders), Buhner chopped down so many runners early in his career that opponents stopped challenging him. Coaches and managers regularly voted Buhner's arm the best among all major league outfielders. One assist on July 22, 1996, against the Milwaukee Brewers at the Kingdome is seared in the memory of anyone who saw it. Trailing 3–2, M's third baseman Doug Strange airmailed a throw to first on a bunt by Fernando Vina. The ball caromed around the bullpen area, and by the time Buhner, after sidestepping over the bullpen mound, had reached the ball, Vina, with good speed, was halfway to third base. For most right fielders, the prudent play would be to pocket the ball. But not for Bone. He wound up and unleashed a 230-foot frozen rope that nailed an incredulous Vina. Said Buhner: "I think a defensive play can ignite a team as much, if not more [than an offensive play]. "It can change the momentum and shut down a rally in a hurry." Indeed, the M's rallied to win the game.

Delivering on the field is something every major leaguer must do. Becoming a leader in the clubhouse is optional. Buhner stepped into that role willingly as a veteran, providing invaluable leadership as the young M's came of age. As the heat turned up in September of 1995, Buhner grew more vocal and active. He calmed his teammates with constant words of encouragement. He pushed them with gentle criticisms and challenges. And he echoed a steady mantra: "We are going to win the division."

Throughout the '90s the Mariners clubhouse consisted of a volatile mix of talent and personalities. Buhner bridged the gaps and helped knit the team together. "He was the one who could get along with everyone but who could still get on me or Randy Johnson or Edgar Martinez when we needed it," Griffey said. "There is one guy on every winning team that makes it all possible." Whether it was the eight to 10-person dinners made up mostly of rookies, for which he paid, or the pranks he cooked up throughout his career, Buhner helped maintain harmony and an effective level of looseness in the clubhouse. His strong relationship with his teammates lent a hand in keeping him in Seattle when he hit free agency. The M's considered letting Buhner walk after the 1994 season. But Griffey, who viewed Buhner as his closest friend on the team, made a threat to management: "If Buhner goes, I go." The M's wisely listened.

As the Mariners grabbed ahold of the city and some players grappled with the consequences of increased public attention, Buhner continued to engage the community and fans, who renamed right field "The Boneyard." Autograph seekers and inquisitive fans had an excellent shot at striking gold with the M's star right fielder. "People coming up to you, asking for autographs, taking pictures, talking about the game, all that stuff—is that such a bad thing?" Buhner told *Sports Illustrated* in a 1996 cover story. "I mean, think about it. Is that supposed to make me miserable? I think it's nice." Every year he invited his Issaquah neighbors over to see his lavish Christmas light display, and he and his family mingled comfortably among the throngs at Salmon Days. He also helped the Mariners with community outreach efforts and was the headliner in one of the M's most popular promotions: Buhner Buzz Cut night.

Buhner retired after the 2001 season, having been done in by the buzzkill of excessive injuries. His wrists, elbows, shoulders, ankles, knees, and feet all succumbed at some point to his hard-charging style. Ten times he hit the disabled list during his career. Buhner finished with 310 career homers, one All-Star appearance (1996), one top five MVP finish (1995), and, in a miscarriage of justice, only one Gold Glove (1996). "Not many people know what he meant to the team and organization," Griffey said. "They don't make many like him. In fact, they only made one, and he was a beauty." Buhner has made Seattle his permanent home. Turn on the TV, and chances are you'll see him hawking some local product—probably a pickup truck. He still matters in the Emerald City and has remained visible with the M's as well, providing occasional color on Mariners TV broadcasts. Said Buhner upon retirement: "Nothing can top us saving baseball in Seattle and having the satisfaction of being part of one of sport's biggest success stories ever."

21 Origin of Mariners Nickname

As a nickname for Seattle's baseball team, the Mariners certainly fits. Or so it seems after wearing it comfortably for almost 40 years. But, as was often the case in the Mariners' early years, the initial reaction to the name ranged from the indifferent to the indignant.

After a months-long contest in the spring of 1976, the Seattle baseball club announced the name of its team on August 24 of that year. The winning entry came from Roger Szmodis of Bellevue, Washington. Many other entries suggested the Mariners as well, but Szmodis' won the contest because the Mariners rated his explanation the best. All entries were limited to 25 words or fewer. Here's what the winner wrote: "I've selected the Mariners because of natural association between the sea and Seattle and her people who have been challenged and rewarded by it."

The Mariners received "approximately" 15,000 entries. Szmodis received two tickets to every Mariners game in 1977 and an expense paid trip to one West Coast series.

The nautical name failed to impress the media. "Mariners?" wondered *The Seattle Times* sports editor Georg N. Meyers. "It has to be a typographical error. Two months of contest. Three months of decision. And Mariners? Try it out: "M-A-R-I-uh—uh-N-E-R-S—whew! What's a Mariner? A Pilot, that's what it is. Pilots? We had that, didn't we?"

The paper also rounded up opinions from around town. Most Puget Sounders responded with a shrug—or worse. Here are a few reactions the paper printed:

"It doesn't ring a bell."

"I thought the name would begin with an S, like the Sounders, Seahawks, and Sonics."

"Mariners? It sounds funny for a baseball team. I thought they would go with something starting with an S. Yes, I was in the contest. I submitted Sovereigns."

"No way I am nuts about Mariners. Looks like they'll sink right away."

"They don't play baseball at sea. The names all right for water polo or a swimming team."

"Well, it's different. But it doesn't lend itself to shortening up. I submitted the Utopias, which could be shortened to Tops."

"Where did they get it? Does it have a meaning? I don't see the connection. It doesn't click with me."

The Utopias? The Sovereigns? Only in Seattle.

Anyway, back to Meyers. He continued ranting for a few more paragraphs before finally wrapping up with these acerbic but prophetic words: "Ah well—like living next to a paper mill—in time we will get used to it. We will, won't *me*." Two years later, in a meeting with new Mariners public relations director Randy Adamack, Meyers confessed that he just didn't like baseball, so it's probable whatever name Seattle chose Meyers would have derided it.

Another story that circulated at the time was that Buzzie Bavasi—president of the San Diego Padres, father of Toronto Blue Jays executive Peter Bavasi, and good friend of Mariners owner Danny Kaye—shared with Kaye that he really liked the name of

San Diego's minor league hockey team, which was the Mariners. This supposedly had some influence on Kaye as the organization reached its decision.

An interesting postscript is that Mariners was one of the five finalists in the naming contest the year before—for the NFL Seahawks. Seahawks was selected over Mariners, Sockeyes, Evergreens, and Olympics.

22 Mr. Mariner

In his 19-year Hall of Fame career, Chicago Cub Ernie Banks never played in the postseason. But that failed to diminish the adoration Cubs fans had for the man they called "Mr. Cub."

In Seattle the same could be said of Alvin Davis. He persevered through eight seasons when the Mariners were mostly a short seller's dream, finishing above .500 just once—during his last season with the M's. But Davis comported himself so exquisitely on the field and with such dignity, grace, and eternal optimism that announcer Dave Niehaus started calling him Mr. Mariner. The name stuck, and to this day, no one—not Junior, not Ichiro, not even Edgar—has usurped Davis as Seattle's Mr. Mariner.

As Davis entered junior high in Riverside, California, he discovered that Atlanta Braves great Hank Aaron taught himself to hit by using a broomstick and rocks. "So every day I was out in the back hitting rocks into the orange groves," Davis said. "Pretty soon I graduated up to an old aluminum bat, which I then proceeded to beat up pretty badly."

The San Francisco Giants and Oakland A's drafted Davis three years apart. Neither could coax him into signing. He finally signed with the Mariners as a sixth-round pick in 1982 after starring at Arizona State. "When he told the Athletics he wanted to remain in school and complete his education, some scouts thought he didn't have the intensity to play in the major leagues," said Hal Keller, Seattle's vice president of baseball operations. "But I saw him in high school, and he was already an outstanding hitter. He just didn't have a position yet. He had tried to play third and he couldn't do that. But we knew he could hit."

Davis rampaged through Double A as a 21-year-old and again as a 22-year-old, exhibiting a sharp eye, high contact skills, and decent power. Heading into the 1984 season, the M's had planned to give Davis, who needed more polish as a first baseman, extensive time at Triple A Salt Lake City. The burgeoning prospect just hoped for a September call-up. But in April Ken Phelps, the Mariners' starting first baseman, hit the disabled list with a broken finger. Davis got the call to replace him. "He's one of the finest young hitters I've ever seen," Keller said days after Davis' promotion.

He showed why two at-bats into his career.

After a lazy fly ball out in his first major league at-bat against Boston's Dennis Eckersley, Davis came up again in the fourth of a scoreless game with two men on. He got ahead in the count, as he would so many times in his career, and then turned on an Eckersley fastball. The ball ripped through the upper reaches of the Kingdome before slamming off the second-deck façade in right. "I felt the contact, and that was it. It was an awesome gift, to have that happen in your first ballgame," Davis said. The home run staked the M's to a 3–0 lead they would not relinquish. Later, the Red Sox intentionally walked Davis in his final at-bat, an incredible sign of respect for someone making his debut. "When I ran back on the field to start the next inning [manager] Del Crandall told me to make sure I tipped my hat to the crowd," Davis said. "I did, but basically, I'm not into the attention. I'd rather just run out and play the game and have fun."

Fun pretty much describes Davis' rookie year. He hit successfully in his first nine games, including four homers and five doubles, and continued tormenting American League pitchers through September. In July he played in the All-Star Game, the first homegrown Mariner to make the Midsummer Classic. The 6'1", 195-pound Davis possessed a classically sweet left-handed swing. But what set him apart from most young hitters was his advanced ability to recognize pitches. "A lot of people look at all the walks he gets and credit it to Alvin's patience, experience, or maturity," explained Mariners hitting coach Ben Hines. "But he was gifted very early in life with exceptional perception of where the ball is going to be pitched. His eyesight lets him wait an extra split second, see the velocity, movement, and direction of the pitch, and that gives him a real edge."

Davis routed the competition in winning the American League Rookie of the Year, the first major national award of any kind for a Mariner. He hit .284 and belted 27 home runs. He also set club records in RBIs (116), game-winning hits (11), and grand slams (two). Davis, who early in his career consistently walked more than he struck out, also drew 16 intentional walks, a major league record for rookies. "He's as good looking a hitter as has come into the league in years," said Toronto Blue Jays manager Bobby Cox.

Patience, power, and poise summed up Davis for the remainder of his career. He averaged about 90 walks his first eight seasons, finished in the top ten in on-base percentage five times and twice landed in the top ten in extra-base hits. Other career highlights included nine grand slams and four homers in four consecutive games. When he retired as a Mariner, he held club records in career hits (despite lead feet that limited infield singles), doubles, home runs, RBIs, total bases, extra-base hits, and walks.

Just as the Mariners' long climb to respectability appeared ready to set sail, Davis' skills abruptly deserted him. He endured his worst season ever in 1991, the year the Mariners posted their first winning season. Eligible for free agency, the M's let him leave without making an offer. He signed with California, but the Angels released him 40 games into the 1992 season so he could join a team in Japan. That ended his major league career.

In his final major league game, played against the Mariners in Seattle, the M's honored Davis in front of 14,219 fans at the Kingdome. His two best friends on the Mariners, Harold Reynolds and Dave Valle, took part in the pregame ceremony. Davis' voice cracked a few times during his emotional farewell speech. "It's good to be home," he told the crowd. "This is my home. Everything good that ever happened to me was right here in front of all of you." In 1997 the Mariners made Davis their first selection to the Mariners Hall of Fame. "I'm still a Mariner in my heart," Davis said.

23 The Kingdome

Just as the Kingdome was opening in 1976, the public's fascination with multipurpose stadiums, which had been in vogue the past decade, began a fast plummet. The stadium, used by both the Seahawks and Mariners, personified many of the genre's worst qualities, especially as a baseball venue: poor sight lines, colorless atmosphere, and dreary aesthetics.

Add it all up, and the result was a stadium obsolete the day the Mariners debuted. The combination of losing baseball and uninviting environs helped depress attendance in the early years and contributed to the national perception that Seattle was at best indifferent to Major League Baseball.

The Kingdome, like the Mariners themselves, grew out of a dispute between Seattle and Major League Baseball. The city scrambled to build the park in an attempt to save the Pilots, but finding land and funding proved troublesome. The city finally broke ground in November of 1972—two years after the Pilots had relocated to Milwaukee. Construction continued uninterrupted, however, as Seattle lured the NFL expansion Seahawks as a tenant and then used the Kingdome's ongoing construction and looming completion to help in a lawsuit against Major League Baseball that resulted in the creation of the Mariners.

Seattle never embraced the Kingdome unconditionally, certainly not as a baseball park. Attracting fans to watch baseball indoors during beautiful Seattle summers always proved a difficult sell, particularly when the losses far outnumbered the wins. "It's especially tough on nice days," said Mariners reliever Jerry Reed in 1988. If the Kingdome was especially tough on nice days, it was mercilessly tough on pitchers every day. The ball easily cut through the dome's artificial air, and the short outfield fences (315 down either foul line, which were 10 feet shorter than originally posted) upended the career of many pitchers.

Not surprisingly, the Kingdome earned a number of unflattering nicknames over the years. The Tomb was one. Others included The Mausoleum ("It's as inviting as a mausoleum," wrote a *Sport Illustrated* reporter in 1988), The Concrete Coffin, and The Accident on Occidental. And decisions made in service of finishing the stadium's construction in a timely manner led to future problems, none more damning and dangerous than when four huge ceiling tiles fell before a Mariners game in 1994. The cost to repair the damage exceeded the cost of building the entire Kingdome 20 years earlier.

Despite the Kingdome's warts, many Seattle baseball fans retain fond memories of the stadium—particularly on its Opening Night in 1977. "The Kingdome, to me, was the most beautiful arena I'd been in in my life at that particular time," recalled Dave Niehaus in a 2010 interview with *Baseball Prospectus*. "It was vibrant, it was alive, and it was breathing. Humanity was there." Tens of thousands of Seattle humanity saw their first Major League Baseball game at the Kingdome, bathed in the thrill of postseason baseball, and watched a quartet of worthy Hall of Famers. And no fan can deny that without the Kingdome Seattle would probably still be a minor league town.

The Mariners fled the Kingdome in July of 1999, and it was demolished to make way for a new Seahawks stadium in 2001. Today, you can see remnants of the Kingdome at the Museum of History and Industry (MOHAI) on South Lake Union. On display is home plate circa 1990. Dozens of other artifacts are stored in MOHAI's off-display collection, including a row of seats and a pitcher's mound.

24 1995 Supporting Cast

Tino Martinez

The lesser Martinez and first-round pick of the Mariners in 1988, the first baseman finally started slugging in 1995. Well, he'd slugged before, but in '95 the 27-year-old mashed in the fashion of other bruising, fearsome first basemen. He hit 31 bombs while batting .293, both career highs. Bases-loaded situations were his catnip. Martinez delivered at a .480 clip. The Sunday before the All-Star Game, which he made as a replacement, Martinez hit a towering grand slam for four of 111 RBIs he collected on the year. When Tino hit another slam against the Detroit Tigers, Mariners broadcaster Dave Niehaus unveiled a call destined to become another trademark: "Get out the rye bread and mustard, Grandma, it's grand salami time." Martinez also had three two-homer games, the last September 24 when the second tater beat Dennis Eckersley in the bottom of the ninth. The M's traded Martinez during the offseason, triggering a mini-revolt among fans.

Luis Sojo
Sojo's cue ball double down the first-base line blew open the tiebreaker against the Angels. Manager Lou Piniella handed the shortstop position full-time to the journeyman infielder in August. Lacking range, he compensated by turning every ball he could reach into an out. "I'm not spectacular, but I make the plays," Sojo said. "I can't make a mistake on the routine play." He hit a career high .289 and also had a game-winning hit in the American League Championship Series.

Joey Cora
The double-play partner of Sojo, Cora was for Mariners opponents the annoying little nephew: a small pest who ruined holidays. He bunted, blooped, and bleeded his way to a career high .297 in '95, including .392 in August and two walk-off hits. Two drag bunts played pivotal roles in Games 4 and 5 of the American League Division Series. He had some flair at second base, though throwing problems plagued him throughout the year and led to a team-high 22 errors. A diving stab of Jim Thome's one-hopper in Game 1 of the ALCS highlighted his defensive skill.

Vince Coleman
Acquired in a waiver deal on August 15, the former St. Louis Cardinals stolen-base king and outfielder was just the medicine the Mariners needed at leadoff. Coleman stole 16 bases, scored 27 runs, and collected 47 hits in just 40 games. One of his hits was his first career grand slam, which helped erase a 6–0 deficit against the Oakland A's on September 22 and set up more dramatics in the later innings. He also scored six runs in the ALDS.

Rich Amaral, Alex Diaz, and Doug Strange

Amaral and Diaz platooned in the outfield while Griffey missed time with an injury. Amaral hit .297 in Griffey's absence and smacked a homer in the 12th to beat the New York Yankees on May 29. Diaz went deep in his first at-bat as a Mariners player, only the second of his four-year career. Then he belted the most unlikely Mariners home run of the year, a three-run, pinch-hit blast to beat the A's on September 22. Strange delivered endless pinch-hit knocks, the biggest a bottom-of-the-ninth two-run homer to force extra innings against the Texas Rangers on September 19.

Norm Charlton

One of the Nasty Boys on Cincinnati's 1990 champions, Charlton missed the entire '94 season due to Tommy John surgery. Fence post digging at home in Texas helped him rebuild strength in his left-handed throwing arm. In his second tour with Seattle, Charlton, traded to the Mariners at the deadline, provided devastating lockdown heat in the late innings. He assumed the closer role in late August and recorded saves in nine consecutive appearances from August 29 to September 16. "I was on the Cincinnati team that won a world championship and I was on the Seattle team that won 116 games," said Charlton in *The Grand Salami* magazine in 2005. "But by far the '95 season was the most enjoyable."

Andy Benes

Another veteran picked up in a trade mid-season (from the Padres), Benes won four consecutive starts in a critical September stretch. He also started Game 5 of the ALDS. When Benes made his first Mariners start, Jay Buhner pulled him aside: "Just keep us within six runs in the first five innings, and we will figure out a way to win." Such was the runaway confidence of the 1995 Mariners.

Jeff Nelson and Bobby Ayala

Ayala held down the closer's job early in 1995, not blowing a single save through early June. Nelson appeared in 62 games, bridging the critical innings between the starter and closer. His three-quarter delivery and wipeout slider kept right-handers especially in check. They hit a measly .191 against him. He was traded to the Yankees the next season and enjoyed a long run in New York before returning to Seattle and the M's next magical year. "All the World Series I've been in," Nelson said, "[1995] was still probably the most exciting two months I've ever been in."

25 Randy Johnson's No-Hitter

Heading into June of 1990, 26-year-old Randy Johnson had yet to achieve consistency in his young career. In the first two months of the season, the Big Unit alternated between good starts and bad, struggling with control of his upper 90s fastball and slider. His ERA pushed 5.00, he walked nearly as many hitters as he struck out, and he allowed home runs at an alarming rate. In Johnson's last start of May, the Blue Jays lit him up for three more homers and five runs. "Not to take anything away from Toronto's hitters, they're good hitters, but [Johnson] makes it a little easier," said Mariners catcher Matt Sinatro. But then the catcher struck a hopeful note: "The pitchers that are successful are the ones who minimize mistakes. He's coming close to becoming a complete pitcher." On June 2 Johnson took a step the size of the Coulee Dam toward fulfilling Sinatro's prediction.

Near the end of an 11-game homestand in which the M's had struggled, the Mariners needed a lift. They had blown an early lead to the Detroit Tigers the night before and had to remove starter Scott Bankhead in the second inning due to an injury. Rumors spread that Bankhead, the M's best pitcher the previous year, could be lost for the season. Visions of past season meltdowns started to elbow out the optimism so pervasive in the spring.

Johnson's opponent, the Tigers, had lost more than 100 games the year before, but they had strengthened their lineup with Cecil Fielder, a 26-year-old thumper who had spent the previous season learning to hit the curveball in Japan. Fielder already had clouted 19 home runs.

The base paths buzzed with traffic early in the game, especially for the Mariners who turned eight base runners, six on walks, into a single run through four innings. Two Tigers reached base, both on walks, but Johnson allowed no damage. Then the M's pitcher, struggling with control of his fastball, loaded the bases in the sixth on three more walks. With two down, Chet Lemon, a notorious Mariners Killer, stepped to the plate. The crowd of 20,000, snoozing through a game with more walks than base hits, suddenly came to life. To this point the Tigers had failed to center many of Johnson's pitches. Ken Griffey Jr. had chased down a long fly ball in the first, and third baseman Edgar Martinez snagged a ball destined for the hole in the fourth. Nothing else threatened to fall in. "He was throwing that slider over for strikes when he was behind in the count," said Fielder afterward on why the Tigers couldn't dent Johnson early.

Johnson fell behind Lemon 2–1 and then threw a breaking ball for a strike. The crowd roared. Lemon fouled off the next pitch. On the sixth pitch of the at-bat, Johnson unspooled a vicious slider, and Lemon swung through it for strike three. Then, abruptly, Johnson found command of his exploding fastball and retired the side in the seventh and issued only a walk in the eighth. "Usually I come in here on gamedays really high strung, but I was really relaxed," Johnson said, remembering. "And then, in about the seventh inning, to get

At Least 15 K

Twice as a Mariners player, Johnson accomplished the rare feat of striking out 15-plus hitters and walking no one. In the first game on June 14, 1993, he fanned 15 Kansas City Royals, including Kevin McReynolds four times, and didn't issue a walk. In the second game on June 24, 1997, the Big Unit whiffed 19 Oakland A's, including Mark Bellhorn four times, without walking a batter. The only Seattle pitcher to fan 15 or more hitters while posting a zero-walk game, Johnson even exceeded those rarefied performances after he left Seattle. He had a 20-strikeout, no-walk game for the Arizona Diamondbacks on May 8, 2001, a 17-strikeout, no-walk game for the D-Backs on June 30, 1999, and a 16-strikeout, no-walk game for the Houston Astros on August 28, 1998.

my mind off the no-hitter, I started tapping the drum beats I'd been practicing. I just got a beat and kind of got into my own world." A nice tag by first baseman Alvin Davis on an errant throw preserved the no-hitter in the seventh. As Johnson dealt in the late innings, the Kingdome crowd grew more attentive and loud. By the ninth every seat was empty, but nary a soul had left.

No Mariners pitcher had ever thrown a no-hitter. Weeks earlier Brian Holman had entered the ninth with a perfect game, but a home run with two outs spoiled any postgame confetti. That fresh wound created a mix of emotions as Johnson took the hill to start the ninth. Fascination. Anticipation. Dread.

Johnson fanned the dangerous Fielder to start the ninth and then retired Lemon on a pop up after falling behind 2–0. He immediately got ahead of catcher Mike Heath 0–2. The noise in the Kingdome peaked. Heath fouled off the next pitch. Then Johnson reared back and threw a fastball up and outside to the right-handed hitter. The Kingdome radar showed 97 mph, the hardest pitch Johnson threw all game. "I'm a fastball pitcher and I'm going down throwing fastballs," Johnson said postgame. "I'm not going to lose this on anything but my best pitch." Heath flailed hopelessly at

Johnson's best pitch to secure history. "Randy went after them with high fastballs and when Randy Johnson has his good high fastball, no one is going to catch up to it," said his catcher Scott Bradley, who had to reach up and way out of the strike zone to catch the no-hit clincher. "The man pitched a great game and deserved what he got," stated Fielder in the visitors' locker room. Heath, accepting his fate with less grace, vented his frustration afterward by destroying a TV set with his bat.

Johnson struck out eight, five in the last four innings, and walked six during the 2–0 victory. "Every time Randy goes out there, he's got the ability and the stuff to throw a game like this," offered his manager, Jim Lefebvre.

For the Mariners the no-hitter represented another step toward relevancy. For Johnson, who won his next six starts with five quality outings and one 10-strikeout performance, the no-no launched him on his way to a Hall of Fame career. "After it was over, I didn't know how to react," he said after the game. "It's the greatest thrill in the world. It's a great joy to do it. It's an accomplishment I'll probably never do again." Two other times in a Mariners uniform, Johnson carried a no-hitter into the ninth before they were broken up. In a different uniform, a decade and a half later, he bested his no-hitter with a perfect game.

26 1977: The First Season

The Seahawks had just finished their inaugural season by losing 12 of 14 games. The SuperSonics, in town now for almost a decade, had fallen far short of the first part of their nickname, logging only three winning seasons in their nine-year history. The Pilots,

Seattle's first Major League Baseball team, vanished after a single season. That summary of the city's sad-sack experience with professional sports set the backdrop to the return of professional baseball to the Emerald City.

But Seattle sport fans approached the Mariners with a mostly open mind and growing anticipation. The day before Opening Day, manager Darrell Johnson participated in a parade down Fourth Avenue with his new team. Despite an afternoon marred by vintage cold and gray, fans quickly filled in every open space along the street.

On April 6 a sellout crowd of 57,762 shoehorned into the Kingdome, a Major League Baseball attendance record for an evening Opening Day. "There was just incredible excitement," recalled the late announcer Dave Niehaus. "Anticipation. A new baby. Hopes. I was nervous. The fans were so happy. I'll never forget that night." U.S. senator Henry "Scoop" Jackson threw out the first pitch. The Mariners ownership group, including entertainer Danny Kaye, shared a box with MLB commissioner Bowie Kuhn.

The M's lost, but the only boos rained down on Kuhn. "What matter the score," wrote *The Seattle Times*. "After seven years of travail, baseball is back in Seattle—to stay." The Angels' Frank Tanana shut out the M's 7–0. Said Shortstop Craig Reynolds postgame: "Yes, we were jittery, so many people and all that. Once we got untracked, we played decently. We'll be back."

The M's didn't win the next night. They also again failed to score a run, getting shut out by Nolan Ryan 2–0. Niehaus started wondering whether the Mariners would ever score a run—let alone pick up a win—and why he had accepted the team's announcing gig. *My god, what kind of decision did I make*, he thought.

That the Mariners lost their first two games and didn't look particularly good doing it was about as surprising an event as the gray skies and drizzle outside the Kingdome that first night. Only Seattle's makeshift spring training facility in Tempe, Arizona,

Those who attended the Mariners' home debut on April 6, 1977, received this certificate. (David Eskenazi)

scarred by rocks in the infield and gopher holes in the outfield, contained more blemishes than the M's roster. Indeed, one reporter covering early spring training scanned the field and concluded that the best looking Mariner was Vada Pinson, who was in uniform as the 38-year-old hitting coach and two years removed from his playing career. Most of the players had been picked up in the expansion draft, which offered slim pickings for the Mariners (and Toronto Blue Jays). They included: veterans near the end of their career, such as outfielder Lee Stanton, catcher Bob Stinson, and third baseman Bill Stein; younger players with a handful of mostly lackluster years, such as first baseman Dan Meyer and outfielder Dave Collins; and the greenhorns, such as outfielder Ruppert Jones.

The pitching staff remained unsettled all year. Seventeen different pitchers started games for the M's. Glenn Abbott, Dick Pole,

Two Highlights of the Maiden Season

July 24, 1977—Mariners pitcher John Montague pitched six and two-third innings of perfect relief, giving him 33 consecutive batsmen retired over two games to tie an American League record.

September 16, 1977— Seattle defeated the Kansas City Royals 4–1 to snap the Royals' winning streak at 16 games, the longest in the majors in 24 years.

Gary Wheelock, John Montague, and Tom House captured the most starts. The payroll stopped just short of $1 million. When a reporter from *The Seattle Times* asked Stinson when the team would be eliminated from the pennant race, the catcher quipped "Opening Day." The M's managed to stave off elimination until September 3, and in a bit of an upset they avoided triple-digit losses by winning 64 games. And in another minor victory, they finished ahead of the Oakland A's and out of last place.

The first win came in game No. 3 against the Angels. Behind 6–5 entering the ninth inning, the Mariners rallied to score two runs on RBI doubles by Stinson and Larry Milbourne. Then, in the fourth game of the five-game series with California, the M's dominated, winning 5–1 behind a four-hit, six-inning start by Wheelock, a rookie who had been rocked in spring training. The M's lost the next three games and never threatened .500 again.

Attendance at the Kingdome tripped along at between 9,000 and 20,000 until the New York Yankees came to town for a two-game midweek series in May. The M's won the first game 5–2 in front of 23,978, the third largest crowd of the season. Then the next night, in front of 42,132, Danny Meyer and Bill Stein hit home runs on consecutive pitches in the first inning to help the Mariners beat the mighty Yankees again. All at once, the Mariners had their first series win and sweep. The back-to-back dingers, line drives both, quieted chatter about raising the right-field fence, which opposing hitters had been clearing at a higher rate than M's hitters. Another 120,631 fans showed up for the weekend Boston series, which the Red Sox swept to drop Seattle to 11–27.

By late August and September, the wins started dwindling as rapidly as the hours of daylight, and the crowds thinned. Those who did show up developed bonds with a handful of players, especially Jones and second baseman Julio Cruz, who made his season debut in July. Final attendance settled at around 1.3 million, a middle-of-the-pack showing. It was solid for a 98-loss team but suggestive of future trouble, should the losing continue unabated. Most of the highlights belonged to the offense. Seattle finished eighth in the American League in home runs. Meyer hit 22, Jones hit 24, and Stanton hit 27. Collins and Cruz almost singlehandedly helped the team finish fifth in stolen bases.

The pitchers, done no favors by the Kingdome, had a miserable year. They surrendered the most runs and home runs in the Junior Circuit. In 1977 home runs nearly doubled in the AL. The Mariners could take a few bows for that, especially on August 9 when M's pitchers allowed six home runs against the Chicago White Sox in a 13–3 loss.

An exchange (recounted in *Tales from the Seattle Mariners Dugout*) in Milwaukee between Stinson and pitching coach Wes Stock encapsulated the M's pitching woes. The Mariners gave Abbott a big first-inning lead, one he coughed up immediately, prompting Stock to visit the mound along with Stinson. Said Stock to Stinson: "How's his stuff?" Replied Stinson: "I can't tell you. I haven't caught any of his pitches yet."

27 Ichiro's Hit Record

For 84 years the record stood. It withstood the offensive eruptions of the 1930s and the years wrapped around the new millennium. All-time hits leader Pete Rose didn't break it. Babe Ruth never came close. George Sisler's record of 257 hits in a single season as a St. Louis Brown survived longer than Roger Maris' home run record and has lasted more years than Joe DiMaggio's consecutive game hit streak.

That's why 45,573 fans crammed into Safeco Field two days before the end of an otherwise dismal 2004 season, one that began an unwind of the glory years. The heroes of 1995 started retiring, others got old fast or injured, resources were misspent, and trades and prospects went awry. Bob Melvin, who replaced Lou Piniella in 2002, lost his job in 2004. The M's hired former Indians skipper Mike Hargrove, but he failed to disrupt the free fall. Over two years the M's lost 192 games and finished last in the American League West.

None of these sobering facts dampened the glow surrounding Safeco Field in the closing days of the 2004 season. Not with one of baseball's longest standing records in jeopardy. Sisler's hit record may have lacked the cachet of, say, Maris' home run record, but as Ichiro Suzuki crept closer to breaking it many in baseball, especially those in Seattle, started wondering why that was the case.

Sisler was one of baseball's greatest hitters for an eight-year period. In 1922 he batted .420, an American League record for left-handed hitters. The luminous Ty Cobb considered him his peer as a hitter. The only knock against the future Hall of Famer, in Cobb's view, was that he was too gentlemanly. He also never played in the postseason, spending his prime years with the nearly anonymous Browns.

After a 10-game road trip, the Mariners returned home for the final series of the season. Ichiro stood a hit shy of tying Sisler's record. The Mariners flew members of Sisler's family in for the game, including his 81-year-old daughter. George had passed away in 1973, the year Ichiro was born. More than 150 members of the Japanese media elbowed their way into the pressroom as well. Everyone wondered how Ichiro would react if he broke the record. "I don't see him running around the stadium and giving high fives," Melvin said.

As Ichiro came to the plate in the first inning of the Friday night game against the Texas Rangers, the sellout crowd rose to its feet. On the first three pitches of Ichiro's at-bat, a strike down the middle and two foul balls, the sky turned white as thousands of flash bulbs burst simultaneously. On the fourth pitch, Ichiro swung and bounced a chopper over third baseman Hank Blalock's head. The vintage Ichiro hit set off fireworks and a two-minute standing ovation. Suzuki stepped off first and tipped his cap.

In the top of the third, Ichiro nearly cut the party short when he appeared to have injured himself after reaching for a foul ball. But it was a false alarm. "Even if I broke a bone here, I was going to get up to the plate," Ichiro joked.

In his next at-bat, he ended the evening's suspense by lining a full-count pitch into center field for the record breaker. His teammates streamed onto the field to congratulate him. Ichiro walked over to greet the Sisler family and bowed to them. "[My grandfather] would be proud of this man, this professional, and the job he is doing right now," said Sisler's grandson, Bo Drochelman, whose family relished the renewed interest in their accomplished but somewhat obscure relative. "[Ichiro's pursuit of the record] brought back the past with the present," said announcer Rick Rizzs.

The fans interrupted play for five minutes with another standing ovation. True to form Ichiro reacted with calm and grace, though he revealed more emotion than usual. "I felt a big relief,"

Ichiro said after the game. "To have the fans involved made it very exciting for me."

Ichiro finished the season with 262 hits and a .372 average, the eighth highest batting average since 1950. Opponents intentionally walked him 19 times, a record for a leadoff hitter.

Some in baseball questioned the significance of Ichiro's accomplishment. "He's just a singles hitter," usually began the argument. *Sports Illustrated* bulldozed over those critics thusly: "[Ichiro and his hits record] is the art-house masterpiece, not the box-office money champ, the simple song sung without dancers and wardrobe malfunctions. Excellence is not always sexy and exciting. This is a PBS record, not HBO."

Five years later during the 2009 All-Star break, Ichiro visited George Sisler's grave and laid flowers at his tombstone, which is located in Des Peres Presbyterian Church Cemetery in Frontenac, Missouri.

A-Rod

First Randy Johnson left in a messy divorce. Then Ken Griffey Jr. Mariners fans mostly blamed M's management for the departures of both superstars. When they returned—Johnson as an Arizona Diamondback in 1999; Griffey as a Cincinnati Red in 2007—fans greeted them with lengthy standing ovations.

Alex Rodriguez, the third exquisitely talented Mariner star to leave in a three-year period, provoked a much sharper response from Seattle fans. They booed him savagely every time he returned—first as a Texas Ranger and then as a New York Yankee.

That Seattle would treat Rodriquez like a pro wrestling heel would have seemed preposterous in the mid-1990s. He debuted at the age of 18 in 1994. He hit .358 as a 20-year-old and finished second and should have finished first in MVP voting. He averaged 42 home runs from ages 22 to 24. And with the glove, he evoked memories of Omar Vizquel. By this time Mariners fans had seen their share of superstars for sure. But they had never seen the likes of Alex Rodriguez, who was so good, so ridiculously young. Said Boston Red Sox general manager Dan Duquette, only half jokingly: "The way he's going, someday he might bat .400 and hit 60 home runs. He's the best young talent I've seen in years." And yet he was so humble and likeable. Wrote *The New York Times'* Murray Chass: "At age 21, Rodriguez is…a phenomenal baseball player. He may be an even more phenomenal person. It is easy to walk away from a conversation with him wanting to take him home to be another child in the family."

Born in New York but raised in Miami, Rodriguez caused a major stir among scouts as the 1993 Amateur Draft neared. As hard as they tried, they couldn't uncover a single gap in his game or flaw in his character. Rodriguez had five-tool potential fused with baseball intelligence, resoluteness, passion, humility, and amiability. The Mariners owned the No. 1 pick, thanks to the ill-fated 1992 season, and targeted Rodriguez and—as a backup—pitcher Darren Dreifort. "Rodriguez is one of those special guys like Griffey, [Darryl] Strawberry, or [Shawon] Dunston," said Mariners scouting director Roger Jongewaard days before the draft. The Mariners wanted Rodriguez, and he seemed open to the idea of playing in Seattle until super agent Scott Boras got involved. Despite a series of awkward exchanges in which Rodriguez requested that the M's pass on him (presumably so he could land in a big market), the Mariners selected Rodriguez anyway. After months of tense negotiations, they signed him for a $1 million bonus just days before the start of classes at the University of Miami. Rodriguez went against the advice of Boras and his sister in accepting the M's offer, which was $2 million less than Boras wanted.

A-Rod, as he was quickly dubbed, sped through the minors, hitting .312 with 21 home runs and 20 stolen bases over three different levels in his first year. The Mariners, desperate to settle the shortstop position, called him up on July 8, 1994. In the M's 4–3 loss to the Red Sox, Rodriguez impressed more with his glove than his bat—as the M's expected. He started a double play with a nifty feed to second base in the fifth inning. On the next batter, he went into the hole to rob Tim Naehring of a hit on "a play not seen since Omar Vizquel left Seattle," wrote *The Seattle Times*. A-Rod was not the only one flashing leather in the game. The Red Sox shortstop John Valentin squashed a sixth-inning M's rally with the 10th unassisted triple play in major league history and only the second in the last 26 years. Said Rodriguez after the game: "I'll never forget it. I loved everything but the score." Days after Rodriquez turned 19 on July 27, the M's farmed him out to Triple A Calgary. He had hit just .204 with no power in 17 games for the Mariners.

Rodriguez received a longer look in 1995, hitting .232 in 48 games. He was mostly background noise as the M's surged to the American League West title. As with many young hitters, Rodriguez was pull happy. So during the spring of 1996, M's coaches worked with the 21-year-old to shorten his swing and concentrate on spraying the ball to all fields. He proved a quick study, putting together perhaps the greatest season ever by someone so young. A-Rod led the league in hitting (.358) and doubles, clubbed 36 home runs, knocked in 123 runs, and fell only three votes shy of winning the MVP. Said his manager Lou Piniella: "It came almost overnight."

In the process A-Rod exploded into a national sensation— almost as much for his staggering youthful production as for his character, which mesmerized the press. Profile after profile, at the local, regional, and national level, stressed the qualities that

Cycle Windfall

Alex Rodriguez became the first Mariners player to hit for the cycle in a nine-inning game in Detroit on June 5, 1997. He secured it with a shallow fly to right that landed just inside the foul line. No one cheered louder when the ball landed fair than Mariners fan Pamela Altazan. She won a contest sponsored by the M's that awarded $1 million to a lucky fan in the event any Mariner hit for the cycle.

so impressed *The New York Times'* Chass: humbleness, loyalty, respectfulness, generosity, politeness. "If I can lose the MVP every year because of my humility, I will lose it every year," Rodriguez said. In a *Sports Illustrated* cover story entitled "The Fairest of Them All," Rodriquez expressed his loyalty to Seattle, his love of baseball and its history, his admiration and respect for Griffey and the other M's star veterans, and his desire to be remembered more as a good person than a great ballplayer. He also revealed his favorite drink: milk.

It all seemed too good to be true—and it was. But not before Rodriguez enjoyed four more seasons in a Mariners uniform that rivaled Griffey. Only the third player ever to exceed 40 homers and steals, he smacked 42 homers and stole 46 bases in 1998. He also hit well over .300 in 15 postseason games as a Mariner, avoiding any prolonged October slumps.

At the end of the 2000 season, which included an American League Championship Series loss to the Yankees when A-Rod hit .409, Rodriguez was 25 years old and a free agent. His career line to date was a .309 batting average, a .374 on-base percentage, and a .561 slugging percentage with 189 homers. "When you look at it, he had the best production of any free agent in history at that time," Duquette told NBC Sports columnist Joe Posnanski in 2013.

During most of the 2000 season, Rodriguez repeatedly issued assurances that he wanted to stay in Seattle, that his priority was to sign with a winner, and Seattle offered that. The fans took him at his word. A few months later, after spurning the Mariners' $95 million offer, he shocked baseball by signing an unprecedented 10-year, $252 million deal with a Texas Rangers squad that had finished 71–91 in 2000. Not since the Pilots heist had Seattle baseball fans felt more betrayed. As additional news leaked about the negotiations, Rodriguez's standing in Seattle plunged quicker than the crashing dot-com stocks of the spring. Word spread that A-Rod had made ludicrous demands that seemed almost beyond the pale. He wanted a marketing team just for him, he wanted a personal merchandise tent set up at spring training, and so on. "Pay-Rod" headlines screamed from newsstands throughout the Pacific Northwest.

The pleasing portrait of Alex Rodriguez, one he carefully nurtured and managed, fell apart over time as well. His humility and affability came to be viewed as false, and reports of petty jealousies and tensions in the Mariners clubhouse trickled out over time. Bob Finnigan, the former Mariners beat writer for *The Seattle Times*, wrote in 2013: "More than anything, [Rodriguez] resented Griffey's popularity. In futile efforts to attain this, Alex stayed approachable, was a great quote, but he could never do anything but try to please, to be all things to all people. He was whatever you needed him to be. And he never realized that by doing this he became unreal and unconvincing." In 1996 Finnigan voted Griffey for American League MVP over Rodriguez, which cost A-Rod the award.

As a Ranger and then a Yankee, Rodriguez continued to beef up his Hall of Fame credentials, leading the league in homers five times and earning three MVP honors. That just buffeted the anger of Seattle fans. On his first visit, someone hung a fishing pole with a dollar bill over his head as A-Rod stood, unaware, in the on-deck circle. It didn't help that he had recently signed his name to a plea directed at Boeing to persuade the cherished local company to move to Dallas. On future visits, detractors floated dollar bills from the upper reaches of Safeco Field.

In subsequent years A-Rod's national reputation took hit after hit, not always fairly, but it cratered in 2009 when *Sports Illustrated* exposed that Rodriguez had tested positive for steroid use in 2003. Between these dates, Rodriguez had on numerous occasions made grand public statements, including a celebrated interview with Katie Couric, insisting he was clean. Shortly after the *SI* piece, he admitted to using steroids as a Rangers player. A chaotic legal battle followed with the Yankees and Major League Baseball that resulted in Rodriguez's suspension.

Rodriguez's legacy is tainted forever now. A first-ballot Hall of Famer before, he will probably join the likes of Pete Rose and Mark McGwire as baseball pariahs—a fall from grace perhaps unprecedented in major sports history.

29 The Peanut Man

The Mariners have issued the most walks in the league three times (1984, '85, and '92). Too many other times to count they have finished among the American League leaders in base on balls. The M's, especially during the franchise's first two decades, have tended to serve up more free passes than a fledgling rock band. While young Mark Langston walked more than a batter every other inning in 1984, Rick Kaminski fired strikes, without fail, all over the Kingdome. And he usually did it with a behind-the-back fling.

From the franchise's inception until 2011, Kaminski sold beer and then peanuts to Mariners fans at the Kingdome and Safeco Field. Yes, Kaminski's weapon was just a bag of peanuts. And there was no one waiting with a bat hoping to send the projectile back at his head (well, not usually). But anyone who ever ordered peanuts from Kaminski must have wondered what the man could have done with a baseball. Surely, it couldn't have been any worse than what they were watching.

A Seattle native and Vietnam veteran, Kaminski started working as a vendor at various Seattle sports venues in the early 1970s. Kaminski also played tennis and competed in many weekend tournaments, which caused him to miss critical weekend games. His bosses fretted, stripping Kaminski of his seniority status and taking away his coveted beer vending gig.

That didn't stop Kaminski, a former student body president at Shoreline Community College. After selling soda pop, he transitioned to peanuts.

A short time later, he devised a plan that would allow him to speed up the pace of his sales. The scheme also made Kaminski a huge favorite among Mariners fans and gave birth to his nickname, "The Peanut Man." "I found the process [of passing peanut bags] was too slow for selling 50 bags of low-priced items from each basket," Kaminski told the *Seattle Post-Intelligencer* in the early 1980s. "I began throwing them to speed up the process and found it was fun. Now I can sell almost as many bags of peanuts as beer."

Kaminski delighted fans with his dead-on accurate tosses to customers, many of whom ordered a bag just so they could be part of the show. He had a full repertoire that ranged from long-distance lobs to quick-strike bullets. He rarely missed his mark. "He knew exactly how to line drive it to someone or how to lob it and have it drop into their lap," said his longtime partner Candi Mindt-Keener to mlb.com in 2011. Kaminski credited his good working knowledge of physics for his remarkable accuracy.

Besides his uncanny precision with a bag of peanuts, Kaminski, warm and witty, knew how to entertain a crowd. When wiseacre fans would challenge him to do the same thing with a beer, he would stealthily stuff a beer cup with napkins and launch it. Those nearby would recoil in fear and then burst out laughing.

As the Mariners continued to walk way too many batters in the 1980s, Kaminski's dazzling display of pinpoint accuracy at high speeds created a buzz that migrated beyond the walls of the Kingdome. Patrons in restaurants and grocery stores started to recognize him. "Nearly everywhere I go," he said, people knew who he was. That helped him land a job, along with another famous Mariners vendor, as a TV pitchman for a local men's clothing store. He even became a national story with his clever tosses appearing a few times on ESPN or *This Week in Baseball* highlights.

Kaminski remained a peanut vendor at Mariners games well into his 60s and was still working when he died unexpectedly of a brain aneurysm in July of 2011. At the time of his death, Mariners president Chuck Armstrong issued a statement calling Kaminski "a fixture at Seattle sporting events [who] will be sorely missed at Safeco Field."

Many fans mourned Kaminski for his affable personality and his status as an icon in Seattle sports. To *The Seattle Times*, one reader summed up the feelings of countless fans: "Rick the Peanut Man needs to be in the Mariners and Cooperstown Hall of Fame!!! The best Goodwill Ambassador the M's could ever have...A genuine Original—a great entertainer—A Great guy!...the guy deserves his own Statue in Safeco!!!!"

30 Jim Lefebvre and the First Winning Season

Amid the turmoil of ownership uncertainty and relocation threats, the Mariners at the end of the 1980s and early 1990s quietly started another roster transformation. And this time the core would drive the franchise beyond anything it had experienced before.

After an implosion in 1988 when the M's canned another manager mid-season and slipped from 78 wins to 68, the Mariners hired an energetic, first-year manager who, some reports said, turned down the Chicago White Sox and California Angels. "Good people in baseball said, 'Don't go there. It is a mess,'" Jim Lefebvre said. "But I also had good people tell me, 'You've got to go. This is a great opportunity.'"

Lefebvre hoped to transfer the winning culture he'd been a part of as a Los Angeles Dodger in the '60s and '70s to Seattle. He also contrasted sharply with crusty, autocratic manager Dick Williams. Lefebvre, slick and new age, relied on inspiration and encouragement. In his first spring training, he issued T-shirts that read "Lefebvre believer" and he started each day in Arizona with an uplifting speech, often quoting famous figures in history. The press dubbed the meetings "the sermon on the mound." Veterans of a few Mariners wars, such as Alvin Davis, Harold Reynolds, and Dave Valle, found Lefebvre's style a revelation. "We needed an attitude sweep and we got a good one," first baseman Alvin Davis said.

The Mariners made incremental improvements each of Lefebvre's first two years. In 1989 they won 73 games. During the offseason erratic owner George Argyros sold the Mariners to Jeff Smulyan, who talked of a new direction, which included earnest pursuit of free agents beyond the discount rack, one of whom—first baseman Pete O'Brien—signed with the M's. In 1990 the Mariners jumped to 77 wins, the second most in team history. They fell out of the race early, but as late as August 17, they were above .500 despite another injury outbreak.

With the pitching rounding into form (the M's set a franchise record for lowest ERA in 1990) and a bevy of good young hitters, excuses had run out. "Our development period is over," Lefebvre said at the end of 1990. "It's time to start winning." Then the Mariners lost their first six games. The fans and media grew restive. But before talk of curses and managerial changes could grow hair, the Mariners won their next eight games, the longest winning streak in franchise history. "We started out 0–6, and the season was over," Reynolds said. "A week later we've won six in a row and we're the greatest thing."

The rest of the first half mirrored the first 16 games—eyesore stretches followed by two weeks of sublime play. They lost seven of nine, then won 13 of 15, and so on until the M's settled two games below .500 at the All-Star break. Then they burst out of the turn faster than Miss Budweiser, winning 17 of their first 23 games to move a franchise record nine games over .500. A sweep of the Angels concluded the hot streak.

In fourth place, five-and-a-half games back of the Minnesota Twins, the M's felt, perhaps for the first time in club history, they could mount a serious charge for the division title. "We realized we were capable of playing with anyone," said Valle in *Tales from the Seattle Mariners Dugout*. "Most of the players were starting to come into their own that year. Junior…Randy Johnson…All of those things colliding at the same time started to make us think, 'We can do this.'"

After losing the next four, though, the Mariners failed to stay in the race. But the possibility of at least winning 82 games never drifted too far. On September 8, a loss to the Boston Red Sox

dropped the Mariners a game below .500. Past M's teams had come
unglued at this point. Not this one. The M's won six of their next
seven games and entered the final road trip of the season in Texas
at 78–77. They split a doubleheader, winning the first game on a
Jay Buhner homer in the ninth. After Dave Burba, making only his
second start of the season, beat the Rangers 8–1 for victory No. 80,
the M's went for history the next night.

History appeared on hold until Valle, enduring a hellacious
year at the plate, doubled in two runs in the seventh to key a 4–3
comeback victory and win No. 81. Lefebvre called it "a World
Series" moment. "This is my proudest day to be part of the
Mariners," said equipment manager Henry Genzale, who had been
with the team since 1977. "This is for all those players who ever put
on a Mariner uniform," added Genzale, who may have laundered
more jerseys stained by tears and blood than the New Jersey mob.

"To beat that curse, we need to win a couple more," cautioned
Davis, the longest tenured Mariner. "Winning tonight was like
righting the ship. Winning one more would be setting the right
course." The M's returned home to set the right course. An amped-
up crowd of 55,000 greeted them at the Kingdome two nights later.
KIRO-TV broadcast the game as well, making the Friday evening
game against the White Sox perhaps the largest audience to date to
ever watch a Mariners game. And the M's sent 'em home happy.

Valle once again was a hitting hero, knocking in the go-ahead
run in the sixth before Buhner belted his 27th dinger to ice the 6–4
win and guarantee a better-than-.500 season. The M's split the final
two games of the series to finish with 83 wins. "Winners...we're
winners," Davis said. "It means so much to those of us who've been
here. The young guys look at our happiness and ask, 'What's the big
deal?' But this means more than winning a pennant. That kind of joy
is in the heart. This emotion comes deeper in the body, in the gut."

One of the young guys befuddled by it all was Buhner. "There
was a champagne toast. I'm thinking, *You're crapping me, we're*

celebrating finishing above .500?" he told a Seattle radio station 18 years later.

Strangely, given the circumstances, rumors had swirled for weeks that Lefebvre's days as manager were numbered. In fact, the M's themselves had been feeding the press negative stories about Lefebvre, suggesting he had lost the clubhouse and respect of his players. Others reported that he didn't get along with general manager Woody Woodward. Whatever the reason, Seattle canned Lefebvre shortly after the end of the season.

Things, though, still pointed in the right direction. Attendance topped two million for the first time ever. And the Mariners had their best season despite the big three in the rotation, Johnson, Erik Hanson, and Brian Holman, all missing time due to injury. Plus, there was no denying that Buhner, Ken Griffey Jr., and Edgar Martinez looked like three of the best hitters in the American League. Fill a few holes, it seemed, and things could get really cooking.

31 Dan Wilson

"I have never thrown a warm-up pitch before with a tear in my eye," a moved Jamie Moyer said after catcher Dan Wilson caught him before the start of the second inning at Safeco Field on September 30, 2005. It was Wilson's last appearance in a major league uniform.

Wilson grew up in Barrington, Illinois, and attended the University of Minnesota. In the upper Midwest, they have a word for folks like Wilson: "Minnesota Nice." He embodies many of the qualities that characterize the stereotype. Wilson is reserved, polite, and selfless. He is also dedicated and endowed with a strong work ethic. "Dan's the single greatest person I've ever met," said his high school baseball coach Kirby Smith in 1997. "I still hear teachers say, 'We'll never have another Dan Wilson.'" The inimitable Wilson began his college career as a pitcher and catcher, but he dropped pitching when he discovered he had an allergy to extreme cold and ice, a palliative critical to the long-term health of every pitcher.

The Cincinnati Reds drafted Wilson seventh overall in 1990, and he moved up quickly, revealing major league-caliber defense at baseball's most bruising yet cerebral position. "A take-charge receiver with a strong arm," read a scouting report in 1991. "He stepped in and immediately won the respect of more experienced pitchers with his ability to handle a game." Hitting proved more of a challenge, but standing in the batter's box didn't completely overwhelm him, so the Reds gave him a cup of coffee in 1992 and a few bigger gulps in 1993. After that season the M's acquired Wilson, along with reliever Bobby Ayala, for Erik Hanson and Bret Boone. Mariners manager Lou Piniella insisted Wilson be included in the deal. He had followed his progress in Cincinnati when he managed the Reds and remembered how pitchers in Cincinnati were keen to have Wilson warm them up.

Piniella gave him the majority of starts in 1994, and then he became the regular catcher starting in 1995. "[Piniella] totally shaped my career by giving me a chance to start every day," Wilson said. Just as in Cincinnati, Mariners pitchers loved to throw to the former Gopher, who spent hours devouring scouting reports and offered his pitchers an easy target behind the plate. Piniella even joked that Wilson forced him to over-prepare for meetings just so he could keep up with his catcher during pregame scouting sessions. "Dan...works well with all the pitchers," said starter Chris Bosio after Wilson landed in Seattle. "He calls a good game. He can adapt to pretty much anybody's style. He understands the game."

A favorite in the entire clubhouse, Wilson became the Mariners' players union representative almost immediately, handling the ticklish period of 1994–1995 with skill and aplomb. His eternally youthful face, which prompted Griffey to jokingly ask the catcher if he was in a boy band, belied a steely resolve and even temper that served him well in the union rep job.

Pitchers and coaches appreciate the subtleties of game calling and pitch framing. "A caring catcher" is how Piniella described Wilson. Fans tend to evaluate catchers based on the more visible aspects of the position such as cutting down base stealers, blocking balls in the dirt, and, yes, offense. On the first two counts, Wilson excelled. That he started his collegiate career as a pitcher served as a testament to his strong arm. And his ability to prevent wild pitches and passed balls probably stemmed from his years as a hockey goalie in high school. Randy Johnson used to say that he could throw his slider, one of the nastiest in the league, in the dirt with the winning run on third base and never worry with Wilson behind the plate.

Wilson developed slowly as a hitter. During spring training of 1996, Piniella and hitting coach Lee Elia worked tirelessly with Wilson on hitting the inside pitch, his biggest weakness. The extra attention worked. Wilson had a career year, socking 18 home runs and driving in 83 runs while hitting .285. In early April he clubbed three homers in a game against the Detroit Tigers and five days later he collected five RBIs and a grand slam. Wilson's uptick in offense helped him make his only All-Star team. Said former New York Yankees hitting coach Rick Down: "[In 1996 Wilson] was more relaxed [and] more aware of how pitchers were working him."

Subsequent years yielded their share of additional offensive highlights. Twice he hit inside-the-park home runs. The second was a grand slam against Detroit. Grand slams and inside-the-parkers notwithstanding, Wilson usually hit eighth in the Mariners' star-studded lineup, and any offense he gave the Mariners was considered gravy. "He would rather call a good game and win than put his batting first," Piniella said.

Wilson retired in 2005 with the highest catcher fielding percentage (.995) in American League history at the time. He holds Mariners records for games caught and home runs by a catcher. He caught 30 postseason games for Seattle, though he scuffled at the plate in October. Wilson's name is scattered throughout the M's top ten in numerous other offensive categories such as hits, doubles, RBIs, and runs scored.

Hits and fielding percentage, though, and games played only tell a sliver of the story. Wilson and his wife—whom he met in third grade, started dating in eighth grade, and married right after college—became pillars in the Seattle community. They took a particular interest in helping homeless children.

All of the 1995 Mariners had moved on by 2005 except Wilson, who was elected to the Mariners Hall of Fame in 2012. He was the last to give up his M's jersey (though Griffey rejoined the Mariners in 2009). "Dan is one of the good guys of the game," manager Mike Hargrove said. "There was nothing phony about Danny. As a competitor Danny wasn't flashy. He was one of those who made people around him better."

32 1993: The Culture Changes

Just about everything went wrong in 1992. The pitching collapsed, especially the bottom of the rotation and bullpen, which spent the season pulling the pin on grenade after grenade. On offense Edgar Martinez won a batting title, and Ken Griffey Jr. continued his ascent. The rest of the offense was as dull as unpolished silver.

Veteran Kevin Mitchell, acquired in a universally praised trade to add more thump, arrived lugging a bat going bad and an attitude souring just as fast.

New manager Bill Plummer, caddy to Johnny Bench on the Big Red Machine and the Mariners' third-base coach under the recently fired Jim Lefebvre, proved to be unready for the job. An early mix-up with the lineup card that included two first basemen and no designated hitter set the tone. Then as the season circled the drain, Plummer grew increasingly detached. A week after the M's finished the year with 98 losses and the second worst record in the majors, Plummer got the flush. Many Mariners fans clamored for a complete housecleaning as well. Their calls went unheeded.

"There have been a lot of frustrations playing with the Mariners: good players leaving, talents and good teams wasted," Harold Reynolds reflected after the season. "But this year, failing to build on our winning team, was the worst. For me, for sure, the worst. Just when it was coming together, it fell apart." In 16 years the Mariners had had 10 different managers. The disappointing results of 1992 notwithstanding, none of them had the talent populating the current Mariners roster. Seattle hoped to find a skipper possessing just the right calibration of acumen, experience, and temperament. After weeks of determined pursuit, the M's actually found that man.

Lou Piniella, a World Series champion player and manager, agreed to take the job. His firebrand, uncompromising style offset by balms of humor and compassion proved just the tonic for a young team taking halting steps forward. But the start was a little shaky. The Mariners, playing every spring training game on the road, as their new Peoria, Arizona, stadium neared completion, started 1–10 in the Cactus League. Piniella, who detested losing of any kind, considered calling it quits. But he rallied and so did the Mariners, ripping off 15 wins in 20 games the rest of the spring. "Piniella's demanding nature and combustible personality are

Brawling in Baltimore

Baseball brawls are often pillow fights. Not this one. When on June 6, 1993, O's pitcher Mike Mussina plunked M's catcher Bill Haselman, who had homered off Mussina earlier in the game, a melee ensued. Both benches and bullpens emptied followed by a fusillade of punches, many of them thrown by Orioles reliever Alan Mills. The brawl lasted 20 minutes. "You don't expect fights to last that long," Haselman said. "You expect the one pileup; then that's it. After the first pile, I thought it was done. Then I looked over, and another fight broke out and then another one." The Baltimore police started heading down to the field, but the umpires told them to make sure no fans came on the field instead. Mills, Rick Sutcliffe, and future Mariner David Segui were ejected for the Orioles. Haselman, Chris Bosio, Norm Charlton, Mickey Sasser, and manager Lou Piniella were tossed from the Mariners. During the fight Bosio re-aggravated a broken collarbone injury. The Orioles won the game 5–2 and, based on the body count, the fight as well.

just what the Mariners need," wrote *Sports Illustrated* in March 1993. "He turned a country club into a working camp where no player's job was safe." Players with key roles in the past—such as Brian Fisher, Greg Briley, and especially former closer Mike Schooler, whose career had been derailed by injuries—learned just how unsafe when the M's cut them. In discussing why he released Schooler during the spring, Piniella was direct. "There was no message…no budget considerations, although I read both of those things," he said. "We had to make changes. Schooler was not pitching well." As he cleared out his locker, Schooler griped to reporters: "That Piniella—all he cares about is winning."

With the roster pruned to Piniella's liking, the Mariners improved by 18 games to notch 82 victories, the second winning season of the last three years and the second greatest victory total in franchise history. Tellingly, no tears or fireworks greeted the accomplishment. "The team played hard to a winning record, and we're going to build from here," Piniella said.

Ken Griffey Jr. went from a star to a superstar in 1993, hitting 45 long balls and tying a record for homers in eight consecutive games. (Six of the homers during the streak traveled at least 400 feet.) A crowd of 45,000 showed up to watch his attempt to break the record. Jay Buhner, who hit for the cycle, which included a grand slam, and sophomore Tino Martinez also rebounded with stronger seasons. And the pitching stormed back as well, led by free agent signee Chris Bosio, Randy Johnson (who won 19 games), and reliever Norm Charlton (acquired for the disappointing Kevin Mitchell). Injuries wrecked havoc. Edgar and Tino Martinez, Bosio, who broke his collarbone in the start after a no-hitter, and Charlton missed time due to injury.

The Chicago White Sox beat the Mariners in the second-to-last series of the year to clinch the American League West. In the visitors' clubhouse, Piniella, his voice cracking, delivered a message as the celebration raged in Comiskey Park. "Everyone listen to that. That is what you play for: to celebrate and win and go to the playoffs," Piniella said. "When you work out this winter, every time you run, every time you throw the ball, every time you lift weight, remember that celebration." Then, as tears slipped down his face, he walked the entire length of the clubhouse and into his office. Said Bosio in *Sweet Lou*: "A lot of us teared up. That was Lou. No parties at our expense. Absolutely not."

"We told the players in spring they could win," Piniella said days after the season ended. "They went out and developed a winning attitude." Then he contemplated the road ahead. "This year was actually the easiest part, turning the direction around," he said. "Going in the right direction and climbing that path is tougher." By all measures, it seemed, the Mariners had found the man who could help them make that climb.

33 Mariner Weird

Following is a grab bag of strange or unusual anecdotes and stories:

Longest Stay by a Drifter in a Seattle Athlete's Apartment

During spring training of 1993, Chris Bosio received news that a drifter had broken into his apartment and lived in it for a week, pretending to be a gardener. The drifter took Bosio's moped out for a spin and crashed it. He also stole Bosio's clothes, fax machine, and kitchen utensils. The police arrested the man but released him. Undeterred, the drifter returned to Bosio's house, kicked in the garage door and stole more belongings. Next, a woman who lived in an apartment below Bosio's shot her daughter and killed herself. Then Bosio's grandfather died. After Bosio threw a no-hitter on April 22, he said, "Things happen for a reason." In his next start, Bosio suffered a broken collarbone while trying to cover first base.

Crowd Noise or Lack Thereof

Attendance during the 1985 season was so awful that the Mariners actually piped crowd noise through the Kingdome's public address system.

Mariner Pitcher KO'd

Seattle pitcher Stan Clarke hopped aboard a flight from Toronto to Seattle in 1987. Two hours into it, an overhead compartment door flew open, and a sleeping Clarke got bonked by a flying bottle of scotch.

Men Picking Fruit

Prior to the opening of the 1988 season, Mariners second baseman Harold Reynolds decided to accept a $200,000 contract offer after watching men pick fruit. "What made up my mind," Reynolds explained, "was driving past a field where men were picking fruit. That put my financial matters in perspective."

The Moose Causes a Balk

On April 15, 1991, Mariners starter Randy Johnson committed a balk in the fourth inning of a game against the Minnesota Twins when the Mariner Moose threw a bag of peanuts onto the Kingdome turf, startling him.

Death Valle

Mariners catcher Dave Valle was taking a muscle relaxant to ease the pain in his back after a game in Oakland in 1991. Valle washed it down with a cup of coffee, which went down the wrong pipe. Valle began coughing and dropped to the floor. The coughing gave Valle muscle spasms, and he had to be rolled out of the Oakland Coliseum in a wheelchair.

Ugly Team of the Year

After a U.S. Marine color guard mistakenly flew the Canadian flag upside down during the 1992 World Series, a Toronto columnist wrote, "The American flag should not be burned, mutilated, turned upside down, or worn on the uniform of the Seattle Mariners (who had lost 98 games)."

Nobody's Home

The Mariners played before a crowd of only 653 fans in Oakland and lost to the A's 6–5 on April 17, 1979.

Earth Day
Registering 5.4 on the Richter scale, an earthquake rocked Seattle and the Kingdome, suspending a May 2, 1996, game between the Seattle Mariners and Cleveland Indians in the bottom of the seventh inning. The Mariners trailed 6–3 when disaster struck, forcing evacuation of the facility. Play was resumed the next day.

Football Fables
For reasons known only to him, Mariners outfielder Al Martin compared a collision with teammate Carlos Guillen on August 28, 2001, to the time he tried to tackle Michigan RB Leroy Hoard in 1986, a year in which Martin claimed to have played strong safety for the USC Trojans. Said Martin: "For some reason, I decided I could make a head-on stop of Hoard. I hit him or rather he hit me. You remember those big tree-trunk legs Hoard had? That's what hit me." Martin not only made this claim for years, but he also frequently talked about making other big tackles in USC games. But some elementary gumshoeing revealed that USC and Michigan did not play in 1986, that he had never attended USC, and that Martin had been an outfielder in the Atlanta Braves' system in 1986.

Bone Chips on eBay
Mariners reliever Jeff Nelson underwent surgery to remove chips from his pitching elbow. KJR sports talk show host Dave Mahler convinced him to put them in an eBay auction. Nelson didn't think anyone would bid on his bone chips. The opening bid, however, was $250. In the span of an hour, 68 more bids were made, and the price reached $12,000. The site stopped the bidding when the price reached $23,600, saying that it couldn't list body parts on its website.

Loco over Coco

Before the bottom of the fifth inning in an August 5, 2007, Mariners game against the Red Sox at Safeco Field, Boston's Coco Crisp jogged out of the dugout to take his position in center field. While driving an ATV around the field on the warning track, the Mariners' mascot, the Moose, drove the vehicle straight into Crisp's knee, nearly knocking him down. He was uninjured, but it marked the second time the Moose had witlessly interacted with a player.

34 Jamie Moyer

Picked up in a trade deadline deal in 1996, Jamie Moyer found his groove in Seattle. Slender and barely six feet, Moyer, a classic soft-tossing lefty, lived on the edges of the plate. Deception, location, and changing speeds offset a fastball so slow it collected moss on its flight to the plate. Before arriving in Seattle, his formula had worked just enough to help him establish a career on the periphery—as a fifth starter, spot starter, long reliever. But it also resulted in three trades and three releases—once by a Chicago Cubs minor league team.

"We brought you here to pitch," said Lou Piniella, Moyer's new manager in Seattle, upon meeting Moyer the first time. "We need pitching. We think you can help us. We didn't bring you here to fail." Those were words the 33-year-old Moyer had rarely heard in his 10-year journeyman career. Piniella, tough as sandpaper on pitchers, instantly liked Moyer's makeup. He sensed the native of a Philadelphia suburb could handle his no-coddling approach and confrontational style. Moyer thrived, especially after a meeting with Piniella in 1997 recounted in *Just Tell Me I Can't*. "You're not throwing your change-up enough," the skipper said tersely when Moyer, in a funk, sought his counsel. "Don't just show it. The change-up is who you are, for chrissakes." In the Mariners' next game, Moyer handcuffed the heavy-hitting Los Angeles Dodgers, inducing bad swings and weak contact on 36 change-ups, most thrown in mid-70s speeds. He allowed only two runs, won his sixth game, and became another member of the Lou Piniella Fan Club.

Moyer's renewed commitment to the change-up, a pitch he developed at St. Joseph College but lost faith in upon reaching the majors, keyed his turnaround. A willingness to aggressively pitch inside contributed as well. Throwing 80 mph fastballs and change-ups at 14 different speeds, Moyer became an indispensable member of the glory year Mariners. He won 15 or more games four times. Twice he won 20, including the historical 2001 season, when Moyer emerged as a staff ace. In the fifth and deciding game of the 2001 American League Division Series against the Cleveland Indians, he befuddled the thunderous Indians lineup with pinpoint location and wicked timing disruptions. "[Hitters] can't wait to pick up their bat and get in the on-deck circle," Moyer once said. "I say, 'Fine. Dig in. And do what you want to do because I'm going to get you out.'"

In 2003 at the age of 40, he made his first All-Star Game during his other 20-win season. Moyer retired National League beasts Jim Edmonds, Albert Pujols, and Barry Bonds in order. The next season he slumped. For years Moyer had worked with sports psychologist Harvey Dorfman, who suspected Moyer had run out of challenges. Dorfman told Moyer to "put something on the line" and then suggested he pitch for his kids. Moyer rebounded the next season, but the Mariners had begun a stubborn decline.

The Piniella era included a number of high-character guys. Jamie Moyer added quantity and quality to the list. A meeting with Erin Metcalf, a 15-year old girl dying of liver cancer, touched the Moyers profoundly. Moyer and his wife, Karen, became friends

Jamie Moyer, the soft-tossing lefty who won 15 or more games four times for the Mariners, pitches against the Texas Rangers in 1999.

with the girl and her family. That relationship led to the establishment of Camp Erin, a grief camp for children who have lost loved ones. Under the auspices of The Moyer Foundation, a model many athletes now use for philanthropy, it grew into the largest child bereavement camp in the country. "Sometimes in life you have these moments, and they change you forever," Moyer wrote in *Just Tell Me I Can't* about a poignant encounter at the camp with a boy whose uncle had recently died. "Baseball has given me many things I'll always be thankful for. That moment was one of them."

Moyer left the Mariners in August 2006 when the Phillies traded for the 43-year-old to bolster their playoff chances. (The ageless wonder won a World Series ring with Philadelphia in 2008.) He could have scotched the deal but worried about the M's future. Moyer was the last of the '90s Mariners to depart. He left a legacy in Seattle matched by few: most starts, innings pitched, and victories in Mariners history. "They were 10 great years here in Seattle," he said.

35 Rick Rizzs

For almost 30 years Mariners fans have been treated to the unbridled enthusiasm and earnest strains of Rick Rizzs on both radio and TV, making him one of the longest tenured broadcasters in baseball.

A native of the South Side of Chicago, Rizzs (pronounced without the "s") developed his passion for baseball and the craft of broadcasting it at an early age. He used to listen to legendary Chicago Cubs broadcaster Jack Brickhouse. As he got a little older, Rizzs would turn down the radio and do his own play-by-play. "I can't remember a time when I didn't think, eat, and dream about baseball," he said.

Rizzs majored in radio and television at Southern Illinois and shortly after college in 1975 he landed a job with the San Diego Padres' Double A affiliate Alexandria Aces of the Texas League. The gig included three innings of play-by-play and duties as the clubhouse attendant. That meant Rizzs also shined the shoes of visiting players and washed uniforms. Later he made minor league stops in Amarillo, Texas; Memphis, Tennessee; and Columbus,

List of Radio and TV Broadcasters
Dave Niehaus (1977–2010)
Ken Wilson (1977–1982, 2011–2012)
Bill Freehan, TV (1980)
Don Poier, TV (1981)
West Stock, TV (1982–1983)
Nelson Briles, TV (1984–1985)
Ken Brett, TV (1986)
Rick Rizzs (1983–1991 and 1995–2014)
Joe Simpson, TV (1987–1991)
Ken Levine (1992–1994)
Ron Fairly (1995–2006)
Chip Caray (1993–1995)
Dave Henderson (1998–2006)
Dave Valle (1998–2006)
Tom Paciorek, road TV only (2001)
Jay Buhner (2002–2005)
Dave Sims (2007–2014)
Mike Blowers (2007–2014)
Aaron Goldsmith (2013–2014)

Ohio, where he called games for the New York Yankees' Triple A affiliate.

In 1983 Mariners owner George Argyros contacted him about the second seat in the Mariners broadcast both. "We talked about an hour, and George was interrupted by phone calls, doing his other business," Rizzs said about his interview with the M's owner. "I didn't know how I was doing. Then after one call, George put down the phone, stuck out his hand, and said, 'Welcome aboard.'"

In his first game as Mariners broadcaster on Opening Day against the Yankees, Rizzs unveiled the home run call he'd used in the minors and continues to deploy even today. When M's outfielder Richie Zisk hit a home run, Rizzs screeched: "Good-bye baseball!"

With the exception of a three-year period, when from 1992–1994 in an ill-fated move he took the lead announcer's job with the Detroit Tigers, Rizzs has been with the Mariners, working in both the radio and TV booth. He calls his time in Detroit, where deposed legend Ernie Harwell returned to the booth for one year, difficult. But he said in an interview years later that, "My three years in Detroit were a great learning experience."

The most memorable call of his career took place in a season special to every Mariners fan. In the oppressively tense 1995 tie-breaker between the Angels and M's, Rizzs, his voice rising in excitement, described the action as Luis Sojo scampered home to clear the bases and give the M's a seemingly insurmountable lead. "I just screamed, 'Everybody scores' [as Sojo crossed the plate], and we were on the way to the playoffs for the very first time in our history," he said.

That was the apex of Rizzs' fulfilling baseball career. "I think a lot about my father," Rizzs said in a 1991 interview. "He told me once, 'If you wake up in the morning, and you're happy to go to work, you've got it made.' I've got it made."

36 1997: A Winning Tradition

As an encore to the magical, franchise-saving 1995 season, the Mariners set a team record with 85 wins in 1996, aided by the first full major league schedule in two years. Seattle also established a franchise attendance record with 2.7 million fans.

But the milestones had a hollow ring.

The M's finished second and out of the playoffs. Shortstop Alex Rodriguez nearly won the MVP as a 21-year-old, and mid-season pickup Jamie Moyer exceeded expectations with a 3.31 ERA and 6–2 record. But Randy Johnson missed most of the season after back surgery, Griffey endured another injury, and financially motivated offseason trades of Tino Martinez and Mike Blowers and free-agent departures of Jeff Nelson, Tim Belcher, and Andy Benes left a few holes unfilled. "The Mariner Way is never easy," uttered third-base coach Sam Perlozzo, who left for a new job in Baltimore.

Johnson returned in 1997 and was better than ever. So was the offense, which led the league in runs scored and featured four All-Stars. First baseman Paul Sorrento, signed as a free agent in the winter of 1995, and third baseman Russ Davis, acquired for Tino Martinez, prospered as well, making the M's lineup from top to bottom nearly bulletproof. "[The Mariners' offense] is ridiculous, and I mean that fondly and respectfully," said Belcher, the former Mariner-turned-Kansas City Royal. Moyer continued to build on his surprising success from the year before, and Jeff Fassero, acquired from Montreal in an Expos salary dump, fortified the rotation. The combination proved good enough to propel the Mariners to 90 wins (another franchise record) and a second American League West crown in three years. A thin bullpen, partially the result of budgetary constraints, forced the Mariners to make two trades, however, they would later regret.

The Mariners' march to the 1997 division title lacked the white-knuckle tension of 1995. In fact, for most of the season Seattle held the top spot. Only the bullpen prevented the M's from sailing far away from the rest of the division. In his first start, Johnson allowed two runs and fanned eight, burying concerns about his health. He turned a 3–2 lead over to the pen. First Bob Wells and then Norm Charlton coughed up leads, and the Mariners fell 8–6. The wobbly bullpen effort was a foreshadowing. By June the M's bullpen ERA had bloated to a gassy 6.72.

Meanwhile, Griffey slugged a major league record 13 homers in April. Joey Cora romped to a team record 24-game hitting streak. And rookie Jose Cruz Jr., promoted at the end of May, radiated with 12 home runs in just two months. At the end of June, the Mariners, despite their rocky bullpen, held a five-and-a-half-game lead in the AL West.

For the first three months, Mariner manager Lou Piniella kept using Charlton to close games, waiting for the veteran to reclaim his effectiveness. But in June Charlton's ERA eclipsed 8.00. Frustration with the pen reached the boiling point in mid-July. On the 17th the M's blew another game late, which shaved their lead over the Texas Rangers to one game. "If you want to know the truth, we need to go out and get some help, okay," Piniella complained after the game. "I do the best I can with what we have. But if we get some pitching help, we'll be a much better club."

The desperate Mariners pulled the trigger on two trades. Seattle lost three young players, including Cruz Jr., in exchange for three relief pitchers. The Mariners had deemed Cruz Jr. "untouchable" only a few weeks earlier. "It's our [the bullpen's] fault Cruz was traded," lamented Charlton as Mariners fans howled over Cruz's departure. In exchange for the exciting rookie, the M's received relievers Mike Timlin and Paul Spoljaric from the Toronto Blue Jays. On the same day (July 31), prospects Jason Varitek and Derek Lowe headed to Boston in exchange for closer Heathcliff Slocumb, who had endured an up-and-down season. But he shined in his last few outings, so the Mariners rolled the dice.

Cruz Jr. developed into a solid major leaguer. Lowe and Varitek later would anchor the Boston Red Sox's first championship in 86 years. Slocumb saved 10 games (and only blew one) for the Mariners, albeit not without raising Piniella's blood pressure frequently with cluttered traffic on the bases. Timlin and Spoljaric provided modest benefits in middle relief. Overall the trades helped though, as the Mariners posted a 3.88 ERA after the moves (down from 5.17).

Seattle pulled away from the Angels in September, clinching the division on September 23. Griffey hit .304, clubbed 56 homers, and won the American League MVP, a Mariners first. Johnson won 20 games and finished second behind Roger Clemens for the Cy Young. Attendance boomed. The Mariners drew more than three million fans, only the 12th team in history to surpass the three-million threshold. No one minded the lack of drama at the end. "Two years ago we came on like Silky Sullivan [an upset winning race horse]," Piniella said. "But getting it done this way is an achievement in its own right, one that bodes well."

Unfortunately, the Mariners' heavy hitting lineup slumbered through the American League Division Series, scoring only 11 runs in the series. The Baltimore Orioles dusted the Mariners in four games as a result. "We never got anything going the whole series," Piniella said. "We never sustained rallies." Asked for final comments, Piniella reflected on the season: "What we'll take out of this season are 90 wins and the feeling we've established a tradition of winning in Seattle."

37 Mike Blowers

By age 28 Mike Blowers, a graduate of Bethel High in Spanaway and the University of Washington, had logged thousands of miles on minor league busses from Jacksonville, Florida, to Calgary, Alberta. He had accumulated 2,826 minor league plate appearances during these travels and had teased just enough to earn a few looks with the New York Yankees. But he failed to distinguish himself in any of them.

On May 3, 1990, in Yankee Stadium, Blowers' professional career hit bottom. Blowers, playing third base, committed four errors, tying a major league record. The notoriously ruthless and profane crowd was merciless. "They were tough on me," Blowers recalled. "I learned a lot that day."

The Mariners, who had drafted Blowers in 1984 out of high school but failed to sign him, rescued the former Husky by trading for him in May of 1991. Blowers had hit .350 in the spring and broke camp with the Yankees. But by May he rode the bench. "Even when I played for the Yankees, I was a Mariner fan," said Blowers, who hoped a change of scenery would change the trajectory of his career. The Mariners viewed the deal as "an insurance policy" in the event third baseman Edgar Martinez flamed out.

Blowers spent most of the next 20 months in the minors. Making his Mariners debut in 1992, he hit a nose below the Mendoza line in 73 at-bats. But Blowers refused to sulk or wave the white flag on his career. Heading into the 1993 season, he worked hard to improve his defense, especially at third, and took reps in the instructional league as a catcher. When Martinez hit the disabled list to start the season, Blowers made the M's as a short-term replacement at third base and emergency catcher. "Lou Piniella [the M's new manager] gave me a chance this spring, and I think I made the most of it," Blowers told reporters on Opening Day.

After a slow first few weeks, Blowers' bat suddenly awakened—with a rumble. In back-to-back games in mid-May, he accomplished something only Babe Ruth, Jimmie Foxx, and 11 other major leaguers ever had. He belted grand slams in consecutive games. The first came in support of a Randy Johnson one-hitter against the Oakland A's and the second in a blowout 16–9 win against the Texas Rangers. "Me and Babe Ruth and Jimmie Foxx," he said after the Rangers game. "You hear those names as a kid and you can only dream of them and now this."

Blowers' bat stayed hot to the touch for the rest of May, cooled slightly in June, and then burned again in July and August. Those expecting the 28-year-old's uprising to imitate a cicada eruption by quickly dying off were surprised. At season's end Blowers had hit .280 with 15 homers. And, incredulously, he had earned the starting job at third base. When Martinez returned he slid into the designated hitter spot, yielding to Blowers' superior defense. He credited his breakout year to increased concentration triggered by the birth of his first child. "I always believed in hard work. Now I'm really grinding," Blowers said. "I'm not giving away any at-bats." On the year, Blowers belted three grand slams. Two years later he would equal this feat—in one month.

When Ken Griffey Jr. fractured his wrist in May of 1995, the Mariners needed Blowers, who tailed off some in 1994, to rediscover his 1993 stroke. At first he sank under the burden of increased expectations. Through June 22, Blowers had only two homers, and his average tangoed with the low .200s. "You'd think as a veteran player you wouldn't press, wouldn't try to do too much," Blowers said. "But you're still human and when you struggle and the average dips some, you press even more."

For years, the Mariners had urged Blowers to adjust his stance by moving closer to the plate. Heeding their advice usually only induced a slump. In mid-June, on the advice of teammate Rich Amaral, Blowers moved farther from the plate instead. The adjustment was a revelation. "It was such a simple thought. It was almost childlike," explained Blowers, who always liked the ball out over the plate.

In July Blowers belted four homers and knocked in 22 runs, a mere appetizer it turned out. In August, as the Mariners clung by their fingernails in the American League West wild-card race, Blowers smoked nine homers, drove in 33 runs (a club record), and posted a Griffey-like .988 on-base plus slugging percentage. Three of the August homers were grand slams, which tied him with just four other major leaguers for most grand slams in a month. The second slam came in Minnesota during a win on August 14, the day before Griffey returned to strengthen an already stout lineup.

Blowers victimized Boston Red Sox knuckleballer Tim Wakefield on August 18 at the Kingdome for his final grand slam of the month. He also belted a three-run homer in the Mariners pivotal 9–3 win. "Obviously, it was the best month of my career," he later said. "I was as locked in as I've ever been at the plate. I felt as though I could hit anyone." With the cooler temperatures in September came a slight frosting of Blowers' bat, but he remained a key cog down the stretch in 1995 and then hammered a ball to dead center field off Dennis Martinez in Game 1 of the '95 American League Championship Series.

Blowers ended the season with a career high 23 homers and 96 RBIs. Establishing himself as major league regular in his hometown and becoming a key figure in helping his city fall madly love with its team was Hollywood stuff. But then the credits stopped rolling, and reality smacked him in the face. The M's couldn't afford to keep Blowers, who was a year away from free agency. As a result, they traded him to the Los Angeles Dodgers in November of 1995. "We hated to let Mike go," said general manager Woody Woodward. Blowers didn't want to leave Seattle, but he understood the financial realties.

Blowers missed the second half of the next season with an injury and then re-signed with the M's in January of 1997 as a free agent. In part-time duty he hit five home runs and helped the M's clinch a playoff berth. After a stop in Oakland, Blowers returned again to the Mariners and retired after the 1999 season. He now broadcasts Mariners games on TV.

38 Ownership Carousel

With a few exceptions, baseball franchises that experience long-term success also enjoy stable ownership. So the stormy first 15 years of the Mariners shouldn't surprise. In that short period, the Mariners changed hands three times. Two of the owners had no history or ties to Seattle, and the first three had money problems.

The original Mariners owners consisted of a group of local businessmen and one well-known entertainer: jeweler Stan Golub, furniture executive Walter Schoenfeld, department store owner Jim Walsh, construction builder Jim Stillwell, broadcast and recording executive Lester Smith, and A-list actor Danny Kaye, who surprised future Mariners general manager Lou Gorman with his rich knowledge of the sport. Perhaps with the exception of Kaye, none of the owners were rich in a New York or oil tycoon sort of way. They paid $6.5 million for the Mariners and then watched the M's struggle on the field, and attendance sag as a result. The combination of lower than expected revenues, increasing player salaries, and lack of deep pockets among the owners meant constant financial bleeding. By 1981 only four owners remained, and the splintered group decided to unload the team. In four years the Mariners went 246–400 under its initial ownership group.

George Argyros bought the M's for $13 million. At first, Seattle cheered the purchase by the real estate developer from Southern California. "Patience is for losers," he blustered. But the joy turned to frustration quickly. Argyros proved to be as tight-fisted as the previous owners, maybe more so. He could also be brusque, intemperate, and a bit of a blowhard.

Almost immediately, he started complaining about the unfavorable terms of the M's lease on the Kingdome. The complaints usually included a threat to move the Mariners out of the Pacific Northwest. In 1985 Argyros resorted to de facto blackmail by announcing his intention to declare bankruptcy, which would undercut the city's leverage in negotiations. Seattle caved, granting the Mariners free rent through 1987 and subsequent lease payments half of what they had been.

On the field, the bedraggled product continued to underwhelm, though signs of improvement emerged, primarily in the form of young players drafted and developed by the M's. But Argyros, a notorious penny-pincher who refused to allow his team to travel via chartered flights as most major league teams did, kept letting the best young talent leave as it reached free agency. Moreover, his players accused him of not bargaining in good faith or, in the case of arbitration, insulting them with lowball offers. "Argyros says he wants to win, but who's he kidding?" asked Mariner Ken Phelps. "Ideally, he'd like to have a .500 club and also have the lowest payroll in baseball."

Argyros also meddled, driving his managers crazy with daily phone calls to discuss lineups and impromptu meetings with players to offer unsolicited advice. Then in 1987 Argyros, embroiled in a nasty divorce, attempted to buy another major league franchise, the San Diego Padres, so he could be closer to his Orange County home. He even called Padres manager Larry Bowa to congratulate him after a game. Baseball commissioner Peter Ueberroth fined him $10,000 for tampering with other teams and put the Mariners in trust until the Padres deal fell through.

Finally, in 1989 with his popularity both locally and among baseball's establishment in shreds (commissioner Bart Giamatti likened him to James Watt, the former secretary of the interior with a reputation for making a fool of himself in public), Argyros decided to sell the Mariners. Seattle rejoiced and then launched a search to find a local owner and one who would be willing to put a superior product on the field. (In nine seasons the Mariners went 614–790 under Argyros and never finished above .500.) Argyros conducted his own search and shocked the city when he sold the Mariners to out-of-towner Jeff Smulyan for $77.5 million. Talk show host David Letterman also had a small ownership interest in the Mariners during the Smulyan era. Wrote *Los Angeles Times* sports columnist Mike Downey: "David Letterman has bought a piece of the Seattle Mariners, confirming once again that he is one of America's funniest people."

Smulyan had made his money as a radio broadcast mogul in Indianapolis. He was younger (42 years old), savvier, and less publically combative than Argyros. He also expressed his loyalty to Seattle and set about to restock the city's interest in the Mariners. And he treated his players infinitely better than Argyros. Privately, however, he told Mariners GM Woody Woodward that he intended to move the team to Tampa, Florida, when the timing was right. Within a year rumors about Tampa surfaced. Then, when Smulyan fired manager Jim Lefebrve in 1991 after the first winning season in club history, speculation arose that Smulyan preferred losing because an unsuccessful and thus unpopular team would be easier to move. And he apparently didn't trust that Lefebrve could keep a secret.

As it happened, Smulyan shared something else with past Mariners owners: not enough wealth, which came to a head when U.S. Bank called in his loan on the Mariners. Smulyan couldn't afford to pay it back, and things deteriorated from there. He intensified his efforts to move the club to Tampa, where a sweetheart financial deal awaited him. He also went public to bash Seattle as a baseball town, hoping to persuade new baseball commissioner Fay Vincent, who opposed franchise movement, that leaving Seattle was the only way to rescue the franchise. Others in baseball agreed with him. "He has no future there; he can't make it," an AL GM told *Sports Illustrated* in September of 1991. "I like Jeff. Everyone in baseball does. He's tried hard. The Mariners have increased attendance, but that's not enough. With a payroll going up and with no support, he's got no chance."

Meanwhile, a local group of Seattlelites led by senator Slade Gorton, who were committed to keeping baseball in the city, quietly conducted a search for a local owner. Because of a clause in the lease with the Kingdome, Smulyan had to first offer the club to local ownership and accept fair market offers. Things looked dire until months later a local ownership group stepped forward. Made up of money from Microsoft, McCaw Cellular, Boeing, and Nintendo of America, it ticked all the boxes of the search team—most importantly local ownership with deep pockets. But one detail threatened to torpedo the deal.

Most of the Nintendo money actually was coming from Hiroshi Yamauchi, chairman of Nintendo in Kyoto, Japan. And Yamauchi's $75 million gave him majority interest in the team. Baseball squawked. The national media pounced. *You can't allow a foreign investor, especially one from a country currently threatening U.S. economic hegemony, to control a majority interest of part of America's Pastime.* Eventually, baseball and Seattle settled on a compromise. The local owners would contribute just enough to give them a 51 percent interest in the Mariners. The other 49 percent would come from Yamauchi but be controlled by his son-in-law Minoru Arakawa, who lived in the U.S. and was president of Nintendo of America.

So, on July 1, 1992, the Baseball Club of Seattle—as the owner consortium called itself—took control of the Mariners. Smulyan walked away with $125 million, almost $50 million more than he paid for the club three years earlier. On July 16 the Mariners hosted Opening Night II, which included numerous dignitaries and ceremonies similar to April Opening Nights. They also handed to every paying customer a button that read, "July 16, 1992: Safe at Home." There have been a few challenges along the way, but the Mariners have had the same owners ever since.

39 Chris Bosio's No-Hitter

"A bulldog" is how a scout described Chris Bosio on the day in 1992 he signed the biggest free agent contract in Mariners history. Bosio, a 16-game winner with the Milwaukee Brewers the year before and a control artist, didn't rattle easy nor hesitate to throw inside—an act of courage considering his 89 mph fastball. But the 6'3", 230-pound pitcher kept hitters guessing with a cauldron full of off-speed stuff highlighted by a split-fingered fastball. "You'll see him make up pitches on the mound," that same scout said.

Not many pitches worked for Bosio in his first three starts for the M's in April 1993. He failed to win a game and had been pounded for six runs in his third start. Ever since signing his deal with the Mariners, life had thrown him a few nasty curveballs. His home had been robbed while Bosio started spring training in Arizona. The burglar even stayed a week while pretending to be the gardener before a contractor discovered him living there. Around the same time, his good friend, Tim Crews, a Cleveland Indians pitcher, was killed in a boating accident. Then a woman living below him in his Phoenix apartment killed her daughter and shot herself. Finally, just as camp was about to break, Bosio's grandfather died. "I couldn't wait for the season to start," he told a *Sports Illustrated* reporter. "Spring training was a nightmare."

Bosio's next scheduled start, against the Boston Red Sox on April 22, was coming on only three days' rest, something Bosio had told Lou Piniella during the spring he could handle. To compound matters he woke up that morning with the flu. No matter, Bosio took the mound that evening after cutting short his usual warm-up routine—and promptly walked the first two hitters. M's pitching coach Sammy Ellis made a quick visit to the mound and dryly (and ironically) suggested that Bosio should get the next hitter and then "throw a no-hitter so we can get the heck out of here."

On Bosio's next pitch—to notorious fastball hitter Mike Greenwell—he threw a hittable fastball that Greenwell got on top of. The hard hit ball bounced tidily to second baseman Bret Boone, who turned the double play. Bosio retired the next hitter to end the rally. He then retired the side in order in the second and the third and every inning after that—until a teammate in the eighth mentioned to Bosio that he had a no-hitter going. He hadn't realized it. In the Red Sox dugout, Boston hitting coach Mike Easler, who was with the Brewers at the same time as Bosio, realized early the BoSox faced trouble. "I knew. I was trying to tell my hitters to stay back and be patient with him," he said. "When he starts getting that breaking stuff and forkball over the plate, he's nasty. Just nasty."

After a clean eighth, Bosio took the mound in the ninth with the crowd of 13,604 in a frenzy. Bosio retired the first two hitters on ground ball outs, two of 16 he recorded on the day. That brought Ernest Riles to the plate. In high school Bosio had thrown back-to-back no-hitters on the same day, which was also his birthday. But this was the closest he had come as a pro to achieving the penultimate. "I knew what was going on," Bosio said. "But in this game you always expect the worst."

The worst almost happened in the fifth inning. Leading off, Boston's Mo Vaughn hit a routine-looking two-hopper to first that suddenly took a funny spin, skipping off first baseman Tino Martinez's glove. Boone pounced on it, though, and with his bare hand made the play to nip Vaughn, the slowest runner in the Red Sox lineup. Ivan Calderon, a former Mariner, hit a screamer to center field that Ken Griffey Jr. ran down.

With two down now, Riles dug in. After the first two hitters of the game, Bosio had gotten ahead of every Red Sox player since. But he fell behind 2–1 to the Boston second baseman. On the next pitch, Riles hit a chopper over the mound into no-man's land. The Kingdome gasped, as the no-hitter looked in jeopardy. But Mariners shortstop Omar Vizquel reacted quicker than a frog's tongue capturing its prey, reaching the ball in a flash and made the play to first using his bare hand. Game over. The Kingdome scoreboard banged out a message as quickly as the bang-bang play that ended the game: "No-Hitter." The small crowd let out a roar louder than the fireworks exploding in the background.

"That was for your grandfather," Randy Johnson whispered to Bosio as they put their arms together on the mound surrounded by their joyous teammates. "It was the first thing I thought of," Bosio shared after the 7–0 win. "It's a feeling I'll probably never have again. Something came over me after we made that last out. I kind of froze. Guys started to mob me. I didn't know where I was at that point."

It was only the second no-hitter in Mariners history. For Bosio, the timing couldn't have been better. "[With] this game coming after the tragedies of the last month, well, my wife and I sat up the night of the no-hitter until about five in the morning," he told Tim Kurkjian a week later. "I said, 'Suzanne, what's going on here?' We both shrugged our shoulders and didn't say a word for about 15 minutes. Then we looked at each other and said, 'This is just unbelievable.'"

40 Sensational Mariners Commercials

One constant of every recent Mariners season is the television ads produced to promote each season. The other constant is the general quality of those ads. They are consistently some of the best in Major League Baseball. Below are six of the top ones.

The Clapper (2004): Edgar Martinez, heading into his final season, invents his own version of the Clapper, which operates the lights at Safeco Field. Teammates Dan Wilson and John Olerud watch spellbound as Martinez claps his hands, and the lights switch on and off.

Blinded (1999): On a sunny day, Jay Buhner directs his bald head toward the hitter, who is blinded by a ray of light bouncing off Buhner's bald dome.

Radar Gun (2002): Notorious soft-tosser Jamie Moyer warms up before a game and the radar gun reads first 97, then 99. *What gives?* wonders teammate Jeff Cirillo. Turns out the radar gun was imported from France and measures speed in kilometers. "Oooh la la," said a smirking Moyer.

Lou the Therapist (1994): Manager and therapist Lou Piniella, gruff and impatient, hears the emotional problems of his patients. "Whine, whine, whine," he complains to them, before finally snapping at one feeble patient: "You are acting like a loser."

Carny Randy (1994): A woman is strapped to a spinning wheel as Randy Johnson, aka El Rando Grando, hurls knives at her. The

6'10" Johnson, wearing a mullet, throws outside and low the first time and then right down the middle the second. "Aren't you glad he decided to pitch for the Mariners?" intones the voice-over.

Sorry (2009): Pitcher Felix Hernandez whiffs a visibly upset Colorado Rockies player. Later Hernandez sends him a note of condolence and a basket of flowers.

41 Bret Boone

Around major league clubhouses his whole life, Bret Boone, a member of one of the few three-generation families of major leaguers, burst with confidence edging toward conceit. Thurston Howell III (the character from *Gilligan's Island*) is what one Mariner nicknamed Boone. Yet, most of his teammates enjoyed being around him. That much of his arrogance was offset by a wink and a smirk helped. "When you talk to Boone, you can always smile," said bench coach John McLaren. He also produced on the field—especially with the Mariners. That enabled him to become a leader in the clubhouse as well.

Drafted by Seattle in the fifth round of the 1990 Amateur Draft, Boone, a standout at Southern Cal, worked his way up the minor league chain a year at a time. He showed some pop, a rare skill for a middle infielder at the time. He walked regularly. And he made all the plays at second base. Yet scouts feared big league pitchers would easily exploit the biggest dent in his game. Boone took gigantic, Ruthian swings. "I'm gonna swing hard. That's the way I've always had success, and I'm not gonna change that," Boone said early in his career. He hit a respectable .251 in 1993 his rookie season and added 12 homers.

But the next year, the Mariners traded Boone to the Cincinnati Reds. Word circulated that he clashed with manager Lou Piniella, who had once pulled him from a spring training game because he ignored a bunt signal and doubled instead. Boone denied friction existed. "I laugh every time I read that Lou and I didn't get along," Boone said. "We got off to a shaky start that first spring training, but I left on good terms." From 1994–2000 for the Reds and San Diego Padres, Boone averaged .257 and 16 homers a year. In 1998 he hit 24 homers and made the All-Star team. A free agent in 2001, Boone signed with the Mariners and reunited with Piniella.

During the offseason, "the Boone," as he called himself, embarked on an intense weight lifting regime and changed his diet. "Up until a couple of years ago, Bret had taken for granted his gift. [Now] he has become a workaholic…and got serious about his body," said father Bob Boone. The new routine added 15 pounds of muscle. His biceps bulged to the size of grapefruits. "He looked like Tarzan," said Piniella when he saw him in the spring.

The results were astounding. He hit .331 and set American League records for second basemen in homers (37) and RBIs (141), almost singlehandedly picking up the slack left by the departure of Alex Rodriguez. "He matured a lot as a player," Piniella said. "He's tempered his cockiness a bit. He's more selective than when we had him before. He's learned the strike zone and he puts the ball in play." There was no denying Boone had dialed down his violent swing and cocky demeanor—but only a few clicks. He still swung from his heels on fastballs down the pipe, and homers always included a sassy bat flip. And for fun Boone wore T-shirts proclaiming—tongue in check—his greatness.

Boone finished third to teammate Ichiro Suzuki for AL MVP. Some Seattle reporters thought Boone deserved the award instead. Ichiro's breathtaking year dominated baseball in 2001 and overshadowed Boone's breakout. Said Boone: "Ichiro is getting a lot of headlines, but so what? I've been around long enough where things don't bother me. It doesn't matter how much press I get."

He disappeared in the 2001 American League Division Series against the Cleveland Indians, but the Mariners survived. Boone charged back in the American League Championship Series against the New York Yankees, including a monster day in Game 3. He tied an ALCS record with five RBIs on three hits and a two-run homer.

Two more productive years followed. Boone hit 120 homers from 2001–2004 while sparkling in the field. In three consecutive years (2002–2004), he won Gold Gloves. Said Mike Morse, Boone's double-play mate for a half season in 2005: "He would tell me on a double play, 'Just get me the ball. You get the ball and just give it to me, and I'll turn it.' That confidence he had was amazing." Once, in a moment of supreme confidence, he predicted he'd hit two dingers in a game against the Detroit Tigers in 2003. He did. "I did the same thing as Babe Ruth, right?" he said while laughing.

The Mariners traded Boone to the Minnesota Twins in July 2005. Many M's fans lost their favorite player. "I love playing [in Seattle]," he said during his last day as a Mariner. "It's been awesome. This is kind of my place." He retired unexpectedly the next spring, succumbing to alcoholism, something he'd reveal three years later.

Whispers of steroid use surfaced during—and especially after—his career. The circumstantial evidence seemed strong. Jose Canseco, with no proof, implicated Boone as a user in his book, saying with his "small frame and big arms [Boone] was an obvious user." Boone denied it, and without a smoking gun, those 37 homers in 2001 and everything else count.

42 1987: Small Steps Forward

Heading into 1987 the franchise found itself fending off criticisms on numerous fronts: a scrooge-like owner, a guileless general manager, and a youth movement that still hadn't borne much fruit. After a full decade, the Mariners had yet to finish above .500, let alone seriously contend into September. Commenting on a sign that hung above the Mariners spring training clubhouse doorway that read "1987 WORLD SERIES CHAMPIONS," *Sports Illustrated* snarked that the sign should have read, "ABANDON HOPE, ALL YE WHO ENTER HERE."

The M's wouldn't reverse many of these trends in 1987. But they did inch closer to respectability. And two key components of the first great Mariners team, one at the major league level and one through the draft, arrived in 1987. Indeed, for the first time, Mariners fans could attend a game at the Kingdome and see in the flesh someone who would be around when it really mattered.

On May 13 the Mariners entered the ninth inning trailing the Boston Red Sox 4–2. The first five weeks of the season had been a raised middle finger to the M's critics, especially those who had derided GM Dick Balderson's 1986 trades. Mariners owner George Argyros was one of them. But pitcher Scott Bankhead, acquired from the Kansas City Royals in the trade for Danny Tartabull, had a 5–2 record and allowed two runs or fewer in five of his seven starts. Outfielder Mike Kingery, picked up in the same trade, hit .291 with some extra-base fizz. Catcher Scott Bradley, acquired for Ivan Calderon, sizzled at the plate, hitting .378, and provided sound defense at a position that had bedeviled the M's for years. The biggest surprise, however, resided in the middle infield, where the M's-Red Sox swap of shortstops appeared to be a landslide win for Seattle. Spike Owen started slowly for Boston and then began a furious plummet that left him at .139 by the time the Mariners arrived in Boston. Rey Quinones, on the contrary, hit safely in 24 of the Mariners' first 33 games and swatted five home runs, a 20-homer pace for the 23-year-old year, 160-pound erstwhile singles hitter. "We seemed to have embarrassed a few baseball people with those trades," Balderson told a reporter in mid-May. "Not the teams we traded with, but people from other teams who were critical."

Entering the Boston series, the Mariners, 17–14, had moved into a three-way tie for first place. They had never resided in the penthouse this many weeks into the season. Seattle won the first game, dropped the second, and then rallied to win the rubber game with contributions from John Christensen, one of the pieces from the Owen trade, and Steve Shields, acquired with Bankhead and Kingery. "I know it's early, but if these guys keep this up, they might get serious, and other people might start taking us serious," M's manager Dick Williams said. A day later, as the M's traveled home, Kansas City lost, leaving the Mariners alone in first place on May 15. More than 100,000 fans then turned out for a three-game series with the New York Yankees, who cooled some of the overheated talk by taking two of three games.

On June 2 the Mariners made a decision that would trump nearly everything else and redirect the course of the franchise. With the No. 1 pick in baseball's amateur draft, Seattle selected and signed Ken Griffey Jr. "I think he's going to be a Dave Parker-type guy. All his tools are good, but his bat, that's the major thing," said Roger Jongewaard, director of scouting for the Mariners, offering an assessment that in retrospect far undersold.

Their shiniest toy ever in the fold, the Mariners hung around the fringes of the American League West race most of the year. "The curve is definitely upward in Seattle," wrote Peter Gammons at the All-Star break. After pounding the Angels by scores of 15–4 and 14–0 in early August, the Mariners leapfrogged Kansas City into fourth place and crawled to within five games of first place. "Although Seattle seems to be ignoring it, this town has a baseball team on the verge of a pennant race for the first time," wrote Bob Finnigan of *The Seattle Times*. Perhaps the M's 56–58 record explained why Puget Sound baseball fans failed to heed the siren call of a pennant race.

Twelve losses in 17 games in late August snuffed out whatever faint hopes the Mariners had of contending. Quinones, an enigma whose dedication to baseball ebbed and flowed and resulted in his retirement two years later, and Bradley and Kingery cooled considerably.

The Mariners closed the season strong by winning eight of their final 10 games to set a franchise record for wins with 78. They finished seven games behind the first-place Minnesota Twins, another franchise best. One offensive record after another tumbled as well: hits, batting average, extra-base hits, slugging percentage, and stolen bases. The Mariners even led the league in fewest walks allowed.

Yes, by Yankee standards, the M's season would have been deemed a failure. But the Mariners didn't really play in the same sandbox as New York—not yet. "We should have done better," Williams said after the season. "But we won the last four to finish with our best record. That's a big deal to this organization."

An even bigger deal took place on September 12, though it's significance went undetected at the time. Edgar Martinez made his major league debut. After going hitless in his first game, Martinez murdered the ball, hitting .400 the last two weeks of the season.

43 Gaylord Perry and 300 Wins

At age 43 the once great Gaylord Perry joined the Mariners for a single reason: to reach the lofty mark of 300 wins—a virtual guarantee of a Hall of Fame berth. That's what Perry was chasing in 1982 when he signed with the Mariners at an age when most ballplayers were cashing pension checks.

After a 20-year career that included stops with six different teams, Perry had compiled 297 wins through perseverance and cunning—not smoking hot stuff. His fastball was as mundane as most Mondays. But his pitches twisted more than a moving snake, and hitters struggled to make good contact. That led to accusations Perry threw a spitball. During the 1960s baseball talked a lot about spitters, and Perry wasn't the only one targeted. He just drew the brunt of attention as the most successful of those suspected. Perry usually responded to questions about the subject with a smirk or sly grin—followed by a denial. And no evidence had yet been uncovered to indict him.

In 1974 Perry published his autobiography, *Me and the Spitter: An Autobiographical Confession*. In it he admitted to throwing a spitball, one he learned from Giants teammate Bob Shaw, early in his career. "I reckon I tried everything on the old apple but salt and pepper and chocolate sauce," he wrote. But he insisted he had reformed. No one believed him. Perry kept on winning despite being dogged by spitball accusations that varied in intensity depending on his success.

Perry signed with the Mariners without a guaranteed contract. "Let's not deny the fact that Perry would get us attention," Mariners general manager Dan O'Brien told *Sports Illustrated* in the summer of 1982. "We're a long way from everywhere up here and, dammit, we need something. Plus, our biggest winner last year [Floyd Bannister] had only nine wins. I honestly thought Perry could help us."

Perry made the team and notched victory 298 with a complete game, 13-strikeout effort against the California Angels on April 20. Two starts later, he beat the New York Yankees to win No. 299.

On May 6 he took the mound again versus New York, this time in the Kingdome. Before the game, Perry, uncharacteristically relaxed especially for the day of a start, talked to both president Ronald Reagan, whom he had helped campaign for in the '60s, and former president Richard Nixon. Then he took some batting practice, even hitting a home run during the session. "That just shows what a tough place it is to pitch," he laughed. In front of 27,369 fans (the underwhelming turnout reinforced a national perception that Seattle was lukewarm about baseball), Perry allowed only three runs through eight innings. Meanwhile, the M's offense erupted for seven. "This opportunity doesn't exactly come along once a season," said his teammate and veteran designated hitter Richie Zisk before the game. "We'll be ready."

As Perry walked to the mound to start the ninth inning, the crowd at the Kingdome, hardly known for its spontaneity or fervor, chanted "Gay-lord, Gay-lord." Said Perry afterward: "I got chills." He retired the Yankees in order, finishing the complete-game 7–3 victory with a ground ball by Willie Randolph to Julio Cruz. The win was Perry's 300th and the 303rd in Mariners history.

His wife Blanche, daughter Amy, and brother Jim, an accomplished major league pitcher himself, watched from behind the dugout. In the locker room, a jersey hung that read: "300 WINS IS NOTHING TO SPIT AT."

Perry's 300th win made him the 15th pitcher all time to breach the triple century mark. That he did it in a Mariners uniform meant reflected glory for the M's and a likely seat at the Hall of Fame table. Perry remembers the game vividly. "It was kind of like

I was in attendance for

GAYLORD PERRY'S

300TH

CAREER VICTORY

GAYLORD PERRY – The 15th pitcher in Major League history to achieve this milestone.

Seattle Mariners

The Mariners honor Gaylord Perry's achievement of becoming the 15ᵗʰ pitcher in Major League Baseball history to reach 300 victories. (David Eskenazi)

the World Series for a lot of players who hadn't been in many exciting games," he told *The Seattle Times* in 2012. A week later, Perry appeared on the cover of *Sports Illustrated*, a Mariners first.

He finished out the 1982 season with seven more wins. But it was a loss that everyone remembers. On August 23 Perry got ejected by crew chief Dave Phillips for doctoring the baseball against the Boston Red Sox. Twice Phillips checked the baseball, once in the fifth and once in seventh. The second time, after a pitch to Rick Miller tumbled in a strange way, Phillips thought he felt "a funny substance on [the ball]." So, he ejected him. "The rule is if the ball does something funny, he's going to look at it," Perry said. "I was throwing a lot of forkballs, curveballs, not many fastballs.

Caught Red-Handed

Two weeks before the end of Seattle's miserable 1980 season (the M's lost 103 games), Kansas City had played the Mariners in the Kingdome. During the series the Royals had noticed something *different* about the baseballs. That put the Royals on high alert when the Mariners traveled to Kansas City a few days later. In the first game of the series, Mariners starter lefty Rick Honeycutt toed the rubber, and through the first two innings, his pitches gyrated like John Travolta in *Saturday Night Fever.* In the third inning, the suspicious Royals asked umpire Bill Kunkel to inspect the baseball. What Kunkel found prompted him to immediately kick Honeycutt out of the game. On the pitcher's glove hand, he had tape with a tack sticking through. As Honeycutt walked off the field, he forgot about the tack and wiped his hand across his brow, opening a gash. Said Honeycutt after he was fined $250 and suspended for 10 days: "I haven't been in trouble like that since the last time I was sent to the principal's office."

We were playing the Red Sox, a great fastball-hitting club, so why throw them fastballs? Rene Lachemann…came out and said, '[sic] put something on the ball.' I said, 'No problem.' Next thing you know, I'm out of there." In typically equivocal fashion, Perry then explains: "I wasn't guilty by the first account. I didn't put anything on the ball. When I got thrown out, I said, 'Thanks Lach.' He said, 'I didn't mean [use an illegal substance].'"

Perry was the first major league pitcher to be ejected for using an illegal substance since the 1940s. (Others, though, such as the M's Rick Honeycutt, had been ejected for illegal objects.) It took 5,128 innings, but Major League Baseball finally found cause to punish the man it had suspected forever of doctoring the baseball. And even in this case the league lacked indisputable evidence.

Perry retired the next year after Seattle released him in the middle of the season and he latched on with the Royals for half a season. Perry ended up winning 314 games and was indeed elected into the Hall of Fame. Former manager Gene Mauch expressed the sentiments of many in baseball, most of whom liked Perry as a person, when he said a tube of K-Y Jelly should hang next to his Hall of Fame plaque.

44 Lou Piniella's Famous Ejections

Few managers enjoyed a spirited row with an umpire more than Lou Piniella. Not surprisingly, many of them ended with his ejection from the game. In a bit of a handicapper's upset, Piniella was on the job in the Seattle more than a year before suffering his first ejection. It occurred in the Kingdome on May 17, 1994. While arguing with the umpire, Piniella spiked his cap then kicked it 16 times before finally getting the boot in the Mariners' 4–0 loss to the Kansas City Royals. The outburst, mild in comparison to future tirades, also included four soccer style kicks of dirt on home plate.

Piniella shoveled even more dirt over home plate in a memorable ejection in a game against the Cleveland Indians in an April 8, 1997. Umpire Derryl Cousins threw out Piniella for delay of game after the M's manager held up play to argue a call in the Mariners' 14–8 victory. Enraged that he been tossed out of the game, Piniella started by dusting home plate with a few furious kicks of dirt then finished by obliterating the chalk lines of the batter's box. The Kingdome crowd of 24,348 cheered throughout Piniella's lengthy tantrum.

Indeed, many of Piniella's tirades against umpires involved moving dirt around and kicking hats. Once, during a 10-game period in the dog days of the 1996 pennant race, Piniella displaced

Known for his hot temper and his obscenity-laced tirades, Lou Piniella argues a call during a game against the Chicago White Sox in 2002. (Getty Images)

more dirt than a gravedigger and soiled more caps than Ty Cobb in his prime. Umpires thumbed him three times during this stretch. The last ejection, in a 2–1 home win against the New York Yankees on August 26, was the most colorful. Piniella blew a gasket when an Edgar Martinez home run was ruled a ground-rule double due to fan interference. Piniella roared out of the dugout and started jawing with umpire Durwood Merrill. Then he tossed his hat, kicked it, returned to chewing out Merrill, kicked at the dirt but missed before finally connecting after another swipe. Two more times he kicked the dirt after Merrill gave him the heave ho. Afterward, he said, "I'm getting tired of getting run out of games."

A few years later, on May 28, 2002 against Tampa Bay at Tropicana Field, Piniella added some variety to his dirt dispersal act when he got into the face of plate umpire John Shulock following a five-run Devil Ray inning. Piniella started with his standard move, kicking dirt on home plate. But Shulock ignored him, which further agitated Piniella. The M's manager then dropped to his hands and knees and used his hands to scoop additional dirt on the plate. When Piniella had finished, Mariners catcher Dan Wilson borrowed Shulock's brush to clear the dirt off home plate. Said Piniella after the game: "If I was the catcher, we would have played with a dirty home plate. I should be in the landscaping business. If I was the catcher, I would have buried home plate. I would have gotten one of those wheelbarrows full of turf and dumped it on the plate."

Two of Piniella's most memorable ejections as Mariners manager involved hat kicking. The first came on August 26, 1998 in a 5–3 loss at Cleveland. After briefly arguing with umpire Larry Barnett after Russ Davis was called out for running outside the base path, Piniella returned to the dugout. Then he learned he'd been ejected—for, in his estimation, no good reason. His cap bore the brunt of his frustration. He hurled it on the field, kicking it repeatedly. After one kick sent the cap flying through the air,

Dave Niehaus declared, "He got some distance on that one! That was a three-pointer right there." Offered Cleveland manager Mike Hargrove afterward: "I don't know how anybody can think of that many things to yell." Said Piniella: "I don't blame anyone for laughing. Everyone likes to see someone make a fool of themselves in front of 40,000 people." Two days later, Piniella told reporters, "You know the andro stuff [androstenedione] everyone's talking about for muscles? If I was on that, I'd have kicked my hat out of the stadium."

The other unforgettable hat-kicking incident occurred on September 18, 2002 at Safeco Field. A close call at first base prompted a nearly three minute jawing session with umpire C.B. Bucknor. Things really escalated when Piniella perceived that Bucknor was smirking. ("The ump had the nerve to have a smirk on his face," Piniella said afterward.) At that point, the M's manager became unglued and needed his assistants to restrain him, which was enough for Bucknor to finally toss him. Piniella greeted the news with two hat kicks and two throwdowns and then a strong boot of his cap that sent the hat 10 feet in the air. Then he turned to first-base coach Johnny Moses and screamed "Get my f…in' hat!"

Moses obeyed and returned the cap to its owner. Piniella kicked it again. Next he marched over to first base and uprooted the bag and carried it over to the left-field line where he launched it. As the crowd chanted "Lou, Lou," he retrieved the base and threw it again before finally heading to the dugout. "My hamstring hurts, and my shoulder is sore," Piniella said the game. Bench coach John McLaren, who had seen most of Piniella's career tirades, added: "That one was the best. Lou had all his greatest hits in it." A few days later someone showed Piniella a photo of him kicking his hat. "I'm going to send the picture to Jon Gruden [then coach of the NFL's Tampa Bay Buccaneers]. I'm ready for the season. That's good form there."

Occasionally, due to injury or circumstance, Piniella would use other props during umpire disputes. For instance, in a game against the Minnesota Twins at the Metrodome on July 25 he attempted to dislodge third base as a protest against Merrill's call that Raul Ibanez had left third base early on a sacrifice fly. Unable to budge the base, Piniella stomped back into the dugout and started hurling bats, seven in all, on the field. When a reporter asked him why he couldn't pull up third base, Piniella blamed an ailing back.

And then there were the comedic moments. In a game against Indians, Piniella raced from the dugout to argue a call but tripped and stumbled on the steps. This generated a hearty laugh from Hargrove. Piniella finally made it to the umpire and ranted long enough and with enough brio that ESPN cut to the tirade using a split screen to show Piniella and the other game being broadcast.

45 2002–2003: Good, But No Cigar

The two years following the epic season of 2001 mirrored each other. Great years by any standard, they both ended short of the playoffs.

Each season the M's started strong—66–42 in 2002, 40–18 in 2003. Each season they tap danced around .500 during the last two months. And in both years, the Oakland A's blazed down the stretch to overtake the Mariners and knock them out of the playoffs despite Seattle's 93 wins each season. Huge crowds showed up both seasons, as did calls for reinforcements at the trade deadline that went mostly unheeded.

The differences were in the details.

A shortage of power and starting pitching depth cost the M's a playoff spot in 2002. Third baseman Jeff Cirillo, acquired in a deal with Colorado to add sock, struggled to match his Rockies All-Star numbers in Seattle. One obvious culprit: swapping the thin air of Coors Field for the dense marine air of Safeco Field. Moreover, Edgar Martinez missed huge chunks of the season. His bat could have made the difference in a few of the 25 one-run games the M's lost. In the rotation only Jamie Moyer and Freddy Garcia provided consistency, as the Mariners failed to replace Aaron Sele, who departed as a free agent. The bullpen, given a facelift in 2000, continued to thrive.

As the race tightened in July, manager Lou Piniella rarely missed a chance to bring up the team's need for help, though he stopped short of demanding a move. But as CEO Howard Lincoln had reminded fans the previous winter, the Mariners had a budget to adhere to. "We have to operate at a profit," he said. "And we have to make decisions with that in mind." That hamstrung general manager Pat Gillick's efforts to find difference-makers at the trade deadline. "We probably could use a starting pitcher, but from the standpoint of budget, we are more than maxed out," Gillick said. The M's made a series of minor deals instead.

At the end of the 2002 season, Piniella asked out of his contract, which had a year remaining. Differences with upper management had escalated to the point that both sides agreed a change was needed. In a rare deal, Piniella was dealt to woeful Tampa Bay in exchange for left fielder Randy Winn, the Devil Rays' All-Star in 2002. Piniella noted the irony of being traded for a left fielder, a position the M's struggled to fill during his tenure.

To replace Piniella, the M's hired Bob Melvin, who had no major league managing experience. The choice of Melvin, by many degrees more mild-mannered and softer spoken than Piniella, surprised the prognosticators. Conspiracy theorists chalked up the hire to the Mariners' diabolical desire for a yes man. Many legitimately wondered why the M's didn't make a run at Dusty Baker, who had taken the Giants to the World Series and was reportedly interested in a new challenge after 10 years in San Francisco.

The pitching in 2003, from top to bottom, shined. Moyer, Ryan Franklin, Joel Pineiro, Garcia, and Gil Meche each made at least 32 starts, and the bullpen stretched five to six deep. But the offense was as shallow as an episode of *Keeping up with the Kardashians*, stopping pretty much after Martinez and Bret Boone. Fans and media agitated for big trade deadline deals to upgrade the offense, but the Mariners couldn't find a match to their liking.

Ten years ago, back-to-back 93-win seasons would have staggered Mariners fans. But as a measure of Seattle's maturity as a baseball town, no one at the time considered a year without the playoffs much of a success—90-plus wins be damned.

46 The 1979 All-Star Game

By the bottom of the eighth inning of 1979's Midsummer Classic the score stood 6–6. The American League started a rally, putting a runner on second base. Then Graig Nettles laced a single to right. What happened next left the crowd and the 34 million watching on TV bug-eyed.

At the time, the annual midsummer game between the best of the American League and the best of the National League represented more than just a friendly exhibition. A rivalry existed between the leagues, fanned by ancient tensions, separate leadership, and, starting in 1973 with the designated hitter, different rules. That the National League had somehow won 16 of the past 17 All-Star Games exacerbated the tensions between them and added pressure to both sides. The National League relished beating the American League and reinforcing the perception of National League superiority. The American League was simply sick of losing. So, within reason, both sides played the game to win.

In part, that's what made Dave Parker's throw on the looping single by Nettles so indelible. Parker fielded the single on one hop about 25 feet from the outfield wall and, as Brian Downing chugged home with the go-ahead run, unleashed a throw that exploded out of his hand like a Boeing 747. Gary Carter caught the ball on the fly in front of home plate and tagged out the sliding Downing. It was All-Star baseball at its best—happening in Seattle in front of a record Kingdome crowd of 58,905.

As usual when it pertained to Seattle and Major League Baseball, the city warmed slowly to the idea of the game's best coming to town. The likely culprit: the Mariners' lackluster first half. At 40–54 and on their way to another 90-loss season, the Mariners sat where they often did, not even within squinting distance of first. But you couldn't blame the offense. Willie Horton, Tom Paciorek, Ruppert Jones, Leon Roberts, and Dan Meyer represented dangerous threats at the plate. Bruce Bochte, the Mariners' lone All-Star representative, led the pack, hitting .326, slugging .505, and clubbing 11 home runs. "This is the best offensive team I've ever been with," Bochte said before the All-Star Game. "I've got good people hitting behind me and ahead of me."

The M's sat buried in the standings because of pitching. Peach-fuzzed starters Mike Parrott, Ricky Honeycutt, and Floyd Bannister (all 25 or younger) offered hope for the future, but in 1979 they and their cohorts delivered mostly despair.

Seattle could thus be forgiven for failing to embrace immediately baseball's big center stage event. A few days before the July 17 game, tickets remained available. But as the players, current and past greats, started filtering into town, interest picked up, and the midsummer spectacle became a sellout. The whole baseball establishment descended on the city—Hall of Famers such as Lefty Gomez, Bob Feller, and Carl Hubbell; media such as Joe Garagiola and Tony Kubek; renowned minor league baseball entertainer Max Patkin; and even former president Gerald Ford. Restaurants and hotels burst with the royalty of the National Pastime.

Part-owner Danny Kaye, surrounded by a group of children, threw out the first pitch. Outside the Kingdome, the sun shined, Elliott Bay glistened, and the thermometer sweltered, reaching 96 degrees. Inside, of course, the dome fought back on every count, with artificial light, blunted views, but a welcome 72 climate-controlled degrees. Red, white, and blue bunting lined the wall divides between the stands and field. Streamers hung from the roof.

As George Brett stepped to the plate, Morganna the Kissing Bandit, a stripper and then ubiquitous figure at major sporting events, slid past security with a wink and, while standing on her tippy toes, wrapped her arms around Brett and planted a big one. Before Brett could blush, the police escorted the buxom Morganna, wearing her usual tight T-shirt and intemperately small shorts, out of the Kingdome. The crowd booed. Then someone else bolted from the stands and tried to shake the unwilling hand of Pete Rose. The interloper suffered the same fate as Morganna.

Bochte had started the game on the bench. He watched Brett, Don Baylor, Jim Rice, Fred Lynn, and others from the American League and Mike Schmidt, Dave Winfield, George Foster, and Larry Bowa from the National League alternate leads until the bottom of the sixth. With the game tied at five and with runners on second and third, the Royals' Frank White was due up against righty Gaylord Perry. Sensing that the timing could be right for their man, the Kingdome crowd erupted: "We want Bochte! We want Bochte! We want Bochte!" AL Manager Bob Lemon complied. He sent Bochte, who slaughtered right-handed pitching, up to pinch-hit.

The Mariner delivered, sending a single over the head of the shortstop on a big bounce. The crowd responded with a deafening roar, perhaps the loudest summertime cheer in the brief history of the Kingdome. "I was particularly nervous the first time I went up to pinch hit," Bochte recalled. "I really wasn't expecting it to happen [referring to his nerves]." One fan, posting his memories anonymously on the www.ussmariner blog, recalled the experience: "My grandma had the extended family over for barbeque. By the time Bochte came up, I was the only one left inside the house actually watching the game, which was probably good because I went nuts—like the M's won the World Series."

The National League rallied to win on a bases-loaded walk. Parker, who also had nailed Rice at third base in the seventh inning with an equally majestic throw, earned the game's MVP honors. As the glitterati of baseball left town, many commented to local reporters that it was one of the finest All-Star Games they'd ever attended—a rare time in the '70s when Seattle heard praise from the movers and shakers of the sport.

47 Dave Henderson and the Year of Regrettable Trades

For all of the Mariners' missteps in those early years, they did nail one very important decision: who to take with the No. 1 pick in their first amateur draft. And they hit the equivalent of at least a triple despite picking from the worst possible position in the 1977 draft. You see, major league owners may have coveted the cash windfall generated by expansion, but they wanted to help their new comrades become competitive as much as they wanted to help MLB increase its growing appeal. In service to this idea, they assigned the two expansion franchises the last two picks of the first round, the last two picks of the second round, and so on.

In at least this one instance, the Mariners outmaneuvered their foes. They took Dave "Hendu" Henderson from Dos Palos High School, California, with their first pick. And he would go on to surpass the achievements of all but three players drafted ahead of him. A football player with the build to prove it, Henderson considered playing on the college gridiron but signed with Seattle when the Mariners made him an aggressive offer. "Give him one full year, and he'll move up fast," said his high school coach, Frank Ball. "He will be a very colorful player and will help the Mariners, which is good. They are a class organization."

Ball was on the mark. Henderson, knock-kneed and pigeon-toed, moved pretty quickly, reaching Triple A by age 21. He flashed good power, once hitting 27 home runs in A ball and a spoonful of that color Ball predicted. "I'm raring to go," he said on the eve of the 1981 season after a white-hot spring earned him a spot on the Opening Day roster. "I have the raring-to-go butter-flies, not the scared butterflies," he said boldly. Then, in a measure of his counterbalancing levelheadedness, he added, "I hope I can make contact."

Making contact wasn't the problem. Making good contact was. So, in early June Henderson returned to Triple A Spokane where he mashed until the M's recalled him in September. He started the next season in the major leagues and never looked back. The first Mariners homegrown player to make an impact in the majors, Henderson lit up the Kingdome with power, neon defense, an eternal gap-toothed smile, and, as forecast, brio. Henderson's home-run trot, for instance, included more loops and flourishes than a '70s-era tuxedo. And he chased after routine fly balls on his tiptoes, high-steeping and grinning along the way. "Playing professional baseball brings a smile to my face," he told *Sports Illustrated* in 1991. "I don't need much else to have a good time."

The Mariners hoped Henderson would be the first of many homegrown players to get the good times rolling in Seattle. Texas Longhorns shortstop Spike Owen, selected in 1982 with the sixth overall pick, was another. His defense received rave reviews, though some doubted his bat. Hal Keller, Seattle's scouting director at the time, loved his potential on the fast turf of the Kingdome. In 1983 the M's gave him a taste of the big leagues. By 1984 Owen became the everyday shortstop. As predicted, he was a death stalker as a defender. Also as expected, he killed many a rally on offense. But most shortstops of this era hit meekly, and Owen drew walks at a respectable rate. He also exhibited strong leadership qualities, which prompted his manager, Chuck Cottier, to name Owen captain.

The Mariners youth movement supercharged over the next few years, as more and more homegrown talent bubbled up to the big leagues. The losing still continued, but the sense of total despair gave way to occasional bouts of optimism built on the backs of the farm-raised talent that kept showing up.

Then came 1986 and a slew of trades. Outfielder Ivan Calderon, coming off an impressive 1985, went first in June. Perhaps the best-looking hitting prospect the Mariners had to date, Danny Tartabull, got shipped off in December. Seattle worried about his work ethic. And in between Henderson and Owen headed to the Boston Red Sox in mid-August. Henderson's playing time had dropped considerably in recent weeks, even though he was enjoying his best year. But old school manager Dick Williams chafed at what he deemed Henderson's casual approach to baseball. He just couldn't brook the endless smiles and touch of lace Hendu added to everything. Even some other managers wondered if Henderson cared. "I mean, you're smiling in Seattle, where you're always getting beat," Tony La Russa, who would later manage Henderson on the Oakland A's, told a reporter. Both Hendu and Owen were ecstatic about the trade to the first-place Red Sox.

In return for these three trades, the Mariners received eight players. None returned any real long-term value to the Mariners. On the flip side, Tartabull, Calderon, Owen, and Henderson all enjoyed many more productive years. Later that season Henderson even pulled the Red Sox back from the abyss with a dramatic ninth-inning home run in the 1986 American League Championship Series against the California Angels that sent the series to a sixth game, which Boston won. And after the trade from Seattle, no one ever again questioned Henderson's dedication to the sport.

The Mariners lost all three trades—and in the process put a stall on their climb to respectability. "Those kids would have been outstanding here," said Chuck Cottier, Mariners manager from 1984–1986, in *Tales from the Seattle Mariners Dugout*. "They had nice careers and wound up as millionaires with other teams. But it cheated the fans in Seattle because when the players left, the fans lost that identity."

48 Julio Cruz

Selected by the Mariners with the 52nd pick in the 1976 Expansion Draft, Julio Cruz fought well above his weight class to anchor second base for six-plus years and thrill Seattle fans with his der-ring-do on the base paths and circus plays in the infield.

Cruz, from Southern California, started 1977 in Triple A Hawaii, where he swiped 47 bases and hit .366 with some extra-base power. His intoxicating play in Hawaii and a massive slump by Mariners second baseman Jose Baez persuaded the M's to promote Cruz on July 4. Much to his surprise, the M's put him in the starting lineup immediately against the Chicago White Sox at home. He picked up two hits and a walk in the Mariners' 6–2 loss to the White Sox. For the next five seasons, Cruz started almost every game at second base for the Mariners. He played like a first-division infielder stuck on a second-division club—at least with the glove and his feet.

One of the best defensive second basemen in the American League, Cruz made the routine plays and the spectacular ones, flashing the range of a migrating whale. Mentored by Hall of Fame second baseman Bill Mazeroski for two years, Cruz never won a Gold Glove nor finished among the league leaders in the vote. Blame ignorance and bias for that.

By the early '80s, Cruz teamed up with another Cruz (Todd) to form a rhapsodic double-play combo. In 1982 *The New York Times* called the duo "the talk of the major leagues [for their] ability to turn the acrobatic double play." What really gripped the "Paper of Record" was a play Julio made on a ball hit by Yankees Hall of Famer Dave Winfield. The M's led the Yankees 6–5 in the bottom of the 12th inning, when New York started a rally against Seattle reliever Bill Caudill, putting men on first and second with one down. Then Winfield laced a sharp grounder up the middle that looked determined to reach the outfield. Todd broke for the bag instead of the ball—the reverse of what he usually did on a smash up the middle. "I always break for the ball," Todd said after the game. "But this time, I instinctively broke for the bag. Why? Because Julio has great range, and I just sensed it was his ball." Julio dove to his right and ensnared the ball with his backhand while sliding on his belly well past second base. Recording any out appeared unlikely, especially because Jerry Mumphrey, running from first, had good speed. But Julio rose to his knees faster than a striking snake and shuffled the ball "over the top, sort of pushed it" to Todd. The throw beat the runner, and then Todd, bracing himself for a collision, pivoted in a flash and completed the bang-bang double play.

It was just one of many Julio Cruz jaw-droppers that today would be splashed all over ESPN. Another feat that would have headlined *SportsCenter* was the single-game American League record he set on June 7, 1981. Cruz recorded 18 total chances in nine innings without an error. The contest went extra innings, allowing him to handle one more chance, which fell a putout shy of the major league record. The evening ended with a little extra frosting, as he singled in the 12th, stole second, and scored the winning run.

Cruz's other compelling asset was speed. In a Mariners uniform, he stole 290 bases. Every time he reached first base, the home crowd would stir, anticipating the cat-and-mouse game to follow. Cruz usually won his dual with the pitcher and catcher, though it took him a few years before he swiped a base against a lefty. His success rate on stolen bases hovered around 80 percent, which consistently ranked in the top five in the league. In 1981 Cruz tied an American League record by stealing 32 bases without being caught. The Angels' Ed Ott threw him out on August 11 to end the streak one short of breaking the record. Cruz's highlight-reel defense and clever style on the bases became one of the best reasons to watch the Mariners in those early years. Shortly after making his debut, Cruz joined Ruppert Jones as a fan favorite.

Modern baseball statisticians would have scoffed at Cruz's bargain basement walk totals and feather light career on-base percentage plus slugging (OPS) of .620. But little about Cruz bothered most Mariners fans. What did rub them raw was when the M's traded Cruz to the White Sox at the trade deadline in 1983 for another second baseman, Tony Bernazard, who owned a better stick but lacked the Baryshnikov moves of Cruz in the field.

The trade was a boon for Cruz, who became part of the White Sox's "Win Ugly" American League West winner. The Pale Hose clinched the division against the Mariners. As the rest of his teammates celebrated on the field, Cruz quietly slipped into the clubhouse out of respect for his former mates. "Usually, you'd give a fist pump, and guys would be jumping on each other," said Cruz in a 2008 interview. "But I felt so bad for those guys. I played six-and-a-half years with them." He played three more seasons for the White Sox before retiring after the 1986 season.

After retirement, Cruz settled in Seattle, where he remained involved with the Mariners as a broadcaster for M's games in Spanish. He was elected to the Hispanic Heritage Baseball Museum Hall of Fame in 2004.

49 Best Trades

Looking for a reason why the Mariners usually end up taking the path of greatest resistance? Start by tallying up the number of trades the Mariners have won in lopsided fashion. The grim results: a three-toed sloth would need only one limb to count up the grand total. In almost 40 years, Seattle has made only three trades, listed below, in which the general consensus is that they fleeced the opposition.

Demolishing your opponent in a trade is found money that often leads to a period of sustained success. Bunch a few of these trades and you're really cooking. That's exactly what happened after numbers two and three on this list. First…

Three Lesser Trades (based on net Wins Above Replacement difference):
February, 2000. Ken Griffey Jr. to Reds for Mike Cameron, Brett Tomko, Antonio Perez, and Jake Meyer (+5.4 WAR). New general manager Pat Gillick pulled a rabbit from his hat on this deal. The

Sein on Big Stein Trade

In a classic 1996 scene from the 1990s hit TV show *Seinfeld*, the Mariners trade for Jay Buhner is rehashed in an exchange between Frank Constanza (key character George's father) and George's employer, George Steinbrenner, owner of the New York Yankees. In typically farcical manner, George goes missing from work. Steinbrenner then visits the parents' house to personally report the tragedy. As George's mother, Estelle, absorbs the grim news, Frank suddenly and indelicately blurts out: "What the hell did you trade Jay Buhner for? He had 30 home runs and over 100 RBIs last year. He's got a rocket for an arm. You don't know what the hell you're doing!" Steinbrenner calmy responds: "Well, Buhner was a good prospect, no question about it. But my baseball people loved Ken Phelps' bat. They kept saying, 'Ken Phelps, Ken Phelps.'"

Reds had all the leverage because Griffey, who owned trade veto rights, kept rejecting every M's trade offer until the options narrowed to one: Cincinnati. Nonetheless, the M's managed to extract value, especially from Cameron, while Griffey's sublime greatness in Seattle failed to transfer to Cincinnati.

August, 1998. Joey Cora to Indians for David Bell (+6.3). The gadfly of a second baseman finally met his demise as a player in Cleveland. Bell gave the Mariners three surprisingly strong seasons at second then third, displaying 20-homer power and slick defense.

May, 1991. Jim Blueberg to Yankees for Mike Blowers (+5.4). Blueberg, a pitcher, never made it to the majors. Washington-raised Blowers helped key the Mariners' mid-1990s renaissance.

The Lopsided Hall of Fame

May, 1989. Mark Langston and Mike Campbell to Expos for Gene Harris, Brian Holman, and Randy Johnson (+22.2). The most celebrated trade in Mariners history, oddly enough, didn't play out as imagined. At the time, Holman and Harris were considered the prizes. Johnson represented an interesting what if, but he was not the main target. Langston remained armed and dangerous for years after the trade, making the M's margin of victory robust but short of a total rout.

July, 1988. Ken Phelps to Yankees for Jay Buhner, Rich Balabon, and Troy Evers (+22.9). The M's most consistent power source at the time, Phelps, after two productive months in New York, bombed in his remaining time as a Bronx Bomber. Buhner became part of the core of the first great Mariners team. Two lopsided trades, 10 months apart, helped to rearrange the fortunes of Seattle baseball.

July, 1996. Darren Bragg to Red Sox for Jamie Moyer (+26.8). This deal kept the good times rolling in Seattle. Bragg was the definition of expendable, a backup outfielder with an expired upside. Boston surely thought the same thing about Moyer, a journeyman lefty who the Sox used as a long reliever. Somehow, through luck and timing, he had accumulated a 7–1 record before the trade. The M's stuck him in the rotation—where he stayed for parts of 11 seasons, had two 20-win years, made an All-Star team, and helped keep the Mariners interesting for most of that time.

50 1982: A Mound Rising

As the Mariners entered the second half of their first decade, ballplayers with real futures started consuming more and more roster spots.

Many of them could be found on the mound. In the starting rotation, the Mariners featured two talented 27-year-olds: the inconsistent lefty and Seattle area native Floyd Bannister and Jim Beattie, who had enjoyed a strong season the year before. The rest of the staff consisted mostly of pitchers 25 or younger: starters Mike Moore, Gene Nelson, Bob Stoddard, and 19-year-old Ed Nunez and bullpen guys Bill Caudill, Bryan Clark, and Ed Vande Berg. One concession to veteran experience was 43-year-old Gaylord Perry, who was signed during spring training.

Manager Rene Lachemann, who had replaced the baffling Maury Wills at mid-season, hired pitching coach Dave Duncan, a former major league catcher who held the same job with the Cleveland Indians the year before. Duncan, as he would do many times over the next 30 years, pulled off the seemingly unthinkable: transforming the Mariners pitching staff from a lamb into a lion.

An early adopter of charting pitches (how many, what type, outcomes), Duncan's philosophy was simple: instead of lecturing his pitchers on the importance of, say, first-pitch strikes, he would simply show them the data, accumulated from the reams of charts he kept. "Pitchers can argue with the philosophy, but not the numbers," he told a reporter that year. "If I can do something to enhance a given pitcher's physical ability just a little, I feel I've accomplished something."

Mariners pitching accomplished a lot in '82, finishing in the top four in ERA, hits allowed, saves, and strikeouts—far ahead of anything achieved by past Mariners staffs. Gopher balls remained a problem (that darn Kingdome), but M's pitchers mitigated the damage by leading the league in whiffs. No one took Duncan's charts to heart more than free-agent-to-be Bannister, who finally harnessed his three above-average pitches to lead the American League in strikeouts and earn an All-Star berth, where he pitched a scoreless inning. "He is a great confidence builder," Bannister said about Duncan. The Mariners ace also finished in the AL top ten in

ERA, hits per nine innings, and shutouts. "He is one of the premier pitchers in the game," said M's catcher Jim Essian.

Other beneficiaries of Duncan's charts and tutelage included rookie Moore, who surged immediately after the All-Star break before fading in mid-September, Beattie, who recorded career highs in wins and strikeouts, reliever Ed Vande Berg, who posted a 2.37 ERA, and closer Bill Caudill, who picked up 26 saves and enjoyed a career year. Livid that AL All-Star manager Billy Martin failed to select Caudill to the team, the Mariners filed a token protest with league president Larry MacPhail.

No one protested about the way the Mariners played for the first four months of the season. As the pitching kept opponents in check or within reach, the Mariners staged a glut of come-from-behind wins. "The Miracles M's," as local papers dubbed them, staged 26 comeback wins in the first half, including 13 when either trailing or tied in the ninth.

Hitting coach Vada Pinson had a theory on the M's sudden competitiveness. "Anytime you've got a bunch of fringe players who aren't under any pressure to produce—because they know you don't have anyone in your farm system who can replace them—it's hard to create any momentum," Pinson explained to *The Christian Science Monitor*. "Six years ago that was probably the Mariners' biggest problem. But now that our farm system is starting to turn out quality, we're in a position to build a winning attitude that can last. Good trades and a strong bullpen have also helped tremendously." One of the young guys was homegrown outfielder Dave Henderson, who was on pace to hit 14 home runs in just 324 at-bats. Veterans Richie Zisk, Bruce Bochte, and Al Cowens provided the rest of the lineup's sock. The Cruzs—Todd and Julio—gave the Mariners airtight defense up the middle.

On July 8 Seattle beat the Orioles 4–3. It marked a franchise milestone, moving the M's seven games over .500 for the first time in history and within three games of first place, the closest ever to the division lead that late in the season. Attendance spiked, which included 36,471 paid customers for a Monday evening game, unprecedented for that night of the week. One desperate fan called *The Seattle Times* asking how he could get tickets. "I can't find *Seattle Rainiers* in the phone book," he said, puzzled. But Lachemann shrugged off the idea that the M's were legitimately in the pennant race. "You're not a contender until September," he said. "Three games out in July don't mean anything unless you're there at the end."

Alas, the Mariners slowly faded from the race. Then dreams of a .500 finish collapsed when they closed the season on a six-game losing streak. The pitching staff, which had been mostly responsible for the M's flirtation with .500, wheezed instead of whistled down the stretch. A club-record 21 extra-innings games, including a 20-frame loss to the Angels in April, taxed the M's bullpen and probably accounted for some of the drop-off. But the 76 wins represented a franchise record, as did the fourth-place finish. "I felt that come October 5," Lachemann reflected after the season, "you'd be talking to somebody else. [Because] I felt we'd probably lose 100 games."

Attendance shrunk in accordance with the M's decline. But 1982 illustrated that Seattle baseball fans would respond, if given a winner. Unfortunately, storm clouds moved in during the offseason. The staff ace, Floyd Bannister, skipped town as a free agent to the Chicago White Sox. Seattle owner George Argyros blamed the short fences of the Kingdome. Then one of the mainstays of the offense, Bochte, retired unexpectedly. The biggest blow, in retrospect, came when Duncan, rebuffed in his attempt to negotiate a multi-year deal with the Mariners, left for the White Sox, leaving Mariners fans to wonder what more the Mound Whisperer could have done in Seattle.

51 The Inspector

"The Inspector's the best thing to happen to Seattle since Boeing and the rain," said Craig Barrick, director of operations at the Kingdome, to *Sports Illustrated* in August of 1982. The Inspector, of course, wasn't a detective solving difficult crimes around the Pacific Northwest. He was Mariners relief pitcher Bill Caudill, who that year put more adversaries in handcuffs than Sherlock Holmes.

On April Fools' Day of 1982, the Chicago Cubs traded the talented but inconsistent 25-year-old mop-up man to the New York Yankees, who then traded him to Seattle. The joke was on Chicago and New York. Caudill transformed into a lockdown closer that year. He saved 26 games while striking out 111 in $95\frac{2}{3}$ innings with a 2.35 ERA. "I just love being here," he said after recording his first save. "I'm finally getting a chance to play."

Back-to-back games against the power-laden Baltimore Orioles in early July spotlighted his overpowering stuff. In the first game, Caudill entered a 7–7 contest in the ninth with a runner on first and no outs. The Birds' Ken Singleton, Cal Ripken, and John Lowenstein awaited him. Running his 90-ish-mph fastball in, then out, and finally elevating it, he whiffed all three. The Mariners eventually won the game. The next night, he protected a 4–3 lead by striking out Singleton and Orioles great Eddie Murray on six pitches, stranding a runner on second base. "That's when I thought we had someone special in Cuffs," said his teammate, Richie Zisk.

"Cuffs" was another of Caudill's nicknames, along with "the Inspector." In a clubhouse crowded with guys seemingly hooked on mischief and pranks, Caudill stood above them all. For him, every day was April Fools' Day, so you could say the joke was on the Mariners as well. "The only word in pranksterism is originality,"

Caudill said. "I want to pull pranks that people will talk about for 10 or 12 years. There's only one time that the looseness ends, and that's when they say, 'Caudill, start throwing.' You've got to smile even if you lose. I can see baseball ruining my sundown, but I can't see it ruining my sunup. Every day's a new one in this game."

Some of Caudill's antics were strategic and intended to help deflate pressure. That's how he received his first nickname, "the Inspector." After losing seven of nine on their first road trip due mostly to anemic offense, the Mariners returned to the Kingdome to find Caudill dressed as Sherlock Holmes in the dugout. He announced to his teammates that he was examining the bats to determine what happened to all the good ones. He would pull out a bat, check it from top to bottom, shake it, and then throw it away. Voila, Caudill had a nickname, "the Inspector," after Inspector Clouseau of *Pink Panther* fame. Almost immediately, Dick Kimball, the Kingdome organist, started playing the theme song from the *Pink Panther* movies each time Caudill appeared. The fans loved it, sending him a deluge of props: inspector badges, magnifying glasses, stuffed pink panthers, and even a calabash pipe.

Caudill's second nickname originated not from a prank but from a bizarre event in Cleveland. Depending on who's telling the story and when, the details vary. Here's the one Caudill told in 1982. Asked to leave the hotel bar at 2:30 AM, he rode the elevator up to his room. Then he rode it back down. Three times he did this before the hotel's security guard slapped a pair of handcuffs on him and threatened to take him downtown. His manager, Rene Lachemann, talked the guard out of it. Eventually, his teammates discovered what happened, and another nickname was born: "Cuffs." Not able to resist the obvious, Zisk bought Caudill a pair of handcuffs. Big mistake.

At first, Caudill suggested Lachemann make a handcuff sign when he wanted to summon the reliever from the bullpen. But Caudill scratched that idea after getting bombed the first time.

Instead, he launched a reign of terror, handcuffing unsuspecting victims all over the ballpark. That included Lachemann's 13-year-old son, who Caudill strapped to a Nautilus machine, and Julia Argyros, the wife of the Mariners' owner, who found herself handcuffed to the dugout bench. "He always had them with him," said teammate Julio Cruz in *Tales from the Seattle Mariners Dugout*, "and he would walk up to you and just slap them on you...or he would come up and say, 'Let me see if these fit, and cuff you.'"

The hijinks didn't end there. Caudill once entertained Tiger Stadium fans during a rain delay by putting on a Conehead mask, the property of eccentric bullpen mate Larry Andersen, and donning a Gaylord Perry jersey stuffed with a pillow. Then he impersonated Perry while standing on the tarp—until Perry stormed out of the dugout and tackled Caudill, yelling at him, "I'm going to kill you," with his face flush with anger.

Another time, during a losing streak, Caudill took the mound with his beard half-shaved. After Barry Bonnell of the Toronto Blue Jays, who were insulted by Caudill's antics, hit a screamer off his chest, Caudill shaved off the rest of his beard and then pitched a scoreless ninth. Whenever Caudill had a bad game, he had a stock reply for his performance: "Even Betty Crocker burns a cake once in a while."

Caudill burned more cakes in 1983 than 1982. His strikeouts declined, his walks increased, and his ERA doubled. The Mariners traded him to Oakland, where he rebounded with an All-Star year for the A's before being traded to Toronto. The man who negotiated that contract: Scott Boras. Caudill was one of the super agent's first clients, and he secured a five-year $8.7 million deal from the Blue Jays. Caudill retired at the beginning of the 1988 season due to injury. He moved back to the Pacific Northwest and for years coached the Eastside Catholic High School baseball team, along with Cruz. He also worked for Boras.

52 Mariners Misplays and Bloopers

No book about the M's would be complete without a look back at a handful of infamous bloopers, blunders, and slips.

Fined While on the Mound

July 10, 1977

Stan Thomas threw four consecutive balls at the Minnesota Twins' Mike Cubbage with the intent of hitting him—and missed all four times badly—accumulating a team-record four wild pitches in the process. Manager Darrell Johnson stormed out to the mound and fined Thomas on the spot.

Running Wild

May 22, 1977

The Mariners had *six* runners thrown out on the base path in a game against the Oakland Athletics and played one of the most embarrassing sixth innings in their history. In that inning the Mariners had two runners, Skip Jutze and Dan Meyer, both thrown out attempting to steal home on the front end of a double steal. Also in that inning, the Mariners had another runner picked off second. Jutze was also nabbed trying to steal home in the fourth inning on the front end of a double steal. The M's were almost thrown out for the cycle: Dave Collins (second base, seventh inning); Jutze (home, fourth inning); Jutze and Meyer (home, sixth inning); Meyer (third base, eighth inning).

A Broken-Legged Double Play

July 9, 1985

It's one thing to get thrown out at home plate—but twice on the same play? And when the catcher has a busted leg and a broken ankle? In the third inning against the Toronto Blue Jays, Seattle's Phil Bradley attempted to score from second on Gorman Thomas' single to right. Jesse Barfield threw to catcher Buck Martinez in time to nail Bradley, but Bradley bowled over Martinez in a collision that broke Martinez's leg. Thomas went to second on the throw and, seeing Martinez writhing in agony, tried to take third. Martinez, prone, threw wildly to third. Thomas took off for home. Left fielder George Bell threw perfectly to Martinez, who caught the ball half-sitting up and tagged out the runner, suffering a broken ankle in the process.

Runner Scores from Second on a Walk
April 18, 1986
Pitcher Mike Moore got into trouble against the A's in the third inning when, with Jose Canseco on first, Alfredo Griffin doubled. After getting the next two outs, Moore walked former Mariner Bruce Bochte to load the bases. Then Moore walked Dwayne Murphy to force in a run. Moore was so upset that when catcher Steve Yeager threw the ball back to him, he bounced it off the turf in disgust. Just before Moore bounced the ball, Yeager turned his back to Moore and walked toward the plate. Griffin, trotting to third on the walk and seeing that Moore and Yeager weren't paying attention, made a dash for home. Moore panicked and fired a throw that sailed into the backstop, allowing Griffin to score. "It was the most bizarre inning I've ever seen," said Seattle manager Chuck Cottier.

Three Runs on Comebacker to a Pitcher
July 24, 1991
With runners on second and third and one out in the fourth, Pat Kelly of the New York Yankees hit a comebacker to Erik Hanson, who trapped Kevin Maas in a rundown between third and home.

But Maas scored when Edgar Martinez's throw hit him in the back. The ball rolled up the first-base line in foul territory and was snapped up by catcher Dave Cochrane, who threw home to head off Alvaro Espinoza, also attempting to score. The throw went into the Mariners' dugout, allowing Espinoza and Kelly to cross the plate with the second and third runs.

Worst Debut by a Mariners Starter
April 6, 1988
Steve Trout, son of legendary flake Dizzy Trout and a veteran of 10 major league seasons, endured one of the more dreadful fiascos in decades in his first start after joining the Mariners in an offseason trade with the Yankees. In two-thirds of an inning against the A's, Trout threw 22 of 29 pitches out of the strike zone, walked five straight batters, made a throwing error, and uncorked two run-scoring wild pitches. M's pitching coach Billy Connors called it "vapor locked." In Trout's third start, on April 17, he self-destructed again in the first inning, giving up five runs, throwing two wild pitches, committing three balks, and walking three hitters. "He was caca. He has no clue," Connors said. "He was hitting guys on 0–2 pitches and not even hurting them."

A Double Record
June 22, 1992
In a 7–2 loss to Oakland, Dave Cochrane of the Mariners tied a club record for most outfield assists in a game with two and set a club record for most errors by an outfielder with three.

Nine Runs Allowed with Two Outs
April 6, 1992
The Rangers scored them in the eighth inning en route to a 12–10 victory. The main goat was reliever Mike Schooler, who allowed

Gene Petralli's pinch-hit three-run homer, a double, and three singles.

Four Runs on a Single

June 11, 1993

The Mariners lost to the Angels 8–2 after allowing four runs—on a single. After Erik Hanson loaded the bases in the fourth, California's Greg Myers looped a single to left. Henry Cotto threw a ball that sailed over catcher Bill Haselman's head, and two runs scored. Hanson, late backing up home plate, rifled a throw far over third baseman Edgar Martinez's head, allowing two more runs to score. "I've seen that play before," said manager Lou Piniella. "Down in Tampa when I was 11 years old, out playing on a playground."

The Cycle (the Bad Kind)

April 8, 1994

Dave Fleming "pitched for the cycle" in the second inning, allowing Toronto a home run (Carlos Delgado and Joe Carter), a triple (Devon White), a double (Alex Gonzalez), and a single (Paul Molitor).

Six Runs without an At-Bat

May 14, 2004

The Yankees scored six runs against the Mariners without the benefit of an official at-bat. Mariners pitchers issued 10 walks, including four with the bases loaded.

53 A Mighty Wind

Playing third base for the Mariners on May 27, 1981, was Lenny Randle. A utility man, the 32-year-old had been signed as a free agent three days before Opening Day. Seattle was his fifth stop in the majors. One of Billy Martin's favorite players, Randle moved all over the diamond for Martin in Texas and New York and played regularly (unlike many utility men). He had great speed, good instincts, and a mosquito-like quality for bothering the opposition. But he lacked natural hitting ability.

After Martin left Texas to become the Yankees manager, Randle snapped one day after losing his starting job and being called a "punk" by new Rangers manager Frank Lucchesi. He confronted Lucchesi and then beat him senseless. Among other injuries, Lucchesi suffered a fractured cheekbone and spent time in the hospital. The attack stunned everyone in baseball especially because Randle had a reputation as an outgoing, friendly guy with no history of violence or insubordination. Texas suspended Randle and then traded him to the New York Mets, where he had a career year on a miserable team.

By the time he arrived in Seattle, Randle had reconciled with Lucchesi and rebuilt his reputation off the field. His baseball career appeared to be regenerating as well. After a poor year with the Yankees, he rebounded in 1980 to steal 19 bases and hit a respectable .276 for the Chicago Cubs. During the first two months of 1981, though, Randle struggled to hit above .240 and ignite his running game. As he and the Mariners waited for an offensive breakout, Randle found himself smack in the middle of two brawls in a doubleheader with Oakland. He left the second game of the

Randle the Rapper

During the baseball strike of 1981, Randle coaxed a few of his teammates into making a dance song entitled "Kingdome." The song was released as a single in 1982 by Lenny Randle and the Ballplayers. Unlike its more famous successor, "the Super Bowl Shuffle" of the 1985 Chicago Bears, Randle's song didn't include a music video. Randle claims, without much evidence, that the rap song was a "huge sensation." Here are the opening lyrics: "There's a dance going around Seattle, and it's moving across the land. All the folks are doing it—they're even doing it in Iran." In 2014, the song was re-released as part of a compilation on *Wheedles Groove: Seattle Funk, Modern Soul & Boogie, Volume II, 1972–1987.*

twin bill after receiving death threats. A's manager Billy Martin didn't approve of Randle's objections to an inside pitch that prompted the first brawl or Randle's hard tag of Tony Armas that precipitated the second rhubarb. But he understood. "Randle is just trying to shake up his club," Martin said after the game.

Then the Kansas City Royals came to town for a four-game series at the end of May. As the Mariners tried to win for the third time in the four-game set, Randle decided to shake things up again. Or to put it more accurately, blow things around. With a man on first and two down, the Royals' Amos Otis took a big swing that resulted in a dribbler down the third-base line. Playing back, Randle couldn't reach the ball in time to throw out the speedy Otis. Two of his teammates arrived at the ball first. But they could only stare helplessly as it hugged the line, staying stubbornly fair. Suddenly, Randle charged in, knelt down, and lowered his body so his face was level with the ball. He started screaming at it to go foul. When that didn't work, Randle puckered up and blew on the ball until—*voila*—it actually curved over the line into foul territory. "Foul ball!" cried the umpire Larry McCoy. Royals manager Jim Frey bounded from the dugout to protest. After a meeting the umpires reversed the call, and Otis was given a single. The M's protested but to no avail. "I didn't blow," Randle said after the game. "I used the power of suggestion. I yelled at it, 'Go foul. Go foul.' How could they call it a hit? It was a foul ball."

But the impish expression on his face as he offered his defense betrayed him. Plus, the video quite plainly shows Randle with lips puckered blowing on the ball. "None of us had ever seen anything like that," said crew chief Dave Phillips. "Lenny did it to be funny," continued Phillips after the game. "And it was funny. But you can't alter the course of the ball. You couldn't throw dirt on the ball and get away with it."

The Royals failed to capitalize on the single but won the game nonetheless. Quick research in the press box revealed that Randle was actually the second professional ballplayer to deploy artificial wind to alter the direction of a ball. In a minor league game in 1940 between Montreal and Jersey City, Woody Jensen, a Washington state native, blew foul a ball topped down the third-base line by Jersey City's Bert Haas. The International League president later decreed the action illegal. In any event Major League Baseball clarified the rule after Randle's histrionics.

Randle never did find his groove during the season and he retired from baseball the next year. But memory of Randle's cheeky move that day in the Kingdome has survived well past his retirement. Randle even profits from it. He created a baseball academy called "Lenny Randle 4 Education" that mixes baseball training and life lessons. The academy's motto is Don't Blow It…Stay in School.

54 2007 and 2009: Hopes Renew

Following the consecutive 90-win seasons in 2002–2003, a lot went wrong. Stars—Jay Buhner, Edgar Martinez, and Dan Wilson—retired. Solid contributors—Bret Boone, John Olerud, Jamie Moyer, Mike Cameron, and Mark McLemore—moved on or bowed to Father Time. Big free-agent signings—Richie Sexson, Adrian Beltre, Carl Everett, and Jeff Weaver—failed initially or eventually disappointed. Trades—Rafael Soriano for Horacio Ramirez; Asdrubal Cabrera for Eduardo Perez; Shin-Soo Choo for Ben Broussard; Adam Jones, Chris Tillman, et al for Erik Bedard turned rancid. And touted prospects—Chris Snelling, Yuniesky Betancourt, Jose Lopez, and Jody Reed—suffered serious injury or ultimately flamed out.

But two seasons interrupted the misery. In 2007 the M's hung in the American League West for five months. On August 25 they trailed the Angels by a single game. Attendance, which had sagged the previous three seasons, spiked, and talk around town about the Mariners revived. "This is a fun team to watch," said Mariners executive vice president Bob Aylward. "They hit, they play great defense, and they play with emotion. The fans like that." It was fun to watch because of the only holdover from the glory years, Ichiro Suzuki, who went on to win another Gold Glove and collect 238 hits. Along with homegrown product Raul Ibanez, other key contributors were 2005 free-agent signee Beltre, who had his best offensive season as a Mariner; Jose Guillen and his .290 average and 23 homers; catcher Kenji Johjima, signed out of Japan the year before; young phenom starting pitcher Felix Hernandez; and J.J. Putz, who racked up 40 saves and won the Rolaids Reliever of the Year award.

After three straight last-place finishes, the Mariners' contention deep into August shocked many. Even more shocking was manager Mike Hargrove's decision to quit on July 1. The Mariners were 45–33 and breathing down Anaheim's neck. Hargrove swatted away conspiratorial theories about his departure, insisting he was simply burned out. The press speculated his decision was tied to his frosty relationship with Ichiro, who had bristled at Hargrove's suggestion he alter his approach at the plate. In any event the Mariners signed Ichiro to a contract extension 12 days after Hargrove's resignation.

Bench coach John McLaren replaced Hargrove, and the Mariners surged, cresting at 20 games over .500 on August 24. Then they lost 15-of-17 to plunge out of both the division and wild-card races. Five consecutive victories to end the season gave the Mariners 88 wins, the most since 2003. "It was a good way to end the year," said Putz on the Mariners' closing-act winning streak. "It was a good year."

With McLaren back as manager, the next season fell desperately short of a good one. The M's lost 101 games, and McLaren lost his job mid-season. Free-agent signee pitcher Carlos Silva and a blockbuster trade for starting pitcher Bedard yielded miserable results. An expose by *The Seattle Times* revealed a clubhouse riddled with dissension, animosity, and jealousy. McLaren couldn't stamp it out nor could his successor, Jim Riggleman, who had a reputation as a disciplinarian. By the end of the season, the Mariners cleaned house, firing general manager Bill Bavasi and Riggleman.

The purge had the desired effect. The Mariners rebounded in 2009 with 85 wins, though they never seriously contended for a playoff spot. Presiding over the strong reversal were new GM Jack Zduriencik, a heralded front-office executive from the Milwaukee Brewers who embraced baseball's new analytics, and new skipper, Don Wakamatsu, Oakland's bench coach who had worked at one time for all three of the Mariners' division rivals.

Leading the revival were center fielder Franklin Gutierrez, a defensive maestro acquired in a blockbuster trade over the winter; free agent Russell Branyan, who slugged 31 homers; Ichiro and his .352 batting average; the 23-year-old Hernandez, who after a stern talk with Wakamatsu in May rocketed to a 19–5 record and superstardom status; and Ken Griffey Jr., who contributed with 19 homers including a thrilling one on Opening Day in Minnesota as part of his return to Seattle. The biggest turnaround occurred on defense, where the Mariners led the league by a wide margin in defensive efficiency. Credit went to Zduriencik and his team of new-stat lieutenants. Many of the M's insisted good chemistry in the clubhouse played a strong part as well. "Since spring training, there was a lot of difference," Hernandez said when asked to compare 2009 to 2008. "A lot of fun."

55 Best and Funkiest Promotions

Seattle M's Relief "Tugboat"
1982

It was the era of the gimmicky bullpen cart, and the Mariners came up with a doozy: a tugboat, one of the larger reliever transport vehicles in major league service. One problem: Mariners relievers refused to use the boat. Bill Caudill even stole the keys prior to Opening Day. He finally gave them back but not before delaying the start of the game. On one occasion Ed Vande Berg ran in front of the boat all the way to the mound. Gaylord Perry finally instituted a $100 fine if any reliever used the boat. "I'll be [bleeped] if anybody's going to come in and pitch for me riding a goddamned tugboat," Perry said. In August of 1982, Caudill and pitcher Larry Andersen stole the tugboat and stationed it outside the Kingdome just before game time, selling pictures and pennants. They made approximately $500.

Mariner Marketing Slogans
1977: We Can Do It Together
1979: It's an All-Star Summer
1980: Coming on Strong All Season Long
1981: Join the Lineup
1982: Playin' Hardball
1983: Playin' Hardball
1984: Anything Can Happen
1985: See It Happen
1986: Big League Stuff
1987: Playin' for Keeps
1988: Playin' for Keeps
1989: I Believe in Baseball
1990: New Seattle Mariners
1992: Safe at Home
1996: Refuse to Lose
2000: You Gotta Love These Guys
2001: Sodo Mojo
2002: Mojo Risin'
2003: Get All of It. Hey Now!
2004: Get All of It. Hey Now!
2005: What a Show
2009: A New Day, a New Way
2010: Believe Big
2011: Ready to Play
2012: Get After It
2013: True to the Blue
2014: True to the Blue

Note: some years didn't have a slogan.

Funny Nose and Glasses Night
1982

Inspired by a Tom Paciorek TV commercial from the previous year promoting "Jacket Night," this ranks high on the list of the Mariners' wackiest promotions. The glasses were given out to fans before the game as they entered the Kingdome. Manager Rene Lachemann wore a pair when he exchanged lineup cards at home plate. Because of the advance promotion, the game drew 36,700 fans, almost 10,000 more than had watched Gaylord Perry's 300th win two nights before.

Dave Valle Days
August, 1991

During the dog days of the 1991 season and with Mariners catcher Dave Valle batting a myopic .136, a restaurant and bar near the Kingdome, Swannie's, launched a special promotion titled "Dave Valle Days." It worked like this: the price of well drinks or beers at the bar cost whatever Valle's batting average was. So if Valle was hitting .136, a drink cost $1.36. The promotion, which ran for six weeks during which drinks (and Valle's average) fluctuated between $1.28 and $1.57, didn't elate Valle, but Swannie's proprietor, Jim Swanson, told reporters he wasn't worried about it. "If Dave Valle ever got mad and walked in the bar to confront me," he said, "I told my doorman to just give him a bat. That way I know I won't get hurt."

Buhner Buzz Cut Nights
1994–2001

During the first-ever "Jay Buhner Buzz Cut Night" held in 1994 near Gate D at the Kingdome, 512 fans happily had their locks, curls, and cowlicks removed in the fashion of the Mariners cue-balled right fielder. Seattle resident Lori Hanson, a redhead, became the first woman to have her head buzzed. In all seven Buhner Buzz

As part of a gameday promotion called "Jay Buhner Buzz Cut Night," Jay Buhner uses the clippers on his father, David.

Cut nights drew 22,302, including 298 women. The last one, in 2001, drew a record 6,246, including 112 women.

Guaranteed No-Hitter Night
1990
Earlier in the week, Nolan Ryan had thrown his sixth career no-hitter. As luck would have it, the Mariners had planned this promotion before Ryan's no-no. More than 37,000 fans showed up, the third largest crowd of the year. Harold Reynolds ended the suspense early with an infield hit in the third, and the Mariners won 5–0. M's fans received a free general admission ticket to a future game against the Angels—all because Ryan failed to pitch back-to-back no-hitters.

Turn Ahead the Clock Night
1998
A spinoff of the popular Turn Back the Clock Night promotions, Turn Ahead the Clock Night imagined Major League Baseball in the year 2027. Ken Griffey and the Mariners donned futuristic uniforms with a 50th anniversary logo. Pregame festivities featured a laser show. The Kingdome was renamed the Biodome, a robot plus actor James Doohan (Scotty from *Star Trek*) threw out first pitches, and the scoreboard showed new teams (Pluto, Mighty Pups, Saturn Rings, and Mercury Fire).

International Mascot Competition
1981
The Mariners staged a mascot competition. Noteworthy entrants included the Bulgarian Rabbit, the Baby (a guy actually dressed like a baby who crawled 100 yards over the turf), the Space Needle, and a rolling-skating salmon. The Space Needle won.

Edgar Martinez Rubber Duck Night
2003
Fans received a rubber duck loosely resembling Edgar Martinez.

Dave Niehaus Story Night
2003
The promotion included a CD with the M's broadcaster reading bedtime stories.

Stitch 'N Pitch
2005–current
This event sets aside a section for fans to knit.

Beard Night
2013–current
Fans receive a knit hat with faux facial hair.

56 2001 All-Star Game

Boy, had things changed. The last time Seattle hosted the All-Star Game in 1979, the young Mariners franchise was a small planet far from the core of the galaxy. Twenty-two years later when baseball returned to the Emerald City for the Midsummer Classic, the Mariners had grown, shifted orbit, and now stood at the center of the sport. They featured a brand new ballpark, a galaxy of stars, and a record almost unmatched in the history of Major League Baseball.

Differences between 1979 and 2001 could be found everywhere. For starters, eight Mariners made the All-Star team compared to the lone M in 1979. Ichiro even topped all major leaguers with 3,373,035 votes. Seattle baseball fans responded differently as well. Although the Kingdome eventually sold out, seats, which started at $5.50, remained available days before the game. In 2001 the game sold out months in advance, and tickets were well over $100. And in 1979 pregame festivities amounted to a salmon bake and a few expensive dinners. Safeco Field All-Star activities included the All-Star Fantasy Camp at Greenlake, Fan Fest at the Stadium Exhibition Center, a fan cruise of Puget Sound, and the Home Run Derby.

Ichiro dominated the pregame conversation, especially when the first three pitches he saw during batting practice ended up in the right-field bleachers. Wearing his hat and sunglasses backward for the duration of the workout, he maintained his usual cool demeanor as fans clamored for autographs and chanted his name. "He's exactly what people should be talking about," said former Mariner Alex Rodriguez. "He'd probably win the Home Run Derby if he entered it."

Ichiro led off the bottom of the first against another former Mariner, Randy Johnson. Then he reached base, fittingly, on an infield single and stole second base. "I'm very honored just to face Randy Johnson in an All-Star Game," Ichiro said reverentially. The other three Mariners in the starting lineup—Bret Boone, Edgar Martinez, and John Olerud—went hitless, not that the home crowd cared. When each Mariners player batted, he was greeted with robust cheering. "Home of the Great Seattle Eight," boasted a sign in the center-field bleachers. Freddy Garcia pitched a scoreless third inning and picked up the win. Jeff Nelson posted a goose egg in the seventh, and Kazuhiro Sasaki nailed down the 4–1 victory with a save. The other Mariners hit belonged to the wide-eyed

Lasorda Goes Down

The other indelible moment from the 2001 All-Star Game involved another legend. Longtime Dodgers manager Tommy Lasorda was made an honorary coach for the National League and in the sixth inning he trotted out to coach third base. But the quick-witted Lasorda proved less quick on his feet. When Vladimir Guerrero's bat shattered on a vicious swing, the barrel headed toward Lasorda. The 73-year-old threw up his hands in a vain attempt to avoid being hit. He then tumbled backward almost landing on his head, and for a moment, many thought he was seriously hurt. But he pulled himself together, stood up, and put his cap back on. The benches and crowd let out a relieved laugh just before Barry Bonds handed Lasorda a chest protector. "I'm not quite as agile as I used to be," Lasorda said. "I'll be 74 in a couple months."

first-time All-Star Mike Cameron. He legged out a hustle double in the sixth inning. "It was an adrenaline thing," said Cameron about stretching his single into a double.

If Ichiro hogged the attention before the game, Baltimore's Cal Ripken Jr. owned it during the game. In the third inning, on the first pitch he saw, Ripken hit a home run to give the American League a 1–0 lead. His blast underscored another difference between 1979 and 2001. The immensely popular Orioles player had announced that this was his last year, and sentimentality about his final All-Star appearance ran high during the week. When he came to bat, the crowd gave him a rousing standing ovation. They even cheered the reviled A-Rod when he offered to switch positions with Ripken, who had been voted in at third base after spending his career at shortstop. The meatball served up to Ripken by Los Angeles Dodgers pitcher Chan Ho Park aroused suspicions that Park grooved the pitch. Not that anyone cared. Unlike the All-Star Game in 1979, which both sides played to win, by 2001 the Midsummer Classic had morphed into a meaningless exhibition designed for moments just like the Ripken homer.

In any event, Ripken was given the MVP award for the game—as much for his historical contributions to baseball as for his solo home run. Subsequent homers by Derek Jeter and Magglio Ordonez helped the American League secure the victory.

57 Father-Son Connections

Ken Griffey Sr., 40 years old and a former great on the Big Red Machine and New York Yankees, cut ties with the Cincinnati Reds on August 18, 1990. His son Ken Griffey Jr., who sparred with his father growing up and still competed with him over everything, lobbied the Mariners to sign him. The M's obliged. They thought a veteran influence might help not just Griffey but the entire team. It was "more than just a marketing coup," explained Mariners general manager Woody Woodward.

Griffey Sr. suited up the first time for the Mariners on August 31. Before the game the media swamped the dugout, but Junior tried to avoid appearing in public near his father. He had heard a bounty of $10,000 existed for a photo of father and son together. That night both Junior and senior collected hits, and Senior nailed the Kansas City Royals' Bo Jackson at second base on a throw from left field. Said Junior: "It runs in the family." For the next six weeks, the sight of father and son playing together captivated baseball fans everywhere—though one day soared above the rest.

Three weeks after Senior's Mariners debut, the duo again made history, in a moment Junior always cites as a career highlight. They hit back-to-back home runs on September 14, 1990, against the Angels' Kirk McCaskill. In Senior's 32nd at-bat as a Mariner, he hit a 402-foot bomb to center field. It was his third homer as a Mariners player and the 151st in his 18-year career. Junior, hitting behind him, worked the count to 3–0 and then blasted a homer just a few rows behind his father's. "I kept looking at [third-base coach Bill] Plummer for a sign just to make sure the 'take' wasn't on. It's something I didn't think we'd ever do." Added his father: "I felt for him then [after I went deep]. I knew he would be thinking home run. I could see it in his eyes when I crossed the plate."

It was the first time in baseball history a father and son had homered in a game, let alone back-to-back. Then again it's rare that a father and son are even active players at the same time. Tim Raines Sr. and Jr. were the only others to play together. But Raines Sr. was activated the last week of the 2001 season just for the purpose of playing with his son, and the whole thing had the odor of a gimmick. Griffey Sr. and Jr. actually brought out the best in each other (how else to explain Senior's sudden power and Junior's blossoming between 1990–91), and the Mariners as a team played better. "The job that man [Griffey Sr.] has done since he came here," said Mariners manager Jim Lefebvre in September of 1990. "It's like they should be written up for a Hollywood movie."

Senior finished the season batting .377 in 21 games in 1990. In 1991 he hit .282 in 30 games but retired due to an injury sustained in a car accident. Senior later credited his power surge to hitting in front of Junior. *I wish I was hitting in front of this kid when I was a kid*, he remembers thinking to himself at the time. Years later in his autobiography, *Big Red*, Senior recalled the overall experience: "It was a really special thing, being able to share a dugout and field with my son. We'll always be the first to ever achieve that."

Other Notable Family Connections
(Mariners in **bold**)

Floyd Bannister
Father of Brian Bannister (2006–2010)

Robinson Cano
Son of Jose Cano (1989)

Joey Cora
Brother of Alex Cora (1998–2011)

Jose Cruz Jr.
Son of Jose Cruz (1970–1988)
Nephew of Hector Cruz (1973, 1975–1982)
Nephew of Tommy Cruz (1973, 1977)

Dave Henderson
Nephew of Joe Henderson (1974, 1976–1977)

Brian Holman
Brother of **Brad Holman** (1993)

Stan Javier
Son of Julian Javier (1960–1972)

Mark Leiter
Brother of Al Leiter (1987–2005)

Mike Maddux
Brother of Greg Maddux (1986–2008)

Dave Magadan
Cousin of Lou Piniella (1964, 1968–1984)

Edgar Martinez
Cousin of Carmelo Martinez (1983–1991)

Gary Matthews
Father of Gary Matthews Jr. (1999–2010)

Kevin Mitchell
Cousin of Keith Mitchell (1991, 1994, 1996, 1998)

John Olerud
Cousin of Dale Sveum (1986–1988, 1990–1994, 1996–1999)

Spike Owen
Brother of Dave Owen (1983–1985, 1988)

Tom Paciorek
Brother of Jim Paciorek (1987)
Brother of John Paciorek (1963)

Eduardo Perez
Son of Tony Perez (1964–1986)

Gaylord Perry
Brother of Jim Perry (1959–1975)

Enrique Romo
Brother of Vicente Romo (1968–1974, 1982)

Danny Tartabull
Son of Jose Tartabull (1962–1970)

Steve Trout
Son of Dizzy Trout (1939–1952, 1957)

Bobby Valentine
Son-in-law of Ralph Branca (1944–1954, 1956)

Jeff Weaver
Brother of Jered Weaver (2006–)

As for Junior, Mariners teammate Harold Reynolds thought he benefited immensely from his father's presence: "Having his father there helped Junior's transition. He was moving into that stardom stage, and he was still only 20. I think having his father there gave him a great buffer and great example of how to handle things."

Bret Boone didn't play with any relative, but he represented a third generation of Boones to play major league baseball. Grandfather Ray was a third baseman and shortstop for the Cleveland Indians and Detroit Tigers in the '50s, and father Bob was a catcher for the World Series-champion Philadelphia Phillies in the '70s and '80s. His brother, Aaron, played in the majors as well.

David Bell's father, Buddy Bell, and grandfather, Gus Bell, were all major leaguers—and pretty good ones. Slick-fielding, power hitting Buddy played third base for the Indians and Texas Rangers and managed the Tigers and Kansas City Royals. Gus was a slugging outfielder for the Cincinnati Reds.

Diego Segui, former Pilot, and his son, David, both played for the Mariners but in different eras. Diego was the starting pitcher in the first Mariners game. David was a first baseman for the M's in the late '90s.

58 1994: Longest Road Trip

Turbulence suffocated baseball in 1994. The players union and major league owners warred against each other from the first pitch of the year. So thick were the hostilities that another strike threatened to interrupt the season—just as it had in 1972 and 1981.

Meanwhile, the Mariners suffered through their own tempest. They lost the first five games of the 1994 season and spent the next few months desperately trying to recover. On the eve of July 19, they stood 16 games under .500. Blame rested everywhere but mostly on the mound, where once again the M's couldn't sustain pitching momentum from year to year. Only Randy Johnson excelled in the rotation. Free agent signee Greg Hibbard flopped, and Chris Bosio's season ended early in July with an injury. Without injured Norm Charlton, the bullpen performed erratically. "We're at a time when this whole organization has to stay positive," said Jay Buhner, fighting a six-week slump. "It looks bad—like things are falling apart."

The next evening, as the Mariners warmed up at home before a game with the Baltimore Orioles, more than just a season started falling apart. Four 26-pound tiles dropped from the roof of the Kingdome. No injuries occurred—since fans couldn't enter for another 20 minutes—but the game that night was canceled. "It sounded like someone threw a baseball bat into the stands real hard," said Mariners broadcaster Ron Fairly, who stood about 30 feet away when the tiles hit. They floated down "like a coin underwater," added a high school boy shagging flies before the game. "You could hear it all over the stadium like thunder [when they landed]." Engineers inspecting the damage eventually ruled the Kingdome unsuitable for use for the remainder of the season. That detonated a debate in Seattle over the future of the indoor stadium and the Mariners themselves.

Meanwhile, the M's still had two and a half months to play, including 37 home games. What to do? Ken Griffey Jr. offered his smart aleck advice: "Don't we have to play in a neutral stadium? How about Tampa? We'll be there in 1997 anyway." The M's lease with the Kingdome expired in 1997, and Tampa had been openly coveting the Mariners for years. The Mariners lobbied to move the

Travel Woes

No major league team logs more miles of travel than the Mariners. Each year they fly roughly 50,000 miles. It's the price paid for living in the far corner of the country, where getting there from here is always a challenge.

M's home games to either Cheney Stadium in Tacoma, Washington, or B.C. Place in Vancouver. Major League Baseball demurred. They wanted the games played in a major league park. That meant the Mariners would have to play all remaining games in their opponent's ballpark.

The Mariners began their never-ending road trip in Boston. Playing as the home team on the road but still batting first, the M's split the series in Fenway Park. The M's, who stood to lose millions of dollars in lost revenues, received only the standard 20 percent of visitors' gate receipts. One of the games in the series was rained out, which made history: the first ever Mariners rainout as the home team.

Following Boston, they headed to Detroit and Chicago and lost all six games.

But then something unexpected happened.

Baseball at large was ruptured by labor discord and growing fan disenchantment. In Seattle the M's and the city exchanged endless barbs, and media and fans ranted about the home team and its status as "the laughingstock of baseball." Moreover, the stadium the Mariners called home was crumbling as was the hope engendered by the previous season. In the midst of all this tumult, the Mariners grew closer as teammates. "If you liked a guy or hated him, it didn't matter. You were with him," said hitting coach Lee Elia in *Tales from the Seattle Mariners Dugout*. "If there were any anxieties between one guy and another, they got cleaned out. It was like being on an island. You had nowhere else to go, and I think the guys bonded."

Ten scheduled dates remained for the Mariners before August 12, the date set for a strike if no labor agreement was reached. That included road trips to California, Kansas City, Texas, and Oakland. The Mariners won nine of those, including the final six. On the morning of the 12th after Randy Johnson struck out 15 A's in an 8–1 win, Seattle, despite a 49–63 record, found itself only two games out of first place. But the strike came as planned, putting the breaks on the Mariners' momentum. "Most times when you've got troubles on the road, losing and stuff, you get your mind going, '*I can't wait to get home*,'" said Griffey, who authored another memorable season with 40 homers. "Well, we couldn't get home. Instead, we had a meeting in Chicago after we lost some games. We decided we had to finish up strong; we had to make the best of it." Added Lou Piniella, "I'm proud of what these kids have accomplished. They've played with confidence and intensity. They've come together and forged something that's tough to beat. To stop now is…sad. Sad but not unexpected."

The Mariners scattered across the country, waiting for the strike to end. It never did. "I really believe they'd have won the division," Dave Niehaus told a reporter years later. In any event the strangest year in Mariners history thus came to a peculiar but perhaps propitious end. Who knows if the M's—with no end in sight to their traveling show (ultimately it included seven cities, 18 games, and 10,425 miles)—could have sustained the feel-good momentum? As it was, the Mariners entered the offseason closer to each other and swelling with confidence.

59 Unselfish Gil Meche's Very Bad Day

The game on May 14, 2004 began auspiciously for the Mariners and starting pitcher Gil Meche. Holding a 1–0 lead against the New York Yankees, Meche struck out the very first batter, future Hall of Famer Derek Jeter.

It nosedived from there.

Bernie Williams singled followed by a double from Alex Rodriguez, the former Mariners shortstop, and a Ruben Sierra fielder's choice. Then started the procession of walks. With the bases loaded, Hideki Matsui, Tony Clark, and John Flaherty were walked in successive plate appearances. Meche had allowed three runs and three straight bases-loaded walks before getting pulled in just two-thirds an inning of work for reliever Ron Villone. Meche had thrown 38 pitches—and just 17 of them were strikes. "I had one of those days," he said. "I hope it never happens again." The Mariners eventually lost 9–5. "What we're going through right now," Seattle manager Bob Melvin said, "it's extremely frustrating."

It was most frustrating for Meche, but the veteran pitcher was used to adversity. On July 6, 1999, Meche made the second youngest debut for the Mariners. He was not even 21; only Ken Griffey Jr. was younger. Meche finished that year with a respectable 8–4 record and 4.73 ERA but then lost his first four decisions of the 2000 season. He rebounded to win four starts and even his record before having to leave a July 4 game with what was thought to be just a "dead arm." It was more than that. Meche underwent two shoulder surgeries and did not pitch again in the major leagues until the 2003 season. He bounced back that year—going 15–13 with a 4.59 ERA—to such an extent that season that he earned *The Sporting News'* American League Comeback Player of the Year award. After three more years with the Mariners, Meche, who went 55–44 during his six seasons in Seattle, signed a lucrative five-year, $55 million contract with the Kansas City Royals in 2006.

Meche spent much of 2010 on the disabled list, starting just nine games and pitching less than 62 innings for Kansas City. But the 32-year-old hurler was still due to make $12 million in 2011. Sure, the starting pitcher with a history of injuries to his throwing shoulder was breaking down and not what he used to be, but he could've pitched from the bullpen, thrown less innings, or taken a buyout. Instead he made a very unselfish decision in a sport where so many put money before all else. He retired, forgoing all those millions. "When I signed my contract, my main goal was to earn it," Meche told *The New York Times.* "Once I started to realize I wasn't earning my money, I felt bad. I was making a crazy amount of money for not even pitching. Honestly, I didn't feel like I deserved it. I didn't want to have those feelings again… This isn't about being a hero. That's not even close to what it's about. It's just me getting back to a point in my life where I'm comfortable. Making that amount of money from a team that's already given me over $40 million for my life and for my kids, it just wasn't the right thing to do."

Mariners' First...
Our friend and longtime Seattle sportswriter, Steve Rudman, helped compile some notable firsts in franchise history.

Ticket Prices
General admission tickets cost $5, $4.50, $3.50, and $1.50 during the Mariners' first season in 1977.

Player Signed
Seattle signed right-handed pitcher David Johnson on September 30, 1976, but it sold "the original Mariner" to the Minnesota Twins before he had a chance to play for the Mariners.

Average Salary
The 1977 Mariners averaged a mere $38,161 per player.

$1 Million Player
In 1989 pitcher Mark Langston earned $1.3 million.

Pitch
On April 6, 1977, Diego Segui threw a called strike to Jerry Remy of the Angels.

Ceremonial Pitch
Senator Henry Jackson threw it in 1977.

Starting Pitcher
Diego Segui would receive the loss in April of 1977.

Error
During that same game, Dan Meyer recorded an error at first base.

Hit
Jose Baez singled to right field against the Angels.

Game-Winning RBI
On April 9, 1980, third baseman Ted Cox sliced a two-run double to give Seattle an 8–6 victory against the Toronto Blue Jays.

Home Run
Juan Bernhardt hit the dinger off Angels pitcher Frank Tanana on April 10, 1977.

Grand Slam
On May 17, 1977, catcher Skip Jutzke blasted one against the Baltimore Orioles.

Cycle
On June 22, 1993, Jay Buhner hit a grand slam in the first inning, a double in the third, a single in the fifth, and a triple in the 14th against the Oakland A's.

Batting Champion
Designated hitter Edgar Martinez won the batting title, hitting .343 in 1992.

Home Run Champion
Ken Griffey Jr. (of course) hit 40 home runs in 1994.

20-Game Winner
Pitcher Randy Johnson went 20–4 in 1997.

Save
John Montague closed out the April 8, 1977, victory.

Strikeout Champion
Floyd Bannister fanned 209 in 1982.

Cy Young Winner
After going 18–2 with a 2.48 ERA, Randy Johnson earned the award in 1995.

No-Hitter
On June 2, 1990, Randy Johnson blanked the Detroit Tigers.

All-Star
Center fielder Ruppert Jones was the Mariners' representative in the 1977 game.

All-Star Starter
Left fielder Phil Bradley earned the start in the 1985 game.

Gold Glove
Pitcher Mark Langston won the award in 1987.

Rookie of the Year
"Mr. Mariner" Alvin Davis won the award in 1984.

MVP
Ken Griffey Jr., who hit 56 home runs that season, won the award in 1997.

60 Ruppert Jones

You always remember your first. Your first hit in Little League. Your first car. Your first love. For Mariners fans Ruppert Jones, taken No. 1 in the 1976 Expansion Draft, was their first crush.

Jones sailed through his first assignments in the Kansas City Royals minor league system. He averaged well above .300 in three lower rung stops from 1973–74 and exhibited power and patience at the plate. In 1976 the Royals called him up after he clubbed 19 home runs at Triple A Omaha. But Kansas City left Jones, after a quiet 51 at-bats with the Royals, off its protected list because they deemed Willie Wilson and U.L. Washington better prospects. The Mariners jumped at the chance to take the 21-year-old, who teased at times with five-tool talent.

The paying customers at the Kingdome warmed to Jones almost immediately. He played baseball with a combination of pluck, skill, and just a hint of spice, hustling on the bases, diving without care in the field, and scaling the center-field wall to steal away extra-base hits. Like his teammates, he didn't always succeed, striking out a team-high 120 times. Occasionally he ran into outs because of overaggressive base running or gambled and missed on sinking fly balls. He didn't even post the best offensive numbers on the team in 1977. But Jones gained the affection of Mariners fans because of his all-out, no prima donna style. "I played a certain way," he said in a 2012 interview with *The Seattle Times* in 2012, "I think they appreciated that."

Highlights that year included a homer off Dennis Eckersley to end the Cleveland Indians pitcher's bid to break Cy Young's 23 consecutive hitless innings streak and an inside-the-parker off the Yankees' Sparky Lyle in the Kingdome. That in itself was remarkable. The Kingdome's snug dimensions made legging out a home run nearly impossible. But Jones' speed made the seemingly impossible possible. He was named the Mariners' first ever All-Star and pinch hit for pitcher Jim Kern in the bottom of the third. Facing the Los Angeles Dodgers' Don Sutton, he flew out to right field, an out that failed to produce a single groan in Seattle, where fans were just tickled to watch one of their own play in baseball's showcase.

Every time Jones came to the plate, especially that first magical summer of 1977, fans chanted "Ruuuuupe." Then the chant started erupting after he made a catch in the field, sometimes even after a routine play. The left-field bleacher fans ultimately named themselves the "Roop Coop" and adapted the seventh-inning stretch song to "Roop, Roop, Roop for the Mariners." "That was catchy," Jones said to the *Seattle Post-Intelligencer* in 2001. "A ballplayer wants to be accepted. It made me feel accepted."

Others around town started getting into the act. One local broadcaster, Ray McMackin on KING TV, referred to him as Ruppert "Two P" Jones. "Ruppert was the first guy to capture the imagination of the Pacific Northwest fans," Dave Neihaus said. "He had a little flash to him and he had some swagger when he went to center field…He was not a superstar by any stretch of the imagination, but he was our superstar."

The Texas native but California-raised Jones sported a Fu Manchu moustache throughout most of his time with the Mariners, becoming one of a growing number of ballplayers to wear the 'stache. It suited Jones well, adding a dollop of extra mustard to a guy with some hot dog tendencies.

Jones struggled in 1978 after having offseason surgery to remove cartilage from his left knee. He slipped to just six home runs and a .235 batting average. An emergency appendectomy in

June shelved him for a month of the season, contributing to his power outage. But as a measure of his continuing popularity and status as one of the few black players on the Mariners, Jones worked for KYAC, an African American radio station in Seattle, over the summer of 1978. He conducted interviews with his teammates and opponents. It wasn't always easy living in Seattle as a young black man, and Jones claims that state troopers stopped him four times for no apparent reason during his career in the Emerald City while he drove his Mercedes around town.

Jones rebounded in 1979, reaching career highs in hits (166), RBIs (78), and stolen bases (33). In addition, he smacked 21 home runs. Alas, as with so many first loves, this one didn't last. The Mariners, not going anywhere fast, felt moving Jones, while his value swelled, could help them get somewhere sooner than if they had kept "Roop." They traded Jones to the Yankees for outfielder Juan Beniquez, catcher Jerry Narron, and pitchers Jim Beattie and Rick Anderson. Only Beattie returned much in value. Shortly after the trade, Reggie Jackson nicknamed Jones "Reggie Jr."

Jones retired in 1987, never reaching his full potential. Injuries denied him of that. He, however, does own a World Series ring. Jones joined the World Series-winning 1984 Detroit Tigers halfway through the season and hit 12 home runs. He also hit a ball out of old Tiger Stadium.

These days, when Jones, who lives in San Diego, is spotted around Safeco Field, fans serenade him with chants of "Ruuuuupe." And for that Jones has always said, and he's never wavered on this, that if he goes into the Hall of Fame, he'd go as a Mariner—proof that the man still has a sense of humor and just a pinch of that swagger.

61 Cano and the Return of Winning Baseball

During a lull in the middle of the final game of the 2014 season, the Safeco Field crowd of 40,823 groaned. Seconds later a few pockets of fans stood up and applauded. And then a few more did the same—until most were on their feet cheering. The crowd was reacting initially to the sad news, as the scoreboard showed, that the Oakland A's had defeated the Texas Rangers to officially eliminate the Mariners from the playoffs. The cheering that followed throughout Safeco was a show of appreciation for the first Mariners team to finish above .500 since 2009 and first to hang in the playoff race until the very last day since 2001. "I thought it said a lot about our fans," said Mariners manager Lloyd McClendon.

The seeds of the Mariners transformation from 90-loss team to playoff contender began during the offseason when Seattle hired McClendon, the Detroit Tigers batting coach and former Pittsburgh Pirates skipper, to replace former manager Eric Wedge, who walked away from the job in frustration. Seattle baseball fans didn't raise a toast to McClendon's hire, but most took a wait-and-see approach. National baseball writer Paul Morosi was more bullish: "The Mariners will be glad they hired him. Great baseball man and commands respect."

One month later the Mariners made a bigger splash, one heartily toasted by locals and most of the national baseball media. Free agent Robinson Cano, an All-Star second baseman for the New York Yankees, signed a whopping 10-year, $242 million deal with the Mariners. He was an instant upgrade to an offense that for years had scored runs at a deadball era level. Spurned by the Yankees, Cano pursued the Mariners more than the Mariners pursued him. Finally, the M's just couldn't say no. "Robinson Cano is a good answer to anything," said M's general manager Jack Zduriencik when asked if the Cano signing was a move to satisfy fans clamoring for significant changes.

Cano didn't solve all of the Mariners' offensive problems in 2014. But his .314 average and .836 on-base plus slugging percentage provided just enough of a lift to help keep the Mariners

Robinson Cano, whose 10-year, $242 million deal with the Mariners helped launch a playoff-contending 2014 season, hits a double against the Houston Astros during that year.

competitive. The pitching and defense is what elevated them into the playoff hunt. Behind perhaps Felix Hernandez's greatest season, the Mariners pitching harkened back to another era, posting a ridiculously low league-leading and franchise record 3.17 ERA. The top of the rotation dominated. Besides Hernandez, Hisashi Iwakuma and Chris Young stifled hitters most of the year. The bullpen performed even better than the rotation, allowing runs about as often as the 2013 Super Bowl champion Seahawks allowed touchdowns. Four Mariners made the All-Star team: Hernandez, Cano, closer Fernando Rodney, and up-and-comer third baseman Kyle Seager, who became one of only seven major leaguers to ever hit a homer, double, and two triples in a game. Seager's feat came in the M's 10–2 pasting of the Yankees in June.

Two slumps bookending the season ultimately kept the Mariners out of the playoffs. In April the M's suffered through an eight-game losing streak. Down the stretch in September, they stumbled five straight games when the pitching uncharacteristically nosedived. Remove those two hiccups, and the M's went 87–62. "We're pretty close," Cano said after the season.

"I told them they're no longer the prey," said McClendon after the bittersweet final game of the year. "They're the hunters now."

62 Five Managers from the Early Days

Darrell Johnson
(managed Mariners from 1977–1980, 226–362 record)
A former catcher under Casey Stengel and World Series manager (with the legendary 1975 Boston Red Sox), he had the thankless task of guiding the expansion Mariners. Old school yet adaptable,

Johnson proved to be an able teacher and a good fit. "He'd gone from the penthouse to the crapper to come here," said the late Dave Niehaus. "But he was an awfully patient guy and he was the right man for the job at the time." Johnson found the sweet spot between sharp criticism and praise, and the players came to respect and admire him.

Rene Lachemann
(1981–1983, 140–180)

He was 35 when the M's promoted him from Triple A, where he had managed since 1978, to clean up after the Maury Wills experiment. A mostly career minor leaguer, he guided the Mariners to their best season ever in 1982, when the M's won 76 games. Popular among the fans and in the clubhouse, the offbeat Lachemann lived almost full time in his office in the Kingdome. "I have all the beer I want and don't have to worry about driving home," he joked. His age and limited time in the majors helped him develop a strong rapport with his players. "He knows that baseball is a difficult game, and that every player struggles from time to time," said outfielder Richie Zisk. Lachemann also engaged the players in banter and the occasional prank—without undermining his authority. "He doesn't demand respect from his players, the respect is given freely," Zisk said. "His ability to have this give-and-take relationship with his players is special." After a slow start in 1983, the Mariners fired him. The King Street Massacre, as the firing became known, steamed many fans.

Del Crandall
(1983–1984, 93–131)

An All-Star catcher for the Milwaukee Braves in the '50s and '60s, Crandall managed the Brewers without distinction in the mid-1970s. By 1983 he was managing Triple A Albuquerque when M's owner George Argyros hired him to replace the immensely popular

Lachemann. "I had no idea we were walking into a hornet's nest," said Crandall's wife, Fran, the day Del first met with the media in Seattle. His press conference resembled an interrogation. "I was the victim," he said later. Before his debut game at the Kingdome, the Mariners, cowed by the hostile reaction to Crandall's hire, didn't announce his name to the crowd. He never enjoyed a honeymoon period and failed to last two years, though the M's flirted with first place in 1984 for three months of the season. After a sharp drop in the standings, Crandall was gone by September.

Chuck Cottier
(1984–1986, 98–119)
The M's closed out the 1984 season with a winning month, and everyone thought they'd found the man for the job. But the next season and a half, the M's spun their wheels, and after a 4–16 stretch in April and May of 1986 in which they hit .172 and whiffed at a record pace, Cottier got the boot. "Firing Chuck is the last thing they [Mariners front office] should do," said M's outfielder Phil Bradley the day before the axe fell. Many of Bradley's teammates agreed, which reinforced perceptions among the press and some fans that Cottier was too soft. His downfall, however, may have been his floridly optimistic preseason predictions. Management, especially Argyros, took him at his word and grew testy when the M's floundered early. Said Cottier a few days after his dismissal: "I keep hearing Seattle does not have good fans. That is not so. They have great fans and they know what's going on. You can't bull them; they know the game. They also know what kind of person owns the team."

Dick Williams
(1986–1988, 159–192)
During his introduction to the Seattle media, Williams, who had led three different teams to the World Series, served up an oblique swipe at his predecessor: "This is the first day of a new beginning

for the Seattle Mariners. I'm demanding. I'm not hired to be a nice guy. There's no reason to make excuses for a ballplayer." The most accomplished M's manager to date, Williams' approach was also more autocratic and inflexible than all of his predecessors. For a year it worked. The Mariners set a franchise record in 1987 by winning 78 games. But Williams' scorched-earth style alienated many of the M's promising younger players, some of whom Williams ran off via trade. The M's started slowly the next season. Williams then lost the clubhouse and finally the support of management. In early June he got the ziggy. "I'm disappointed," Argyros said, "and I'm tired, tired of this losing." Jim Snyder replaced Williams and went 45–60 to close out the season.

63 The Ultimate Grand Slam

Dave Niehaus called every inning of every critical game in the Mariners' glory years. Yet, he always listed a moment from 1985 near the top of his all-time highlights.

The M's had started the season 4–0, the best start in their history. That piqued the interest of Seattle baseball fans. Almost 25,000 of them showed up for the Saturday game against the Twins, an unusually large crowd for the second home series of the year. The Mariners fell behind in the sixth inning and trailed in the bottom of the ninth 7–4. Then they loaded the bases with a walk to Ivan Calderon. "I was standing in the on-deck circle, thinking that if Ivan got on and I got up, the bases would probably be loaded," Phil Bradley said. "Then the natural thought process started. *You know how great it would be to hit a grand slam and win this thing?* Then I got realistic and wondered what are my chances…"

The Mariners had drafted Bradley, a college All-American, in the third round of the 1981 Amateur Draft. He signed with the M's, even though he had starred as a dual-threat quarterback at Missouri. (His prospects in the NFL suffered from the biases against running quarterbacks at the time.) In the minors Bradley racked up big stolen-base numbers (20, 58, 36) and bloated batting averages (.301, .336, .323). He also ran down everything in the field. Power was the only thing missing, but the Mariners figured that would come and promoted him to the big leagues at the end of the 1983 season. In the majors he aped his minor league performance, stealing 21 bases and hitting .301. But not even the Kingdome could solve his power problem as Bradley failed to hit a home run.

That changed just three games into the '85 season. After putting on 10 pounds and working with hitting coach Deron Johnson specifically to add power, he went deep against the Oakland Athletics in the Mariners' 14–6 drubbing to complete a series sweep.

Now, here he was facing Twins closer Ron Davis with the bases jacked and the game on the line. Forget about hitting a home run, Bradley told himself: "I used that one the other night." On Davis' first pitch, though, he defied the odds. Bradley connected so soundly that Twins left fielder Mickey Hatcher gave up on the ball early, watching flat-footed as it landed in the bleachers. "I knew I hit it good," Bradley said. "I wanted to see it go and never did. But I was so busy looking I nearly ran over D.J." While Bradley almost bowled over Johnson, who was the third-base coach as well as the hitting coach, his teammates rushed from the dugout to surround home plate, an act of spontaneous joy common these days but rare then. Just as jazzed as the players were the fans, who demanded a curtain call and chanted Bradley's name long after the M's had evacuated the field. "You know I'm not real big on showing emotions, or anything else," Bradley said. "But once in a while…"

Only 16 times in baseball history had a player belted a grand slam under similar circumstances: down three runs in his team's last at-bat. Bradley's "Ultimate Grand Slam," which lifted the Mariners to 5–0 on the season and gave them a three-game lead in the division, caused a swell of dreamy thinking. "It may be early in the season," said the M's designated hitter Gorman Thomas, no stranger to magical moments during his career in Milwaukee. "But we've got people hitting well and making plays and everyone is starting to believe. You never know…"

The M's continued hitting all year. Thomas clouted 32 homers, a franchise record. Jim Presley added 28. Most surprising of all, however, Bradley, who in 389 at-bats prior to 1985 had never gone deep, found the seats 24 more times in 1985. The next day he even hit a bases-loaded triple to lead the M's to a 5–1 win and 6–0 start.

Besides the 26 homers Bradley belted in 1985, he also hit .300, stole 22 bases, made the All-Star team, and finished in the top 20 in

Five Moments to Remember from 1985

April 11, 1985—Gorman Thomas hit three home runs in a 14–6 rout of the Oakland A's, and Seattle set a club record with seven home runs.

April 29, 1985—Donnie Scott became the second Mariner, following Larry Milbourne, to homer from both sides of the plate in the same game. Scott's shots came in a 9–7 Mariners win against the Milwaukee Brewers.

May 8, 1985—Mike Moore no-hit the Texas Rangers for eight innings. Although driven from the game on four hits in the ninth, Moore beat the Rangers 4–2.

June 15, 1985—The Seattle infield recorded 21 assists in a 2–1 victory against the Kansas City Royals, tying a major league record last accomplished by the Brooklyn Dodgers in 1935.

August 13, 1985—The Seattle infield once again tied the major league record for assists in a game with 21 against the California Angels.

MVP voting. It was perhaps the greatest all-around season to date by a Mariner. Despite Bradley's full flowering, the M's still failed to contend or even finish above .500, falling seven games short. The pitching proved their undoing.

Bradley never again exceeded 20 home runs. But he continued to hit for average, steal bases, and play strong defense. "[Hitting .300 is] the one thing I try to set out to do every year when I start the season," he told a reporter from Florida before the start of the 1987 season. Thoughtful and quiet, Bradley studied hitting like a science while adopting a philosophy from the Eeyore playbook. "I'm a pessimist," he once told a reporter. "It's real easy when you're going good to think that everything is going to work out. But it's not. It's not like every time I hit the baseball I get a base hit," he continued. "If that's the case, I'd be hitting a thousand, wouldn't I?"

Over time, the Mariners' losing started to weigh on Bradley, leading him to publically criticize some teammates for what he considered their indifference. Management's ham-fisted tactics during arbitration, when Seattle twice argued for 10 percent salary cuts, alienated him as well. As he neared free agency, Bradley openly expressed his desire to leave, which prompted some in the press to attack him. After the 1987 season, the Mariners finally traded Bradley to the Philadelphia Phillies.

He has since buried whatever hard feelings he had about Seattle. "I really liked playing for the Seattle Mariners," he told www.baseballtoddsdugout.com. "I had some success there, and they really gave younger players an honest opportunity to get to the big leagues. They allowed you the chance to get established as a major leaguer, and I really admired that."

After retiring in 1991 as a player, Bradley is now a special assistant for the MLB Players Association.

64 2001 Supporting Cast

David Bell

Acquired for Joey Cora in August of 1998, Bell surprised the M's with 20-homer power in 1999. His glove was as good as advertised, too, at both second and third base where he split time. In 2001 Bell's power dropped, but his defense, this time mostly at third, continued to glisten. One play, remembered by first baseman John Olerud in *Mariners Magazine*, dramatized his steady and spectacular play at the hot corner. "[My favorite play] was the ball Bell dove for in the hole against Oakland and—as he was rolling—threw a perfect strike to me without looking." Bell wasn't a total stiff with the bat either. His ninth-inning home run to tie the San Francisco Giants in the first game after the 2001 All-Star break served notice that the Mariner Express was still at full throttle, as the Mariners won in extra innings. And he collected five hits against the Detroit Tigers in late August. One of the friendlier guys in baseball, Bell's public persona masked his fiery competitiveness. "Bell is…a hard-nosed player who gave us everything he had," said M's manager Lou Piniella the day the Mariners, who sought more offense at third, traded Bell in January of 2002.

Carlos Guillen

The Venezuelan, acquired in the Randy Johnson trade, shifted from second base to shortstop, his natural position, to replace the departed Alex Rodriguez. After Guillen came up with two, two-out knocks to help beat the New York Yankees in April, M's reliever Arthur Rhodes clucked: "We don't need Alex Rodriguez. We've got a pretty good shortstop here." Guillen and David Bell formed an impenetrable left side of the infield—until Guillen hit the disabled list with tuberculosis in September. He missed the remainder of the regular season and the American League Division Series against the Cleveland Indians. His teammates hung his jersey in the dugout during his absence. Guillen played sparingly against the Yankees in the American League Championship Series. He never hit his stride offensively with the Mariners, who traded him to Detroit for Ramon Santiago before the 2004 season. Guillen developed into an All-Star shortstop in Detroit.

Mark McLemore

The 36-year-old veteran floated around the field, playing nearly every position but catcher. Ping-ponging up and down in the batting order as well, McLemore enjoyed a career year at the plate. In 125 games Seattle's first McLemore (pronounced the same as Seattle's even more famous second Macklemore) hit .286, slugged over .400, and stole 39 bases. When tuberculosis sidelined Guillen, McLemore filled in ably at shortstop. "It's not a high-profile thing he does," teammate Bret Boone said. "But he's been a very unsung hero." Piniella agreed: "I hate to think where we'd be without the way he's played and the versatility he provides."

Stan Javier and Charles Gipson

At the end of a 17-year major league career, Javier, like McLemore, enjoyed one of his best seasons ever, hitting .292 and filling in at every position in the outfield. Gipson saw limited action but made a spectacular throw after Piniella inserted him in center field as a defensive replacement in a game the Mariners led 3–2 over the Minnesota Twins. After fielding a single on one hop, Gipson gunned down the potential tying run in the eighth inning to help preserve the July win in Minnesota. M's catcher Dan Wilson didn't think Gipson had a chance to peg the runner, Chad Allen. "Then [I saw] him coming in, and the throw is right on the money," Wilson said. "It hit me right where I wanted it with both feet in position to block. It had to be perfect."

Aaron Sele, Paul Abbott, and John Halama
Forming the back end of the rotation, this trio, without flash, consistently kept the Mariners in games before turning the keys over to the M's nearly leak-proof bullpen. Sele, from local Poulsbo, Washington, won 15 games. In his first 13 starts, the Mariners won all 13. Later, he shut out the Arizona Diamondbacks on two hits in mid-July. Abbott started the year on the disabled list but won 17 games nonetheless. In June he went 4–0 with a 3.34 ERA. Halama contributed 10 wins, none more impressive than a seven-inning scoreless outing against the San Diego Padres in June. "When you get behind this team," said the Twins' Eric Milton, "it's pretty much impossible to come back."

65 Combined No-Hitter

Scoring runs has haunted the Mariners for most of general manager Jack Zduriencik's tenure. But then again, opponents have often been just as spooked by M's pitching during this same period.

The Mariners lost 101 games in 2010 despite a pitching staff that finished third in the American League in ERA. Stud starters Felix Hernandez and Cliff Lee set the pace, allowing runs as frequently as a Prius needs refuels. The M's dreary year, which cost manager Don Wakamatsu his job, was the fault of the offense, which posted historically foul numbers. This theme continued for the next two years: rancid offense and solid, sometimes spectacular pitching. One of the Mariners' best mound efforts occurred on June 8, 2012.

Already seven-and-a-half games behind the Texas Rangers, the Mariners attracted a modest crowd of 22,000 for the Friday evening interleague game against the Los Angeles Dodgers, who sported baseball's best record. Kevin Millwood, signed as a free agent during the offseason to a short-term, low-risk deal, was cooking heading into the matchup against L.A. In his last five starts, the veteran had only allowed six runs total. Continuing his strong run, Millwood kept the Dodgers off the scoreboard for the first six innings. He'd struck out six, walked one, and not allowed a hit. Only Dee Gordon's bunt in the fourth, brilliantly bare handed by third baseman Kyle Seager, had posed a serious threat. Meanwhile, the Dodgers young phenom, Nathan Eovaldi, had blanked the M's as well, an all too familiar script.

When Millwood began his warm-ups to start the seventh, the crowd hummed knowing he only needed nine outs to make history. Then the crowd gasped, as M's manager Eric Wedge trotted to the mound and gave the signal for a reliever. "No one knew what was going on," said M's broadcaster Rick Rizzs. It turned out Millwood had hurt himself the inning before on his second-to-last pitch to Tony Gwynn Jr. "I couldn't push off," he said after the game. "It would have been stupid to stay out there." Sighed his 22-year-old catcher Jesus Montero: "He was throwing the ball amazing."

Wedge summoned Charlie Furbush, a tall, lanky lefty acquired the year prior for the popular and now very successful Doug Fister. Furbush retired the first batter and then fielded a grounder that he threw wildly to first, allowing Elian Herrera (who reached first base on an error) to get to second base. Furbush recovered to fan the next batter, and then Stephen Pryor replaced him and whiffed Juan

Rivera to end the inning. "Yeah, we knew about the no-hitter," Pryor said. "But we weren't talking about it [in the bullpen.]"

The M's cobbled together a run on a Seager single in the bottom of the seventh inning to take a 1–0 lead. Then Pryor walked the first two batters of the eighth. Wedge quickly summoned Lucas Luetge, who left after the Dodgers bunted the runners over. Up next was Brandon League, the deposed M's closer. He pitched like Mariano Rivera on this day, inducing a soft fly to left and whiffing Gwynn Jr. "As good as I've seen him," Wedge said.

New M's closer Tom Wilhelmsen, back in baseball after five years as a bartender, took the ball for the ninth. Gordon greeted him with a dribbler toward short. Shortstop Brendan Ryan charged the ball and just nipped the speedy Gordon. "Pretty close," said a relieved Ryan afterward.

With the crowd on its feet and cheering wildly, Wilhelmsen took a deep breath before retiring the final two hitters. It was the third no-hitter in M's history and the 10th all-time combined. Montero, who caught the entire game, became the youngest catcher to catch a no-hitter since 1971. "No one knew how to react or who to celebrate with," Furbush said. "We got to all celebrate together because everyone got to do their job and be part of it."

66 The Mendoza Line

So many players came through Seattle in the early years. In the first three seasons alone, the Mariners used 70 different ballplayers. A few left a mark, but most just passed through—like sediment at the bottom of a stream.

Mario Mendoza certainly seemed to fit the profile of the latter. Acquired in an offseason trade with the Pittsburgh Pirates, Mendoza also fit the profile of the good fielding/poor hitting short-stop. In his native Mexico, he had earned the sobriquet "Manos de Seda," which translated to "silk hands." But his countrymen bestowed no such elegant nickname for his offense, which could be charitably described as limited.

For the Pirates, Mendoza saw action primarily as a defensive replacement. When he did get a start or make a trip to the plate, it usually ended with a sober trot back to the dugout. In part-time duty over four seasons, he yo-yoed around .200 with a crest of .221 and a floor of .180.

But the Mariners didn't pick up Mendoza for his bat, and after Seattle traded their popular shortstop Craig Reynolds for Floyd Bannister three days after the deal with the Pirates, Mendoza sud-denly became the starter. He played in 148 games for the Mariners in 1979, swallowing every ball in his zone like a ravenous shark. As advertised, though, he hit like a minnow, finishing the year at .198.

Mendoza wasn't alone that year flirting with the nether regions of .200. Baltimore Orioles shortstop Mark Belanger, for instance, hit .167 in almost 200 at-bats. Five other players with at least 200 plate appearances hit .211 or worse. Among the subterranean offen-sive performers, however, Mendoza had the most at-bats. That meant his name often appeared in the Sunday morning sports pages at the very bottom of the list of players with enough at-bats to meet the threshold of a regular. Any other year and Mendoza's offensive futility would have been mostly forgotten.

But at the start of the 1980 season, Kansas City star George Brett slumped badly. On April 22 his batting average dipped to .209, yoking him with the likes of Mendoza. What happened next is murky. The only thing known with certainly is that shortly after Brett's slow start in 1980 the "Mendoza Line," the line between a batting average of .200 and below it, became a catchphrase in a few clubhouses. A short time later, it took on a more existential meaning. To be just above the line represented mere struggle. To be below it meant a crisis, the type that prompts alternative career planning.

Who coined the expression is unresolved. Some accounts suggest it was Brett himself. "The first thing I look for in the Sunday papers is who is below the Mendoza Line," he told a reporter in late April of 1980. But Mendoza, a popular figure in the clubhouse with a good wit and easy manner, says Brett heard the line from two of his Mariners teammates. "My teammates Tom Paciorek and Bruce Bochte used to make fun of me," Mendoza told the *St. Louis Dispatch* in a 2010 interview. "Then they were giving George Brett a hard time because he had a slow start that year, so they told him, 'Hey, man, you're going to sink down below the Mendoza Line if you're not careful.'"

Eventually, ESPN, especially Chris Berman, started using the Mendoza Line in broadcasts to refer to hitters straddling the notorious .200 mark. Almost immediately it became part of the sport's lexicon. Berman credits Brett for telling him about the Mendoza Line; Paciorek credits Bochte for creating it.

Many other theories exist about the expression's origin, some even asserting another Mendoza, Minni Mendoza, a light-hitting infielder for the Minnesota Twins in 1970 was the true inspiration. But the evidence for this is thin.

These days the Mendoza Line has leaked into popular culture and is used generically in business and anywhere else numbers matter. Not surprisingly, the man whose name has come to represent a substandard performance isn't too crazy about it. "It did bother me at the beginning, to be honest," Mendoza said in 2010, "because people would come up to me, like making fun of me, so it used to make me mad, but I don't care anymore."

Just as Abner Doubleday did not invent baseball, Mendoza was not the worst hitter in Major League Baseball history. Check former Pilot Ray Oyler's numbers for proof of that. Nor was Mendoza the clear winner as worst hitter of his own era. Heck, he even hit .245 the year the Mendoza Line was christened. But timing and circumstance conspired to tag Mendoza with the mantle of baseball's most inept man with a bat.

Mendoza did exact a bit of revenge against Brett. The Hall of Famer recovered from his slow start in 1980 to spend most of the season dancing around .400. In late September the Royals traveled to Seattle for a three-game series. Brett's batting average stood at .394. In 11 at-bats, however, he only picked up two hits, even though he kept hitting line drives. Three of those well-hit balls should have been singles, if not for nifty defense by Mendoza. "I remember Mario Mendoza making two or three diving stabs up the middle," Brett told mlb.com years later. "You're hitting line drives at someone, and guys are diving for balls and catching them. You're like, 'What is going on here? A month ago that was a hit.' Now all of a sudden, I can't buy a hit. Then you start trying too hard." Brett left Seattle hitting .389 and fell five hits shy of finishing at .400.

Mendoza's major league playing career ended in 1982 after two years with the Texas Rangers and went on to manage in the minor leagues and the Mexican League. He would like to see the Mendoza Line put into a mothballs. "We should come up with something different—a lot of other guys have played the game and hit below .200, much worse than me," he reasons. "Thirty years—it's enough."

67 Other Mariners Characters, Oddballs, and Pranks

The Mariners employed a number of flakes especially in their early years when pranks, it seemed, often outnumbered wins. Among the most colorful:

Jim Colborn
1978

Colborn, a pitcher, was an incurable impersonator who often masqueraded as an umpire, team mascot, groundskeeper, peanut vendor, or ball boy—usually while the game was going on.

Colborn launched his career as an imposter during a 1975 game when he pitched for the Milwaukee Brewers. Back then the stadium ground crew wore Bavarian costumes—bright yellow lederhosen or short pants with long socks that came up to the knees. After the top of the fifth inning, the crew would race out onto the diamond and drag the infield. Colborn put on one of the outfits and ran out with the crew. When manager Del Crandall saw Colborn, he ordered him to "get his ass off the field."

The following year, Colborn masqueraded as an umpire for the lineup exchange before the final game of the season, going through the routine with Detroit Tigers manager Ralph Houk and Milwaukee's Alex Grammas. Then Colborn (wearing an umpire's mask) marched toward the Brewers' dugout and tried to eject the ballplayers who were giving him a hard time.

Another time, Colborn dressed up as the team mascot, Bernie Brewer, and even slid down a chute in the center-field stands into a giant mug of beer.

Colborn continued his impersonations with the Kansas City Royals. One time he sat in for the ball boy on the first-base foul line and played catch with the Angels' Bobby Bonds between innings.

Colborn was traded by Kansas City to Seattle on June 1, 1978, in exchange for Steve Braun. In 20 games, Colborn fashioned a 3–10 record with a 5.35 ERA. He spent his last day in the big leagues with Seattle in 1978, hawking peanuts in the Kingdome stands.

Larry Andersen
1981–82
The Mariners reliever is widely credited with inventing the "Rally Cap" while loitering in the Mariners bullpen in May of 1982. The Rally Cap did not gain MLB-wide popularity until 1986. Andersen teamed with Bill Caudill in several "Conehead" stunts. (See chapter No. 51.)

Pat Putnam
1983–84
Pat Putnam was traded to the Mariners from the Texas Rangers on December 21, 1982 for Ron Musselman. He had a weird sense of humor.

Putnam once played a game with a dead frog in his back pocket. Asked why, he said, "I didn't have anything else to do with it." Putnam entertained Mariners teammates with his "Shamu the Whale" routine. Putnam would completely immerse himself in a whirlpool and then leap out and snatch a hot dog with his teeth.

Although Putnam put up decent numbers in his brief stint in Seattle, Argyros sent him to Minnesota for a minor leaguer on August 29, 1984.

Salome Barojas
1984
Barojas arrived in Seattle on June 29, 1984. To land him the Mariners traded Gene Nelson and Jerry Don Gleaton to the

Chicago White Sox. When the reliever joined the Mariners, he insisted on working with second-string catcher Orlando Mercado. Miffed, starting catcher Bob Kearney once refused to warm up Barojas in the bullpen. When pitching coach Frank Funk retaliated by tossing Kearney's glove in the bullpen toilet, Kearney slugged Funk in the face.

Rey Quinones
1986–88
Quinones, Mike Trujillo, John Christensen, and Mike Brown were traded to Seattle by the Boston Red Sox on August 19, 1986, in exchange for Dave Henderson and Spike Owen.

Quinones had a fine arm and made spectacular plays, but was guided by the proverbial 10-cent control tower. Quinones once refused to pinch hit because he was on the last level of Super Mario Brothers in the clubhouse. In 1988 he was the subject of controversy when he left the Mariners without consulting the team to attend the funeral of a relative in Puerto Rico. Quinones hit .276 and .248 in his two full seasons in Seattle but committed 48 errors. The Mariners sent him to the Pirates in 1989.

JELL-O Gate
1982
After arriving in Chicago to start a road trip, Andersen, Richie Zisk, and Joe Simpson of the Mariners went to a grocery store and purchased 16 boxes of JELL-O. After finagling their way into manager Rene Lachemann's hotel room, they poured the JELL-O into the toilet, sink, and bathtub and then stuffed all of the furniture into the bathroom. According to an interview Andersen gave years later to Astrosdaily.com, the players also unscrewed the telephone, removed all the light bulbs, and strung toilet paper all over the room. When Lachemann returned he was so determined to find out the identity of the culprits that he threatened to call police.

That wasn't the end of it. JELL-O pranks followed Lachemann all season. (Once, when he went to take a swig of beer, he discovered that someone had poured the beer out of the can and replaced it with JELL-O,) and it wasn't until the end of the year that Andersen, Zisk, and Simpson revealed themselves—by showing up at a team party wearing giant JELL-O boxes over their heads. Though there's no evidence Lachemann retaliated, he admitted it was one of the best pranks he'd ever seen.

Griffey-Piniella Wager

1995

During spring training Mariners manager Lou Piniella made a bet with outfielder Ken Griffey Jr. that he couldn't hit a home run to each field on three swings. The wager: a steak dinner. Griffey hit one to right and then one to center but missed the one to left. The next day Piniella arrived at the ballpark to find that a live 1,200-pound Hereford cow had been placed in his office. "There's his steak," Griffey said, laughing. The cow had slobbered all over and left another "present" for Piniella that almost made him gag.

68 John Olerud

John Olerud epitomized the 2001 Mariners. Both succeeded with quiet efficiency and unspectacular but well-rounded skill. Both also overcame large odds on their path to greatness.

In Olerud's case, the odds were flat-out scary.

He grew up in the Seattle area as a baseball prodigy. "John never tired of swinging a bat," said his father Dr. John Olerud, a former Washington State baseball All-American who also played for the minor league Seattle Angels. "He would spend hours hitting balls of all sizes. Even at age three, he could draw a crowd." The natural-born hitter drew huge crowds to watch him play as a WSU Cougar in 1988, when he enjoyed one of the greatest seasons in college baseball history. A sophomore, Olerud hit .464 with 23 home runs (after hitting .414 as freshman). He also pitched and went 15–0. The season generated a national stir and earned him consensus All-American honors at two positions. Just before his junior year, however, Olerud suffered a brain aneurysm. Most never survive an attack. Olerud did. "It was a frightening thing," his father said. "But we were fortunate the aneurysm was found within a few weeks." Olerud even returned to complete his junior season. Wearing a protective helmet in the field as well as at bat, he hit .359 and was drafted by the Toronto Blue Jays in June of that year.

Beating the odds again, he went straight to the major leagues—just the 17th player since the amateur draft to skip the minor leagues all together. Olerud continued to wear his helmet at all times throughout his career, which sputtered in the beginning but hit hyperdrive in 1993. He won a batting title (.363) and flirted with .400 through the season's first four months. "I've been around a lot of great hitters, but John has been the most impressive I've ever seen," said his teammate and Hall of Famer Paul Molitor. Olerud won two rings with the Blue Jays.

The Jays traded Olerud, who had backslid for a couple of seasons, to the New York Mets in 1996. In 1998 he set a Mets franchise record by hitting .354 and became part of what *Sport Illustrated* called the "Greatest Infield Ever."

After the following season, he signed as a free agent with Seattle, where he proved an excellent fit in his hometown. As sturdy and reliable as his trademark helmet, Olerud solved the Mariners ongoing issues at first base. "Ole," as his teammates called him, won over fans with consistent offensive production, ironclad defense, and a personality as even and pleasing as his textbook swing. "Ole's just a steady Eddie guy. He's just the kind of guy you like in your lineup," said his manager, Lou Piniella, in 2002.

A spray hitter with uncommon power, Olerud fortified the middle of the M's lineup from 2000–2003, hitting a robust .289 with a .392 on-base percentage and .448 slugging percentage. He also nabbed three Gold Gloves and was one of eight Mariners to be named to the 2001 All-Star team. While hitting for the cycle that year against the San Diego Padres in a 9–2 Mariner win, Olerud flexed his muscles by blasting a home run that traveled 464 feet. It was the second cycle of his career.

After his batting average and power dipped considerably, the Mariners released Olerud in July of 2004. He exited with grace and was picked up by the New York Yankees. In 2010 the NCAA created the John Olerud Two-Way Player award granted to the best combined college pitcher and hitter each year.

69 Young Guns

Over the course of 35 months, the Mariners drafted or acquired four pitchers who would form the core of what became known for a time as the "Young Guns." By the middle of the 1989 season, all four had moved into the starting rotation. Only Randy Johnson failed to produce sterling results. Scott Bankhead (25 years old), Erik Hanson (24), and Brian Holman (24) enthralled with ERAs below 3.50 and poise beyond their years.

Johnson, of course, went on to greatness. The others flirted with it. But injuries, the bugaboo of many pitchers, rolled over Seattle's dreams of a Temple of Doom starting rotation.

Alas, 1989 would be the only year in which the entire group pitched together for a lengthy part of a season. Bankhead, a 1984 member of the U.S. Olympic team, had the most experience of the '89 rotation and he set the pace that year. A control artist, Bankhead went 14–6 and established a franchise record by winning games in seven consecutive starts. Bankhead made only four starts, however, in 1990 before a shoulder injury ended his season. He never fully recovered and was let go at the end of 1991. He resurrected his career as a reliever for the Cincinnati Reds.

Holman was considered the prize of the Mark Langston trade. In parts of three seasons as a Mariner, he displayed why. But never more so than on April 20, 1990. Holman put on such a mesmerizing show that night that the crowd in Oakland, 44,000 strong, stood up and cheered for him as he faced his 27th batter of the game. Holman had retired the first 26 A's and needed just one more out for a perfect game. "When the opposing fans cheer you, it's a pretty deep feeling," he told *The Seattle Times* 20 years later. "Very neat. I'd never experienced that as an athlete. Usually, they're booing and throwing batteries at you or yelling at your mom."

Throughout the game Holman had pinpoint command. He only went to a three-ball count three times. Canseco came the closest to ending the perfecto, lining a ball past third base that landed a foot foul. Holman struck him out on the next pitch. For the final at-bat, the A's sent up a pinch-hitter, Ken Phelps, a former Mariner and Seattle native. "When I had two outs," Holman said, "I stepped off the mound and I was literally thinking, *Oh my gosh, I'm going to be in the Hall of Fame. They're going to want my hat, jock, underwear…*"

The scouting report on Phelps was that he never swung on the first pitch and couldn't hit the high fastball. "Tony [La Russa, the A's manager,] said to go up swinging," Phelps recalled in the same *Times* interview. "There was no sense taking pitches off him." On the first pitch, Holman threw Phelps a fastball up. The former

Mariner ambushed him, swinging at the pitch and sending it deep into the right-field seats. The perfect game, no-hitter, and shutout all ended in painful harmony, though Holman retired the next batter to preserve a 6–1 win. "At least it was a home run," he said. "[If it was] a broken bat or a blooper, I would have lost my mind."

Holman didn't get his perfect game, and his career ended two years later when he tore his rotator cuff. Since then Holman has suffered a few more hardships, none worse than losing a daughter at age 11 to leukemia. "A perfect game is a great thing and wonderful, but it's just baseball," Holman offered. "We've dealt with a lot harder things than baseball." Holman now lives in his native Kansas, where he works for an investment firm. His son, David, pitches in the Mariners organization.

The fourth member of the ill-fated young guns was Hanson. He exhibited the most promise initially. Courted to play college basketball in the ACC, Hanson lost his major league debut in 1988 despite not allowing an earned run and then beat the Milwaukee Brewers in his second-ever start with a shutout through seven innings. In 1990 he dominated the American League, especially in the second half, winning 18 games, striking out 211 batters, and finishing ninth in the AL in ERA.

Hanson featured a big, bending curveball, one many compared to the lethal bender of Hall of Famer Bert Blyleven. He also had a low 90s fastball and a change-up that could "make people take funny swings," according to his pitching coach in Seattle, Mike Paul. Hanson had all of his pitches working and coaxed a flurry of funny swings against the Bash Brother A's in a memorable Oakland Coliseum pitchers' duel in August of 1990. Hanson and Oakland ace Dave Stewart matched zeros for 10 innings. "It was as good as I could possibly throw," he told the *Seattle Post-Intelligencer* in 2007. Hanson fanned 11, walked none, and allowed two hits. But the M's lost in 11 when Mike Schooler relieved Hanson. "How did he ever lose a game?" wondered A's slugger Mark McGwire afterward. M's manager Jim Lefebvre, recalling the game years later, considered it "one of the finest duels I've ever seen."

Injuries torpedoed Hanson's remaining years with the Mariners. After losing 17 games in 1992, Hanson was dealt to Cincinnati. In 1995 he managed one last hurrah, going 15–5 with the Boston Red Sox and earning his sole All-Star appearance. Three injury-filled seasons later, he retired. "It was kind of like the Clint Eastwood movie, *The Good, the Bad and the Ugly*," he said in reference to his star-crossed career.

70 Mike Cameron and Four Homers

Seattle's hot start to the 2002 season (the M's stood 18–9) overshadowed a slow one for Mike Cameron. Mired in a 4–37 slump on May 2, the M's center fielder just hoped to scratch out a hit or two in the upcoming game against the Chicago White Sox. Instead, he scratched off a winning lottery ticket.

Cameron, 29, came to the Mariners under stressful circumstances—as part of the 2000 Ken Griffey Jr. deal. Frank Thomas had called him "a potential superstar" during his rookie season with the White Sox in 1997. But when the LaGrange, Georgia, native arrived in Seattle, he was still more potential than super, even though Cameron clouted 21 homers in 1999 after being traded to the Cincinnati Reds for Paul Konerko. He also fanned 145 times. "Imagine the pressure Mike Cameron will feel coming to Seattle as Griffey's replacement," wrote Steve Kelly, columnist for *The Seattle Times*. "What happens when he doesn't get to that ball in the left-center field gap? The one Griffey always got?"

In the first week of the 2000 season, Cameron proved Kelley's concerns overblown. On April 7, he scaled the center-field wall at Safeco Field to rob Derek Jeter of a home run, catching it ice cream cone style. The crowd saluted him with a sustained cheer and later a standing ovation—after he struck out! The catch was a dramatic signal that Griffey's defense would be replaced without a beat. "A little déjà vu," teammate Jay Buhner said after the game.

In the same week, Cameron hit a home run and sparked rallies by getting on base. Over the next four years, he fell well short of replacing Griffey's offense—not that anyone thought he would. Low batting averages and gargantuan strikeout numbers plagued him the entire time. But what he could do with the bat was hit homers, none more timely than the bomb he delivered to end a 19-inning game against the Boston Red Sox in August of 2000. Then a year later in the middle of the M's scorching hot 2001, he went 4-for-4 and belted a grand slam en route to a franchise-record eight RBIs in a 10–2 Mariners victory at Yankee Stadium.

A great influence in the clubhouse, Cameron became one of Ichiro's favorite teammates; a favorite of fans for his community involvement, engaging personality, and accommodating nature; and beloved for what happened on May 2, 2002. Cameron tied a major league record by hitting four homers in a game. (That mark is tied with 15 others, but he became the first American Leaguer to do so since Rocky Colavito of the Cleveland Indians in 1959.) Two of the homers came in the first inning, when he and teammate Bret Boone set an MLB record by homering twice in the same inning back-to-back. Three were bombs to dead center. The first came off rookie Jon Rauch; the other three came off Cameron's former Sox teammate, Jim Parque. After the fourth homer, the Comiskey Park crowd gave him a standing ovation. As Cameron circled the bases, he grinned like he'd just won his 10th straight hand of blackjack. "It's like my son when he played his first little league T-ball game.

That's how I felt. I felt like I was king of the hill." Cameron's bid for a fifth homer died at the warning track, but he also stole a grand slam from Magglio Ordonez with an over-the-wall-catch.

Cameron left Seattle at the end of the 2003 season. He claimed he wanted to return to the M's, but general manager Bill Bavasi let him walk because he was uncomfortable with Cameron's struggles at Safeco. (He hit .224 in his home park.) In his four years in Seattle, Cameron's superior defense (he won Gold Gloves in 2001 and 2003) and timely power helped the M's go 393–255 overall with at least 91 wins every season.

Cammy called it quits after 17 years before the 2012 season. He asked the M's if he could retire as a Mariner. They obliged by signing him to an employee-services contract. On Opening Day of that year, he threw out the first pitch. "The days that I played here and replaced a legend and the fact that the people took hold and took shape of me and walked me through everything gave me a great opportunity to start my career off right," he said that night. "That's why I feel like it should end here."

71 Harold Reynolds

Every year from 1977–1986, the Mariners sent one representative to the All-Star Game. In 1987 this streak, though honestly earned, finally ended. Two Mariners made the team, and they both played. One of them pitched two innings. The other entered the game in the fourth inning—and never left the lineup. Even when the game entered extra innings, he continued playing. Four plate appearances and 10 innings later, he had accumulated more All-Star innings than all previous Mariners All-Stars combined—no doubt fouling

Second baseman Harold Reynolds was known for his speed on the base path.
(Getty Images)

up the plans of Pacific Northwest baseball fans accustomed to dipping into the Midsummer Classic to catch the quick Mariners appearance and then getting on with their evening.

At the end of spring training in 1986, future 10-inning All-Star Harold Reynolds' career stood at a crossroads. In his major league starting debut on September 5, 1983, the 22-year-old switch-hitting second baseman went 2-for-5 with a double and a triple against the Kansas City Royals. But he failed to establish himself permanently, yo-yoing back and forth between Triple A and Seattle for three years. Big stolen-base numbers in the minors plus a respectable batting average and gilded glove kept the Corvallis, Oregon, native on the M's radar. In 1985 Reynolds sizzled at Triple A Calgary, hitting .363 in 52 games. The M's promoted him in July, but he flopped, prompting Kingdome fans to turn against him. In one infamous incident, the home crowd booed Reynolds as he stood on third base after hitting a triple. His crime: not being scrappy favorite Jack Perconte, the incumbent second baseman who was losing playing time to Reynolds.

Given another chance to win the starting job during the spring of 1986, the 25-year-old failed to make the Opening Day roster. Resilient as always, Reynolds tore up the Pacific Coast League once again. And he fine-tuned his mental approach. A born-again Christian considered one of the nice guys in the game, Reynolds became less passive. "You have to find out how to play as a Christian athlete. You can do that and still be aggressive," he told a reporter in late spring. In May the Mariners recalled him again—this time to replace shaky incumbent second sacker Danny Tartabull, who suffered from a strange case of fatigue. Reynolds survived the year, though mostly by default.

During the offseason he went through a baseball detox. "So many people had given me so much different advice that I just decided to wash my mind of everything and just go to work,"

Reynolds told *The Seattle Times*. "I decided I just had to see the ball and do what I could do." Working with his brother, former Padres outfielder Donnie Reynolds; Oregon State baseball coach Jack Riley; and San Francisco Giants farmhand Todd Thomas; Reynolds lifted weights, ran, and took swing after swing. He had everything videotaped and spent hours analyzing the film. The arduous regiment emboldened Reynolds to predict that he would make the All-Star team. "When he told me his decision to make the All-Star team, I wanted to tell him he needed to worry about making the Mariners because he hadn't had a great year yet," said his brother in a 1990 interview. "But he had that look."

With the M's threatening to sign former Mariner Julio Cruz, Reynolds returned to camp in 1987 and won the job—and then soldered it shut with a blowtorch. He played 160 games, hit .275, and stole 60 bases. He also stole the heart of Mariners fans, not just with his league leading stolen bases, slick glove work, and All-Star game appearance. "Harold Reynolds captivated the community," said announcer Dave Niehaus.

Reynolds became actively involved in the Seattle community at a level previously unseen. He won the Roberto Clemente Award for community service—the first Mariner to earn that prestigious distinction, created a Youth Foundation devoted to helping inner city kids, and also won the Martin Luther King Humanitarian Award. Reynolds never big timed anyone either. He chatted up fans in the elevator, made small talk with batboys and stadium crew, rode the subway to games on the road, and moved about Seattle as if Columbia Center was his office and not the Kingdome.

The breakout year proved to be just the beginning for Reynolds. He returned to the All-Star Game in 1988, won three Gold Gloves, stole at least 25 bases in four consecutive years, and hit .300 in 1989, perhaps his finest season. Extra-base power eluded Reynolds, and he had irksomely high caught-stealing percentages, but his defense never wavered and neither did his commitment to community service.

A free agent at the end of 1992, Reynolds, unable to say no, starting feeling pulled in too many directions in Seattle. Some in the Mariners' organization kvetched that Reynolds' performance had slipped as a result. A short time later, his playing time dwindled. Feeling a fresh start could help him restore balance and reignite his career, Reynolds signed with Baltimore. In Maryland's largest city, he could share the role model limelight with other stars, such as Baltimore shortstop Cal Ripken. That concluded a career in Seattle that spanned parts of 10 seasons, making him the longest-tenured Mariner ever at that time. On April 9, 1993, the Mariners honored him before that evening's game.

Reynolds' profile increased after his major league career ended in 1994. He joined ESPN as a baseball analyst and won an Emmy. He left in 2006 after being fired for an offense for which he was later vindicated. In 2009 he landed at the MLB Network, where he promotes his traditional view of baseball and spars regularly with the network's acolytes of Bill James and his statistical revolution.

72 Seven Sensational Firemen

Enrique Romo

A lean slice in a slab of gristle, Romo saved 16 games for the otherwise pitching-challenged first Mariners team in 1977. Purchased from the Mexico City Reds, where he starred, the 29-year-old rookie pitched a whooping 114⅓ innings mostly out of the pen with a 2.83 ERA and eight and one-third whiffs per nine innings. He was a fireman in the true sense of the word—deployed to put out emerging rallies instead of starting an inning with no one on base. After the 1978 season, the M's traded Romo for Mario Mendoza.

Mike Schooler

There weren't many leads to protect in the late '80s and early '90s, but Schooler usually salted away the leads the Mariners managed to take. In 1989 and 1990, he saved 30 games each year while posting sub-3.00 ERAs. Every time he came into the game, the Mariners played (what else?) Alice Cooper's "School's Out." Injuries wrecked the remainder of his career, which was haunted by a painful and career destroying habit of surrendering grand slams.

Kazuhiro Sasaki

The Mariners won a lot in Lou Piniella's first seven seasons as skipper. They would have won a lot more if the bullpen hadn't frequently collapsed as easily as the Maginot Line. Sasaki, signed as the M's first free agent from Japan before the 2000 season, helped shore up the Mariners' last line of defense. Featuring a forkball that could drop sharper than the temperature in the Artic, he transitioned seamlessly to Major League Baseball by racking up 37 saves in 2000, each one followed by a bow. The 32-year-old struck out more than 11 batters per nine innings and earned the American League Rookie of the Year award, making him the second oldest to win the award. (Sam Jethroe in 1950 was the oldest by a few months.) "At times [his forkball] is unhittable," Piniella said. Sasaki made the All-Star team the next two seasons while averaging 41 saves. He saved two games in the 2000 American League Division Series and closed out the Cleveland Indians in the 2001 ALDS. Sasaki walked away from his contract with the Mariners prior to the start of the 2004 season. He wanted to spend more time with his two young children in Japan.

Arthur Rhodes

For years the M's had sought an effective left-hander reliever. Rhodes, who arrived via free agency the same season as Sasaki, didn't solve that problem for the Mariners immediately. But in 2001 he teamed with Sasaki to give the M's a devastating lefty-righty combo in the back end of the bullpen. In 71 games he went 8–0 with a 1.72 ERA. In a bit of gamesmanship on August 25, 2001, the Indians, prompted by former Mariner Omar Vizquel, requested that Rhodes remove his shiny diamond earring. The next year Rhodes again shined as brightly as his jewelry, going 10–4 with a 2.33 ERA. In four seasons with the Mariners, he averaged 10 strikeouts per innings.

J.J. Putz

For two seasons, about the shelf life for most closers not named Rivera, Putz (pronounced "puts") used a split-fingered fastball and four-seam, 98-plus screamer to confound hitters and pile up saves. "[His splitter] is the best I've ever seen," said Detroit Tigers bench coach Jeff Jones. In 2006 the 6'5", 250-pounder saved 36 games with a 2.30 ERA. Putz bested that in 2007 by notching 40 saves in 42 chances while allowing only 11 runs in 68 appearances. For his efforts he made the All-Star team and earned the Rolaids Relief Man of the Year. "When I see Putz, I see dominance," said legendary closer Dennis Eckersley in 2007. The Mariners traded Putz, who missed parts of the 2008 season with an arm injury, to the New York Mets following a 101-loss season.

Shigetoshi Hasegawa and Rafael Soriano

Signed as a free agent in 2002 from the Angels, Hasegawa, who almost signed with the Mariners right out of Japan in 1997, moved from middle relief to closer in 2003. Relying primarily on a sinkerball, he put together an All-Star season, saving 16 games and registering a pimple-sized 1.48 ERA. Unlike other Japanese imports, Hasegawa spoke fluent English. He also read *The Wall Street Journal* and shared stock tips with teammates and the press. Soriano provided lights-out duty as Hasegawa's set-up man in 2003. He struck out 11½ batters per nine innings and allowed only nine runs in 53 innings. After battling arm injuries the next two seasons Soriano was sent to the Atlanta Braves for Horacio Ramirez in an ill-fated trade.

Amateur Draft: The Good, Bad, and Ugly (1977–2006)

Best First-Round Picks (by career Wins Above Replacement (WAR))

1. Alex Rodriguez, 1993 (116)
2. Ken Griffey Jr., 1987 (83.6)
3. Tino Martinez, 1988 (28.8)
4. Mike Moore, 1981 (28.5)
5. Dave Henderson, 1977 (27.6)

Best Value Picks (rounds 11 or lower)

1. Buddy Black, 17th round, 1979 (21.1)
2. Ryan Franklin, 23rd round, 1992 (11.6)
3. Ed Vande Berg, 13th round, 1980 (6.7)

Best Overall Drafts (three or more players with 5 WAR or greater signed by M's)

1. 1981: first round, Mike Moore (28.5); second round, Mark Langston (50.7); third round, Phil Bradley (18.5)
2. 1990: third round, Dave Fleming (5.3); fifth round, Bret Boone (22.6); sixth round, Mike Hampton (29.0)

3. 1991: first round, Shawn Estes (11.2); third round, Jim Mecir (8.2); eighth round, Derek Lowe (34.5)

Worst First-Round Picks

1. 1978: Tito Nanni, No. 6 overall pick (did not play in major leagues). M's could have had Kirk Gibson (12th overall) (38.3)
2. 1979: Al Chambers, No. 1 overall pick (0.5). M's could have had Andy Van Slyke (sixth overall) (41.2)
3. 1989: Roger Salkeld, No. 3 overall pick (0.3). M's could have had Frank Thomas (seventh overall) (73.7)
4. 1997: Ryan Anderson, No. 19 overall pick (did not play in majors). M's could have had Jayson Werth (22nd overall) (31.1 and counting)
5. 1999: Ryan Christianson, No. 11 overall pick (did not play in majors). M's could have had Alex Rios (19th overall) (28.4 and counting)
6. 2005: Jeff Clement, No. 3 overall pick (-1.2 to date). M's could have had either Ryan Zimmerman (fourth overall) (34.3 and counting); Ryan Braun (fifth overall) (36.0 and counting); or Troy Tulowitzi (seventh overall) (37.6 and counting)

Worst Overall Drafts

1. 1983: Top four picks were Darrel Akerfelds, Terry Bell, Micky Brantey, and Dave Hengel. The overall WAR from entire draft was -2.0.
2. 2000: Top four picks were Sam Hays (No. 116 overall pick), Derrick Van Dusen, Jamal Strong, and Jaime Bubela. The overall WAR for players signed by Mariners was 0.0.

74 Freddy Garcia

"One of the saddest, most disgraceful nights in team history." That's how Steve Kelly, a columnist for *The Seattle Times*, described the deal that brought Houston Astros minor league pitcher Freddy Garcia to the Mariners at the trade deadline in 1998. Garcia and minor leaguer Carlos Guillen (and later John Halama) arrived in exchange for Randy Johnson. The trade traumatized Seattle, which struggled to understand the seemingly pitiful return for what locals considered the greatest pitcher on Earth. "It was more a surprise to hear that they basically gave him away for nothing," Mariners first baseman David Segui told a reporter.

The tall Venezuelan quickly pulverized fears that he was a "nothing" by winning a startling 17 games in 1999, which tied a Mariners rookie record. Griping about the loss of Johnson soon gave way to praise for "the Chief," who nearly matched Johnson's production.

A power pitcher with finesse, Garcia's fastball touched 96 mph. His high-arching curveball provided the finesse. "He's 6'5" and he really gets his arm over his head. The [curveball] comes at you hard, then it breaks fast," said teammate Paul Abbott. Garcia also possessed a 78 mph change-up that he masked superbly. In his prime years with the M's, Garcia became a pitcher hitters feared. "He's physically intimidating, his stuff is intimidating, and his attitude is intimidating," said former opponent and one-time teammate Pat Borders.

Garcia spoke English haltingly during his time with the M's, limiting his ability to establish a strong rapport with Pacific Northwest fans. He let his mastery on the mound tell his story instead. In Venezuela, however, Garcia served as a source of inspiration for many young Venezuelan pitchers, including Felix Hernandez, who idolized Garcia and requested his vacated jersey number when he joined the Mariners.

Garcia beat the New York Yankees twice in the 2000 American League Championship Series (the only M's wins), allowing only two runs in 11-plus innings. He turned 24 four days before Game 1, a contest in which he tossed six and two-third shutout innings against the Yankees in Yankee Stadium. As many noted, Garcia's performance that day was better than any postseason outing Johnson ever had. "Absolutely awesome," said M's pitching coach Bryan Price.

In 2001, like many of his teammates, Garcia soared, going 18–6 and topping the AL in ERA. In his best start, he silenced 53,000 fans at Dodger Stadium with a complete-game 13–0 shutout. After scuffling in Game 1 of the American League Division Series against the Cleveland Indians, the Chief took the ball in Game 4 hoping to extend the series. An Indians fan taunted Garcia as he warmed up pregame: "116 wins are about to go down the toilet." The Chief flushed the Indians instead, defeating them 6–2. "That's why he's the No. 1," said teammate Norm Charlton.

The next two years Garcia's effectiveness slipped—perhaps due to burst eardrums he suffered on a flight in 2002, which likely affected his balance. His troubles snowballed to the extent that Garcia lost faith in his abilities and became a nibbler.

Finally healthy and confident as a result, Garcia, a pending free agent, was having a bounce back year in 2004 when the M's traded him to Chicago. "He was the man in Seattle back then," said former teammate Raul Ibanez. "If there was a big game, we wanted him on the mound." In 2005 Garcia won a World Series ring with the White Sox.

75 Seattle Pilots

Like a home-run ball off the bat of Hank Aaron, the Seattle Pilots were here one minute, gone the next. They lasted only a single season in the Northwest, becoming just the second big league franchise to play one year in its founding city. Ironically, the first, Milwaukee in 1902, became the new home of the Pilots.

For years Seattle had been the home of the Rainiers, one of baseball's most successful minor league franchises—both on the field and at the turnstile. By the 1960s, as Major League Baseball revved up expansion, Seattle entered the picture as a strong candidate for a big league club. A swelling economy, driven by Boeing, and baseball's desire to increase its presence on the West Coast aided the city's cause. Thus, in 1967 Seattle was granted one of Major League Baseball's four expansion franchises. Brothers Dewey and Max Soriano, both with deep ties to the Rainiers and the Pacific Coast League, and former Cleveland Indians owner William Daley formed the ownership group.

The Pilots were slated to debut in 1969 and play their games at Sicks Stadium, the former home of the Rainiers/Angels. As a condition of receiving one of the expansion franchises, Seattle had agreed to build a new, domed stadium ready within three years and to pay for a retrofit of Sicks Stadium. To bring the minor league ballpark up to major league snuff, even as a temporary home, the park needed vast renovations—none more pressing than expanding the field from 11,000 seats to 30,000. That proved to be too expensive, though, so the city eventually settled on adding 10,000 seats to bring capacity to 21,000. But a particularly harsh winter bolloxed attempts to finish the stadium upgrades by the start of the season. On Opening Day 1969, only 6,000 new seats had been added, and workers were still putting in benches as the crowd filed in. Other improvements remained unfinished as well, including basic enhancements to the plumbing.

Against this backdrop the Pilots started play. Managed by Joe Schultz, a coach with the 1968 National League champion St. Louis Cardinals, Seattle beat the Angels 4–3 in California. Right fielder Mike Hegan (who would hit .292) blasted a home run, and Marty Pattin picked up the win. After a loss the next night, the Pilots opened at home against the Chicago White Sox. Clear skies and 60 degrees drew an almost capacity crowd of 16,000. They watched the Pilots win 7–0. Gary Bell pitched a complete-game shutout, and Don Mincher hit his second homer of the year. The blast landed in the right-field stands that contained no seats. "A story book start," wrote *The Seattle Times*. The Pilots won the next day as well 5–1. Future Mariner Diego Segui pitched seven and two-third innings and allowed just the one run. Shortstop Ray Oyler, who had hit eight home runs in four seasons with the Detroit Tigers, homered to pace the offense.

Through the expansion draft, the Pilots had acquired a smattering of decent, proven talent still in their prime, such as first baseman Mincher, third baseman Tommy Harper (who led the American League in stolen bases with 73), and outfielder Tommy Davis. One player acquired in the draft was dealt a week before the season. The Pilots traded outfielder Lou Piniella to their expansion brethren, the Kansas City Royals. In exchange for Piniella, the Pilots received John Gelnar, Steve Whitaker, and a nasty case of heartburn. Piniella, to the Pilots' chagrin, went on to win Rookie of the Year that same season and almost cost Pilots general manager Marvin Milkes his job.

Having played reasonably well for three months, the Pilots went 15–42 in July and August, including a winless 10-game homestand. Attendance crashed in response. So did the resources of the owners, who, even before the first pitch of the season, had money problems. As a result they set ticket and concession prices high, which drew the ire of the local press. Plus, the Pilots failed to reach a TV broadcast deal, so no games appeared on the tube locally.

The city dropped the ball as well. The plumbing issues at Sicks never got resolved, resulting in water pressure so low that the visiting team showered in their hotels. Moreover, when attendance in the park topped 10,000, the toilets in the restrooms didn't flush. And the plans for the new stadium progressed slower than rush hour traffic.

The owners complained to the city about broken promises. Then Daley held a press conference in September and unloaded. He warned the Queen City and its fans that "Seattle has one more year to prove itself." Any goodwill the organization had before Daley's outburst had evaporated. Attendance sank even further, and pressure started to build for the Sorianos and Daley to sell. Twice it appeared the Pilots had found local owners, but both deals eventually fell apart, scotched in each case by American League executives.

Heading into spring training in 1970, the Pilots' ownership status remained uncertain. In October the Pilots had filed bankruptcy. By March they faced the real possibility of not making payroll, which would have made everyone on the roster a free agent. Finally, on April 1 a federal bankruptcy judge declared the Pilots insolvent. Milwaukee car dealer Bud Selig had for years coveted a franchise that he could move to his city. When Seattle's last-ditch effort to secure local ownership failed, the Pilots, who had finished spring training, were sold to Selig. The trucks carrying the team's uniforms and supplies north, which had reached Utah, turned east and headed to Milwaukee for the start of the 1970 season. Renamed the Brewers, the ballclub wore the Pilots' old uniforms on Opening

Day with the logos simply replaced by a Brewers patch. All along, Major League Baseball could have said no to the Pilots move. But, on the assumption Seattle's ardor for baseball was lacking, MLB just let the phone ring as the Pilots slipped out of town.

The Pilots story had one last hurrah. Jim Bouton, a former 20-game winner picked up from the New York Yankees, had a mostly forgettable season in middle relief. A year later, however, he became the toast of New York literati when the diary he had been keeping on the 1969 Pilots was turned into a best-selling book. *Ball Four* offered a raw, profane glimpse of baseball behind the curtain. The revelations about the sport, which exposed the drinking and drug use rampant in America's pastime, shocked the nation and helped accelerate the end of the age when fans considered ballplayers heroes.

Jilted Seattle didn't need to read a book to be shocked by baseball. It had already been burned.

76 Expansion Draft

In 1976 the Mariners had no farm system. They were prohibited from participating in the first ever free-agent draft, which would have given them a chance to select and negotiate with the best free agents available. And they would be picking last in the 1977 Amateur Draft in June. All of this put a huge onus on the November 5 Baseball Expansion Draft. In terms of player procurement, it was their biggest bite of the apple.

For the other 12 American League teams (National League teams were exempt), it was a dodge. Each existing junior circuit franchise could only protect 15 players from its entire organization. But every time one of them lost a player, they could protect three additional players. So the talent thinned exponentially as the draft proceeded. And a few loopholes allowed teams to augment their protected lists. For instance Boston left Carl Yastrzemski unprotected knowing—because of his five-and-10 status—he had the right to veto any deal and that he would. Thus the Red Sox could put the 37-year-old future Hall of Famer on the unprotected list without the risk of losing him.

With director of operations Lou Gorman in charge, Seattle started its draft preparations four months in advance. Gorman had led the Kansas City Royals expansion draft in 1968. So this wasn't his first rodeo. The Royals also had a deep farm system, one Gorman knew intimately from his years in the Kansas City organization. It wasn't a surprise when days before the draft speculation surfaced that the M's, who picked first, had targeted Jamie Quirk, a highly regarded 22-year-old rookie infielder the Royals had to leave unprotected because of a roster crunch.

"We will come out with the best 30 players we possibly can," Gorman said three days before the draft. "We know what we are doing. I think we'll come out with some good young talent from the early rounds." Other names surfaced as well, such as future Hall of Famer Brooks Robinson, who the Baltimore Orioles considering leaving unprotected. Sources suggested he was very open to playing in Seattle.

With the first pick in the draft, the Mariners selected a Royal as expected, just not the one rumored. Ruppert Jones went to the M's instead. The Blue Jays, the other expansion franchise, then took Bob Bailor, a highly touted shortstop from Baltimore. Seattle claimed afterward Bailor was the only player selected by the Blue Jays that the Mariners had wanted. Each side then picked 29 more players in five rounds of six players each. The Mariners didn't go as young as many expected, especially in the early rounds. Three of their first six picks were older than 26, including 34-year-old lefty reliever Grant Jackson from the Yankees. (They passed on Lou Piniella to take Jackson.) A month later the Mariners used Jackson to complete their first ever trade, dealing him to Pittsburgh for future starting shortstop Craig Reynolds and second baseman Jimmy Sexton. The M's went younger at the end of the draft, making the average age of their selected players 25.4, just a notch above the Blue Jays' 25. Six players picked in the draft started on Opening Day in 1977: Dave Collins (DH), Steve Braun (LF), Lee Stanton (RF), Bill Stein (3B), Dan Meyer (1B), Jones (CF), and Bob Stinson (C).

Most lauded the Mariners for picking Jones, an exciting out-fielder with five-tool potential. Kansas City farm director John Schuerholz told a reporter privately: "Jones has a chance to be a superstar." Braun, an outfielder/infielder from Minnesota, created the most buzz among the M's choices. No one had expected the 28-year-old career .284 hitter to be available. But he had played the previous year without a contract and signed the final day of the season on the condition the Twins would leave him unprotected. The M's tabbed him with the first pick in the fourth round.

The consensus around baseball was that the M's creamed Toronto. "If I had my choice, say, to manage either club, I'd have to pick Seattle," said Texas manager Frank Lucchesi. Roland Hemond, White Sox personnel director, agreed. "You are 2–1 over Toronto," he told a Seattle reporter. "You're already better than the Brewers," laughed one reporter. "Than the White Sox, too," added another.

Hy Zimmerman, who also covered the Seattle Pilots expansion draft, writing in *The Seattle Times* cautioned that many thought the Pilots had cleaned the clocks of the Royals in 1968 as well, but that didn't turn out to be the case. But overall, he was impressed. "In context, the belief here is that the Mariners did walk out with the better blend of talent…Though stung before, one crawls the limb to predict that the Seattle Mariners, judging by their efforts and attitudes hitherto will be a class organization. One has to be impressed."

77 1986: The Sublime and the Ridiculous

After two consecutive years in which the M's avoided the stigma of 90 losses, 1986 represented a setback. The Mariners lost 95 games and panicked, firing another manager midstream and spinning off some of the young talent they had cultivated. The season included a dash of the sublime but heaps of the ridiculous—none larger than what occurred on a cool April night in Boston.

Opening Night fit squarely in the former. Trailing 4–2 in the ninth inning to the Angels, Jim Presley, one of the Seattle young guns whose bat had the power of a howitzer, blasted a two-run homer to tie the game. What remained of a crowd of 42,000, which like the Mariners had slept through most of the game, shot to their feet and demanded a curtain call from Presley. He demurred, saying after the game he didn't want to show up the pitcher. An inning later, Presley let his bat do the talking once more, ending the game with a grand slam. The crowd again went bananas, and Presley again declined their invitation for a curtain call.

Flash ahead a few months to July 17.

The M's were tied 1–1 with the first-place Boston Red Sox in the bottom of the 11th inning. The season had already taken a gloomy turn, as the Mariners sat 12 games under .500 and 10½ games behind California. But this was the first game after the All-Star break, and hopes renewed that the season could turn around. With the bases loaded, 15,000 Kingdome fans rose at once.

Everyone remembered Opening Day but Presley, who said straight-faced afterward that his focus centered solely on getting a base hit perhaps by shooting the ball through the hole on the right side.

Instead, Red Sox pitcher Bob Stanley hung a breaking ball, and Presley pounced on the mistake, hitting a rocket that carries only a few rows from where his Opening Night grand slam descended to Earth. The crowd again refused to leave until Presley made a curtain call. This time he obliged them with a brief wave. "That Opening Night [homer] was pretty exciting," he said. "We had a big crowd here, but tonight is pretty exciting in itself."

Presley hit 27 home runs in 1986. He also made the All-Star team and even received votes for MVP. Three years later, the M's traded him for fringe prospects. Two years after that, at the prime age of 29, his major league career ended, done in by a lack of patience and astronomical strikeout rates. Presley's high strike-out totals hardly set him apart from his teammates in 1986. The Mariners offense led the American League in whiffs, which helped set the stage for an April perfect storm.

Failing to capitalize on Presley's Opening Day thunderbolts, the Mariners had slogged through a difficult first month. The offense, in particular, struggled—rooted in the team's inability to make contact. The M's had more trouble connecting than a hiker making a cell phone call at 10,000 feet. Against Oakland in mid April, for instance, the M's struck out 18 times, 16 at the hands of Jose Rijo, which set an A's record.

As the M's strikeouts mounted, Roger Clemens, the young Boston ace just then establishing himself as the most feared pitcher in the league, had barreled through the month with an ERA under 2.00. His best weapon: a wipeout fastball that helped him collect more than seven strikeouts a game. The collision course between Clemens and the whiff masters from Seattle, scheduled for April 29th in Boston, tickled the imagination of baseball fans intrigued by the possibilities.

Baseball, as any longtime fan knows, often blows up the script. This time, however, the narrative and the results harmonized like mustard and a Fenway Frank. Facing a lineup without its best fastball hitter—Alvin Davis was out with an injury—Clemens regularly dialed up his heater to 95 mph and occasionally 97, a notch higher than his season average. He threw 138 pitches, 97 for strikes. He opened the game by striking out the side. Then he fanned two in the second inning and one in the third. The M's still had some fight in them—until he struck out the side in the fourth and again in the fifth. The strikeouts kept coming, and by the ninth inning, Clemens, who had surrendered a run on a Gorman Thomas long ball that put the M's up temporarily, needed one whiff to tie and two to break the all-time major league strikeout record. Going on mostly adrenaline he admitted afterward, Clemens fanned Spike Owen on a checked swing and then rung up Phil Bradley (for the fourth time) to set the record with his 20th strikeout of the game. "To be mentioned in the same class as [Tom] Seaver, [Nolan] Ryan, and [Steve] Carlton is something I don't have words for," Clemens said.

"I saw Catfish Hunter and Mike Witt throw their perfect games and I can tell you this is the most awesome performance of pitching I have ever seen," gushed Red Sox manager John McNamara about the three-hit, no walk, one-run effort. M's manager Chuck Cottier, who probably felt the noose tightening, delivered a more colorful if bitter assessment. "Not Big Cy [Young], not Big Walter [Johnson], not anyone ever struck out 20 men in nine innings. Just one guy, only one. Tonight. Against us." Nine days later, Cottier met the same fate as his four predecessors: a pink slip.

78 Maury Wills

For years Maury Wills had been lobbying for a job as a major league manager. The former National League MVP who once stole 104 bases in a season with the Dodgers had written a book in 1976 entitled *How to Steal a Pennant*. It was essentially a lengthy job resume, outlining in detail how Wills could turn any pretender into a contender. His formula, as the title suggests, was heavy on base stealing and other small-ball tactics. But Wills had failed to land a job managing at either the major or minor league level by 1980. His only managing experience came from a few winters in the Mexican League.

Nonetheless, what Wills advocated in his book struck a nerve with Seattle management. They hoped his emphasis on playing smart, sound baseball built around speed and athleticism would rouse the franchise to respectability. So on August 4, 1980, the Mariners made their first managerial change, firing Darrell Johnson and replacing him with Wills. "I am totally prepared for the Seattle job—mentally, emotionally, and spiritually," he said. "I honestly feel I can do a terrific job. I am not just going to be another manager. I am going to be an outstanding manager." Wills proved to be terrific and outstanding—just not in the way the Mariners had envisioned.

He blundered through three of the most wretched baseball months in Mariners history (a bar quite high). The M's ended the 1980 season finishing with a worse winning percentage than they had under Johnson. And then they opened the 1981 season losing 18 of their first 24 games. Worried that the new direction under Wills meant turning bad into execrable, Seattle hurriedly canned the self-professed wunderkind. Wills' final record was 26–56, a

.317 winning percentage. The drumbeat of losses only partially explains why the Mariners cut bait so quickly. Giving a manager, especially one with severe talent deficiencies, only 83 games to turn things around is, on the face of it, unfair and counterproductive. Unless you detest how the sausage is being made.

Wills was just completely unprepared for the job, stumbling into more mistakes than a first-year foreign language student. Strategy, managing a pitching staff, handling the clubhouse, and massaging the press all seemed beyond his grasp. Then, as the listing ship filled with too much water, he publically lashed out at his players and coaches and made a series of facile moves designed to persuade his critics he was on top of things.

Following are just some of the lowlights:

- When Wills arrived at spring training in 1981, he held a team meeting in which he stated he wanted to build a winning attitude. Later that afternoon Wills decided the Ramada Inn (where the Mariners were ensconced) was not to his liking, so he moved to the Fiesta Inn, leaving the team behind.
- Wills told the press in spring training that year that he intended to bring outfielder Steve Stroughter in as a non-roster player. Stroughter had been traded to the Milwaukee Brewers two weeks earlier.
- In the sixth inning of a game against the San Diego Padres early in spring training, Wills left the field without telling anyone and hopped a plane for California.
- Wills decided to crack down on the Mariners during that spring training, insisting on a strenuous conditioning program and not allowing his players to golf on their free time. At this point Wills began to lose the support of his players. He lost his players completely with a string of bizarre actions/decisions.
- At a press conference announcing George Argyros as the new Mariners owner, Wills was asked who would play center field

the following season. "I wouldn't be a bit surprised if it was Leon Roberts," Wills answered. Roberts had been traded to the Texas Rangers five weeks earlier.

- Wills stopped a game in order to have a conversation with Julio Cruz, who later reported: "[Wills] hated Rickey Henderson, and Rickey had stolen second. He told me to hold him on second like I was a first baseman. So there I stood, my foot on the bag, my glove stretched out to the mound. Rickey said, 'What are you doing?' And I told him I was following orders. Then on the first pitch, he stole third."

- During a road trip in Oakland early in 1981, Wills posted a list of 18 new team rules in the Mariners clubhouse. One said: "No Dogs In The Stadium." No dogs had ever been brought to the stadium.

- Wills once made out a lineup card that had two third basemen and no centerfielder.

- Wills held up a game for 10 minutes while he searched for a pinch-hitter. When he finally discovered he had no pinch-hitter available, he tried to send a pinch-hitter to bat who had already appeared as a pinch-hitter.

- Wills placed Willie Norwood on waivers before a spring training game against the Oakland A's, but he didn't tell Norwood about it until after the game. Wills used Norwood in the ninth inning.

- During a game against Milwaukee, Wills called for a relief pitcher but had forgotten to tell any pitchers to warm up.

- After the first game of a series against the A's at the Kingdome, Oakland manager Billy Martin complained to the umpire that Tom Paciorek kept leaving the batter's box on his swing and should have been called out. The wily Wills concocted a scheme to counter that. He had the groundskeeper extend the batter's box several inches toward the mound. That would allow Paciorek to inch up a bit and hit breaking balls, which were a specialty of that day's pitcher, Rick Langford. Martin sniffed out the ruse. He complained to the umps who, after measuring the batter's box, had the line redrawn. The league suspended Wills and fined him $500. Two weeks later the Mariners suspended him for good.

Years later, in his third book, *On the Run*, Wills admitted that during his time as Mariners manager he had a drug abuse problem, which doubtlessly contributed to his erratic behavior and decisions. But he mostly blamed the media for his troubles in Seattle. Wills never managed in the big leagues again. "The Wills regime was just a nightmare, an absolute nightmare, from start to finish," Mariners broadcaster Dave Niehaus said. "Some of the things he did. I expected more of a baseball man like that and I felt sorry for Maury Wills."

79 1998–1999: Transition Years

For a two-year period following the 1997 division title, the wins dried up. Big names skipped town. Stars succumbed to Father Time. Role players failed to play their role well. Management also made a secret decision to retrench financially to make a big splash in their new park, slated to open mid-season in 1999.

That didn't dim manager Lou Piniella's optimism heading into the 1998 season, at least publically. He declared this the best Mariners team of his tenure. Dominated by the Randy Johnson saga and the bullpen's encore performance, the season instead soured into one of Piniella's worst in Seattle.

Over the winter the Mariners announced they couldn't afford to re-sign Johnson. Not wanting to lose the Big Unit to free agency without receiving talent in return, Seattle attempted to trade him, but a deal with the Yankees for closer Mariano Rivera fell apart when New York refused to include starter Andy Pettitte in the swap. Johnson became understandably upset. "If I had my wish, I would have already been traded by now," Johnson complained in December. "It's an uncomfortable situation, knowing I'm not going to be here next year."

For the first four months, Johnson pitched as if his mind was elsewhere. At the All-Star break, he was 7–8 with a 5.07 ERA. Of course the Mariners beleaguered bullpen spoiled many of his outings. Piniella had hoped the bullpen would revive in 1998. But holdovers Heathcliff Slocumb, Bobby Ayala, Paul Spoljaric, and Bob Wells all faltered. Said an American League scout in defense of the Mariners: "Those guys have ability. You can't blame Seattle for trying to go with them this year."

In May the M's nearly traded Johnson to the Los Angeles Dodgers. Team president Hiroshi Yamauchi, who rarely inserted himself, allegedly killed the deal because Dodgers pitcher Hideo Nomo, who had rejected an M's offer in 1995, was part of it. The Mariners lost 12 of their next 15 games and staggered the rest of the season. Seattle finally dealt Johnson to the Houston Astros on July 31.

Despite a historic season from Alex Rodriguez and typically strong years from Ken Griffey Jr. and Edgar Martinez, the Mariners skidded to a 76–85 season. Most of the damage came at the hands of the AL's best. The M's went 19–45 against the top teams. For the first time, public carping about Piniella surfaced as well. The chief complaints: his inability to develop young pitchers and failure to rein in Johnson's emotions.

Then during the offseason, some of the older veterans met with management and lobbied for aggressive upgrades. But the Mariners set their budget at $53 million, the same as the previous year. "Our window of opportunity only lasts so long," Jay Buhner grumbled. M's president Chuck Armstrong retorted: "What is $65 million going to bring that you can't get with $54 million?"

Fifty-four million, as it turned out, brought bullpen help in Jose Mesa, Mark Leiter, and Japanese import Mac Suzuki—but not much relief. The Mariners' ongoing bullpen problems persisted in 1999 and contributed to another sub-.500 season. On July 15 Safeco Field debuted. Mesa, on cue, blew a ninth-inning lead.

It wasn't a lost year, however. Freddy Garcia, Carlos Guillen, and John Halama, all acquired in the Johnson deal, made their debuts. Halama and especially Garcia sparkled. Third baseman David Bell and rookie starter Gil Meche joined the team as well. The Mariners also entertained Japanese superstar Ichiro Suzuki for a game. As was the plan, the Mariners loosened the budget as they moved into Safeco Field, which ended the brief spell of losing and launched the winningest four-year period in Mariners history.

80 Mark Langston

Does the mention of any Seattle Mariner bring more conflicting emotions than left-handed pitcher Mark Langston?

The Mariners drafted the lefty pitcher from San Jose State in the second round of the 1981 draft. He intimidated minor league hitters with a menacing mid-to-upper 90s fastball but struggled with control. In three years in the minors, Langston never really tamed the walking beast but showed enough stuff that the M's, in the middle of a youth movement, had him skip Triple A and start in the Mariners' 1984 rotation.

Langston rocked. He competed with Alvin Davis for Rookie of the Year honors, eventually finishing second but taking home *The Sporting News* Rookie Pitcher of the Year. The 23-year-old won 17 games. He led the league in strikeouts. But not everything about Langston's rookie year had the smell of freshly baked cinnamon buns. His old nemesis in the minor leagues migrated with him to the majors. Langston led the American League in walks allowed.

Base on balls continued to bedevil Langston over the next few years, especially his sophomore season, when he walked 91 batters against just 72 strikeouts in 126.2 innings while fighting a sore elbow. Langston slumped to seven wins and a 5.47 ERA. Sentiment grew to return him to the minors for more seasoning. Langston's manager, Chuck Cottier, resisted the idea and prevailed.

Over the next three-and-a-half years, Langston did his part to make the M's entertaining if not competitive. In 1986 he topped the league in Ks again, punctuated by a 15-strikeout effort against the Cleveland Indians that brought out the immoderate best in M's broadcaster Dave Niehaus, who went nuts calling the game.

The next season, Langston kicked down the final barrier to becoming an ace. Shaving his walks while increasing his strikeouts, he won 19 games, led the league in strikeouts again, completed 14 games (fourth in the league), won a Gold Glove, made the All-Star Game—where he pitched two perfect innings, and finished fifth in the Cy Young voting. "Sometimes they'll be up there against Mark saying, 'I don't even know why I'm up here,'" Mariners catcher Scott Bradley told a reporter. "'I don't have a chance to hit some of his stuff.'"

Langston—who moonwalked in the dugout during a rain delay in Kansas City, bringing a great cheer from the Royals crowd and subsequent heckling from teammates—possessed a rubber arm, another quality of an ace. He regularly pitched into the seventh and eighth innings and bested 225 innings most seasons. The

M's bullpen, usually underfunded and overtaxed, appreciated the breathers.

After another strong season in 1988 (including a 16-strikeout game against Toronto), Langston faced free agency at the end of the 1989 season. Following a familiar pattern, the Mariners and their star pitcher played chicken, and Seattle eventually bailed by trading Langston, who was off to a great start, in May of 1989. According to multiple quotes Langston has made since retirement, the timing of the trade shocked him. Based on a conversation he had with his agent only days earlier, Langston thought he and the M's were close to reaching a contract extension.

Everyone panned the trade, which brought back a few arms from the Montreal Expos. (Brian Holman was the most notable one at the time.) Also included was a project the size of Quebec, a tall, gangly left-hander with a roaring but ungovernable fastball. Langston cut bait in Montreal after a half-season and a scintillating 2.39 ERA. He signed with the Angels, where he battled against the Mariners for six seasons, none more coldly redemptive than when he teamed with Mike Witt to no-hit Seattle in his first start ever against the M's.

Then came October 2, 1995. The day Randy Johnson, the project from Montreal, beat Langston and his Angels 9–1 in a tie-breaker to win the AL West. The victory, of course, set off a series of events that kept the M's in Seattle. Langston is philosophical about being traded for the Big Unit. "Heck, with Randy, I feel almost privileged that one worked," Langston told *The Seattle Times* in 2012. "And I was a part of [the pivotal trade that rebooted the Mariners]."

Langston retired a few years after losing that playoff game against the Mariners and now broadcasts home games for the Angels, though another AL team remains close to his heart as well. "I thought I would play my whole career in Seattle," he told Jim

Street at MLB.com in 2003. "When you first come up with a team, there isn't another team out there. Seattle has always been a special place to me and always will."

81 1984: A Rookie Rush

Dave Niehaus once referred to the Mariners' 1984 season as "magical," a curious word to describe a year when a team finishes 74–88 and in fifth place. But consider Niehaus' sentiment in the context of the age-old saying: "One man's trash is another man's treasure."

For years the M's had fielded a team of mostly aging veterans and cast-offs in their prime. Such was their fate as an expansion franchise. Any success the Mariners enjoyed tended to be the result of someone else's garbage, recycling into something surprisingly useful. By the mid-1980s, however, players drafted and developed by Seattle started popping up in the M's lineup. The homegrown talent generated a different vibe around the Mariners. No one expected immediate contention, but the hope that some of the youngsters would develop into frontline players created genuine optimism for the future.

A handful of promising rookies debuted as early as 1981, such as outfielder Dave Henderson. Pitchers Mike Moore and Edwin Nunez followed in 1982. First-round draft pick Spike Owen, second-round pick Matt Young, and outfielder Phil Bradley received their baptism in 1983. But 1984 saw a wave. Infielders Alvin Davis and Jim Presley plus pitcher Mark Langston, all 23, became eventual starters. Ivan Calderon, 22, Danny Tartabull, 21, and Dave Valle, 23, killed it in the minor leagues all year and received brief but promising looks late in the season. Twenty-three-year-old Harold Reynolds had received a cup of coffee in '83, put together a strong season at Triple A Salt Lake City, and joined the gang of late-season promotions in '84. "We aren't asking for a World Series this year. We're asking for hope," wrote *The Seattle Times* columnist Steve Kelly at the beginning of the season.

Hope was on display almost immediately. The Mariners won six of their first seven, highlighted by a four-hit, 3–2 victory by Langston, who stymied the thumping bats of the Milwaukee Brewers in his major league debut. "He just kept bringing the ball to them, an express," said veteran catcher Bob Kearney. "He said, 'Here, hit it.' It was a pleasure to catch him." Four days later Davis clobbered a ball 450 feet for a home run in only his second major league at-bat to help the M's beat the Boston Red Sox 5–4.

The M's slipped back a bit from their hot start but, bucking a franchise trend, managed to avoid the type of cliff-diving stretches that had derailed past seasons before Memorial Day. Indeed, heading into a three-game holiday series against the Detroit Tigers, Seattle hovered around .500 and stood only two-and-a-half games out of first place. Detroit arrived in Seattle on an epic run, winning 35 of their first 40 games and riding an MLB-record-tying 17-game road winning streak. Not only did the Mariners end that streak, but they also swept the Tigers—in pillaging fashion. Outscoring Detroit by 13 runs, Seattle moved into second place and within a half game of first place. The Kingdome crowd, which on Saturday swelled to 41,342, waved brooms and serenaded the Tigers with a chorus of "Sweep, sweep, sweep." Just the week before, the Tigers had swept the M's in Detroit. "We went into Twilight Zone when they beat us three times there," Kearney told a reporter. "We traded them one Twilight Zone for another."

Never before had the Mariners been as high as second place this late in the season. They hung on to second place for another week, but a six-game losing streak knocked them down to fifth.

"Mr. Mariner," Alvin Davis, hits his 20th homer in 1984, a season in which he won Rookie of the Year honors.

Although they failed to recapture the dominant glory of the weekend against Detroit, the season never deteriorated into a complete mess. The Mariners even stayed on the cusp of the American League West race, pulling to within five games on July 29 after sweeping Oakland to go to 49–56. "Anything can happen," mused Randy Adamack, the Mariners' director of public relations, on the inability of any team in the West to salt away the division and the Mariners' unprecedented distance from first this late in the year.

Through the season's first four months, Langston and Davis continued to row in the same direction: toward contention for Rookie of the Year. Besides Davis, veterans Ken Phelps, a designated hitter; Al Cowens, an outfielder; and 25-year-old Henderson paced the offense. Rookie Presley, called up in June, flashed some power early. On the mound, Jim Beattie provided veteran consistency, and the young Moore started having more ups than downs. The 21-year-old Nunez sparkled in the bullpen.

August proved to be the Mariners' Waterloo. They skidded to a 10–18 record, which cost Mariners manager Del Crandall his job. But then Chuck Cottier grabbed hold of the trident and the Mariners finished strong, going 15–12 in September. No Mariners team had ever played better than .500 in September. The late-season call-ups, who performed admirably, added color back to a season that had started to turn pale.

Langston topped off the year by beating the Chicago White Sox 5–3 and wrapping up the league strikeout title on the final day. "For yesterday, as Langston pitched his way into the record book and his team into a share of fifth place, there was as much a sense of beginning as there was of ending," wrote *The Seattle Times'* Bob Finnigan. "The emotions were mixed because for the first time, really, there is a future for the Mariners."

It was a future that included Davis, who edged Langston for Rookie of the Year, and a host of talent 25 and younger. Some, such as Henderson, Owens, Presley, Bradley, Moore, Nunez, and

Young, had already started contributing. Others, such as Calderon, Tartabull, Reynolds, and Valle, were just a step away. For the first time, really, the Mariners could sell hope. And there are few tonics more "magical" than that.

82 Bruce Bochte

Off the bat, the ball slammed immediately into the hard surface of the Kingdome turf. Then it took a bounce, which even the Sonics' 6'11" Jack Sikma couldn't have snared, and carried over the shortstop for a base hit. No Mariner had ever recorded a hit in an All-Star Game. Bruce Bochte's awkward looking chopper in the 1979 All-Star Game off Gaylord Perry became the first. And it seemed so fitting. A junk pitch that dropped four inches, a fake grass-induced high hopper, a ballplayer with an unusual perspective, and a franchise with more oddball moments than great ones. The first hit in Mariner All-Star history was as quirky as the franchise itself.

Bochte grew up in California and spent his first three-and-a-half seasons playing for the Angels before the Halos traded him to the Cleveland Indians. The Angels ran out of patience waiting for Bochte to fulfill the potential California manager Dick Williams trumpeted in 1976. "The swing, the desire, the concentration, the ability to consistently get a piece of almost every pitch," Williams said, "makes the kid a natural to win a batting championship."

Instead, Bochte never even hit .300 or clouted more than seven home runs. That prompted his trade to the Indians early in the 1977 season. The trade awakened his bat. He hit over .300 for the first time and started looking like the hitter Williams envisioned. What failed to awaken, however, was Bochte's affection for Cleveland.

The Indians really wanted to re-sign the first baseman, but Bochte spurned them, choosing to try the re-entry draft (free agency) at the end of the season. "I didn't want to live in Cleveland," he said two years later. "I didn't think the team had any future." The Indians' pitch to Bochte included the strong scent of desperation. "They said the future of America is in the Midwest because there is no water in California," he recalls. "They also said there would be no money left for the guys who went into the re-entry draft because the teams had given it all away the year before."

The Mariners actually had some money, so, as they often did in those early years, they took a chance on a guy with unrealized potential. Drafted in the third round of the re-entry draft (which no longer exists), Bochte signed a three-year deal for $325,000.

Things didn't fall into place right away for Bochte in Seattle. He took a step backward in 1978 before finding his stride over the next two years. "I expected to win games singlehandedly," he said about the '78 season. "In the beginning I was the only one hitting the ball. It got to the point that I felt if I didn't get two hits and drive in two runs, we wouldn't win the game. It gets to be mental torture." With Ruppert Jones, Tom Paciorek, and Willie Horton fortifying the lineup the next year, Bochte enjoyed a career year. That year included selection as a UPI All-Star and career highs in home runs (16), RBIs (100), and OPS (.878). Bochte finished in the top ten in batting average and provided smooth defense at first base. "He's a natural hitter—opposite field, up the middle, pull if you have to," said his batting coach Vada Pinson. "I've always liked that type of hitter. That real estate out there isn't owned by anybody."

This made Bochte somewhat of an anomaly as a first baseman, men known more for raw power and huge, unapologetic swings and misses. Instead, Bochte walked more than he struck out. Like many first basemen, though, he ran as if wearing rain boots instead of cleats. That contributed to his league-leading 27 ground-into-double-play outs in 1979.

There was another anomaly about Bochte. "He was kind of a nerd," said teammate Tom Paciorek in a 2001 interview with *The Seattle Times*. "He was more intellectual than the rest of us grunts." His Einstein qualities notwithstanding, Bochte related well to his teammates. "He had a great sense of humor," Paciorek continued, "but it's like he was closet crazy, less obvious than the rest of us." Bochte also took a keen interest in life outside of baseball, especially ecology. "He loved the game," Paciorek said, "but at the same time he was just as happy working on environmental issues."

That probably explains in part why Bochte suddenly quit baseball at age 31 after a strong season with the Mariners in 1982. A players' strike had rocked baseball the year before, and Bochte was the Mariners players' representative. It chipped away at his passion for the game. "The labor trouble and strike in 1981 was disillusioning, so many successful businessmen and players who want to play wouldn't reach a reasonable settlement without a strike," he lamented years later. "I didn't like dealing with [Mariners owner George] Argyros. Ultimately, I just didn't want to work for him any more." So, Bochte retired for a year to clear his head and soul. He returned to baseball in 1984 and played three more years with the Oakland Athletics.

After baseball, the California native moved back to the Seattle area before settling permanently in the Golden State. Today, he is a mathematical cosmologist and works for the Center for the Story of the Universe, which focuses on the origin and evolutionary dynamics of the universe. Or something like that. It's not exactly mainstream stuff. And it's why some in the game today insist Bochte was a bit of a flake, a moniker he furiously rejects. "I'm always walking a fine edge between conveying that I'm doing something substantial and solid—and being like Bill 'Spaceman' Lee," Bochte said to the *Seattle Post-Intelligencer* before the 2001 All-Star Game. "I'm hoping not to end up in the category of Spaceman."

83 Mariners Uniforms Through the Years

The Mariners' 1977 home jersey
(Courtesy: David Eskenazi)

The Mariners' 1978 road jersey
(David Eskenazi)

The Mariners' 1983 road jersey
(David Eskenazi)

The Mariners' 1985 home jersey
(David Eskenazi)

The Mariners' 1989 home jersey
(David Eskenazi)

The Mariners' 1995 home jersey
(David Eskenazi)

The Mariners' 1997 home jersey
(David Eskenazi)

The Mariners' 1997 home jersey
during Turn Ahead the Clock Night,
a spinoff of the popular Turn Back the
Clock promotions (David Eskenazi)

84 Tom Paciorek

The Kingdome certainly had its share of detractors. Don't count Tom Paciorek as one of them. A cast-off from the Los Angeles Dodgers, he signed with the Mariners in 1978 and surged. He also loved the Kingdome. "You knew you'd be able to start the game on time in air-conditioned comfort," he said in a 1997 interview with *The Seattle Times*. "No rain delays, snow delays or any of that other stuff."

The Hamtramck, Michigan, native played football and basketball at the University of Houston. The Miami Dolphins drafted Paciorek in 1968. Months later the Dodgers picked him in the fifth round, and Paciorek, a two-time baseball All-American, opted to sign with L.A.

Two years later, after impressing in the minor leagues, the Dodgers promoted him to the major leagues, where he spent six years pushing up Sisyphus' rock. Paciorek never had an above-average season, failing to hit higher than .262 or top five home runs. Eventually, the Dodgers traded him to the Atlanta Braves, but his results aped those in L.A., so at the start of the 1978 season, the Braves released him. Paciorek was 31 years old. His track recorded suggested his next job would be selling insurance.

Thank God for expansion and the Mariners and the 98 losses they had suffered the year before. Only a lemon would be interested in another lemon. The M's took a flyer on Paciorek, signing him to a minor league deal. He raked for a couple of weeks at Triple A San Jose, California, and when Seattle's Ruppert Jones needed emergency appendectomy surgery, Paciorek got the call.

It's little wonder he adored the Kingdome. Like smelling salts it revived him. The strapping 6'4" Paciorek, who had struggled to hit home runs, suddenly started hitting them. Shortly after being recalled, Paciorek went deep off Milwaukee Brewers ace Mike Caldwell, just one of his four hits. "Thank goodness for Mike Caldwell," Paciorek told baseballtoddsdugout.com. "That was fortunate for me because he was an outstanding pitcher that year— one of the aces of the American League."

Paciorek's good work against Caldwell earned him a start the next day. He smacked another home run and added a single. The man who had never clubbed more than five home runs in a season now had two in two days. When Jones returned from the DL, the M's decided to keep Paciorek. "It was just a fortunate series of events for me. After that I was able to play in the majors for quite a long time."

He finished the 1978 season with four home runs and a .299 average. Over the next three years, Paciorek hit another 35 home runs in a Mariners uniform. One of them recalled the feats of Babe Ruth. After promising to hit a home run for an 11-year-old boy with cerebral palsy, he actually did. Someone retrieved the home run ball, and Paciorek gave it to the boy, just as in the movies. "It was an emotional thing for me," he said.

"Wimpy," as he was nicknamed because of his love for hamburgers, had a whopper of a year in the strike-shortened season of 1981. In just 104 games, he set career highs in batting average (.326) and RBIs (66) and hit 14 home runs. The season earned Paciorek a spot on the All-Star team where the magic continued with a single, only the second All-Star Game hit in Mariners history.

For pure drama nothing matched Paciorek's memorable two days in May against the New York Yankees at the Kingdome. On Friday night Paciorek hit a walk-off home run to break a 2–2 tie. For an encore and in front of 51,903 fans lured by Free Bat Day, he homered in the ninth again. Only this time, the game-winner came with two outs, two on, and the Mariners down two runs. "Those were games you'll never forget if you were a fan back then," Dave

Neihaus remembered in *Tales from the Seattle Mariners Dugout*. "When he hit that home run off Ron Davis, everyone in the Kingdome went crazy." The crowd refused to leave, banging their bats in delirium on the cement aisles and demanding a curtain call. Paciorek obliged. As a thank you, the Mariners sent a limousine to pick up Paciorek and take him to the ballpark for the Sunday afternoon game.

"The fondest memories I had in my entire baseball life were here," said Paciorek, who was also one of many guys from that era addicted to clubhouse hijinks and fun. "I'm glad now I was released by Atlanta so I was able to come here."

The Mariners traded Paciorek after his big year. He insists they dumped him because he turned down their three-year $250,000 contract offer. Paciorek continued to ride his late-career rebirth by playing six more seasons in the major leagues, which included earning an American League West division title with the Chicago White Sox, who that year also acquired his former Mariners teammate Julio Cruz.

To this day, Paciorek calls Seattle "a special place." It wasn't because of the Mariners' record but because of the men he played with. "It was a unique bunch of guys," Paciorek said in 1997. "We had a lot of fun and played hard."

General Managers

Dick Vertlieb
1977–1978
He quit his job as a stockbroker in the mid-1960s to focus on bringing an NBA team to a city without one, even though he had

no ties to the sport. That landed him in Seattle, where he was instrumental in the SuperSonics' creation. Vertlieb served as the Sonics' general manager the first year and traded for the legendary Lenny Wilkens. Later he helped bring the Seahawks to Seattle as well. Sporting a handlebar mustache and booming voice, Vertlieb was high-strung, hyper-emotional, and possessed many eccentric qualities and ideas. When he became the Mariners' first GM, for instance, he wanted to dress the M's in black and nickname them the "Men from the Moon." "He had some wild ideas," said Dave Niehaus in 2004 to the *Seattle Post-Intelligencer*. "He had a little bit of rogue in him. He was a hustler himself." Vertlieb handled primarily marketing matters for the Mariners before resigning in a dispute over the firing of an employee. "He was a giant in Seattle sports," said Bob Walsh, a former Sonics executive.

Lou Gorman
1979–1980
A former executive of the expansion Kansas City Royals, Gorman provided the baseball acumen during Vertlieb's time as GM and then took over all management responsibilities in 1979. He oversaw the expansion draft, established the farm system, and set up the spring training facility. Dave Niehaus later said the biggest mistake the Mariners made in the early years was letting Gorman leave. He bolted for the Orioles because Dan O'Brien, named president in 1979, shut him out of many decisions while encroaching on Gorman's turf time and again.

Hal Keller
1981–1985
A former scout, Keller nurtured the Mariners farm system to life only to see parsimonious owner George Argyros undermine much of his work.

Dick Balderson
1986–1988
He's remembered primarily for a series of ill-fated trades—most notably when he shipped Dave Henderson to the Boston Red Sox—in 1986.

Woody Woodward
1989–1999
Under his stewardship, the Mariners posted five winning seasons—the only above-.500 teams in Mariners history at the time, won two division titles, and helped establish baseball as a winning proposition in Seattle. He and Lou Piniella overlapped in New York and were strong friends. Often hamstrung by the budget, Woodward managed to trade for such stalwarts as Randy Johnson, Jamie Moyer, David Bell, Joey Cora, Freddy Garcia, and Carlos Guillen. The Mariners also selected Alex Rodriguez No. 1 in 1993. Some deals, of course, went sour such as the trade that brought Kevin Mitchell and deals that sent Omar Vizquel, Tino Martinez, David Ortiz, Jason Varitek, and Derek Lowe to other destinations. Not known as a nose-to-the-grindstone GM, he retired in 1999 on his own terms despite news reports that Mariners president Howard Lincoln wanted him gone. Seattle fans, stung by recent questionable trades and two straight playoff misses, cheered his departure.

Pat Gillick
2000–2003
One of the best GMs in baseball at the time of his hire, Gillick's tenure in Seattle further burnished his reputation as a shrewd operator. He managed to extract value for Ken Griffey Jr. in the gun-to-his-head trade with the Cincinnati Reds. That same offseason, Gillick signed a strong group of free agents who helped boost the Mariners to the playoffs in 2000. Later acquisitions of Ichiro

and Bret Boone set up the historic 2001 season. Gillick resigned at the end of the 2003 season. The Mariners averaged 98 wins during his four seasons, but they failed to make the World Series. "I've had four kicks of the can, and we couldn't get over the hump," he said. The press speculated Gillick was leaving due to frustration with upper management, though he denied it.

Bill Bavasi
2003–2008
The Mariners nosedived under Bavasi, who was considered by many the most inept GM in M's history. Seattle finished in last place four of his five years. He flubbed trades, free-agent signings, and draft picks and left the franchise in near ruin.

Jack Zduriencik
2009–Present
Named Executive of the Year in 2007, Zduriencik is still working on the rebuild, which charged into motion in 2014. On the plus side, he helped coax Robinson Cano to sign with the M's. On the negative ledger, he traded away Doug Fister.

86 Notable Major Leaguers Buried in Washington

Two Hall of Famers
Earl Averill (1929–1941): Grand Army of the Republic Cemetery, Snohomish
"The Earl of Snohomish" was a lefty power hitter mostly with the Indians. He played in the first six All-Star Games. Averill was so

feared as a hitter that the Red Sox once walked him five consecutive times.

Amos Rusie (1889–95, 1897–98, 1901): Acacia Memorial Park, Seattle
The primary reason baseball moved the mound from 50 feet to 60 feet, Rusie won 36 games in 1894 as a New York Giant and led the National League in strikeouts five times.

Others of Note
Dick Barrett (1933–1945): Holyrood Catholic Cemetery, Seattle
"Kewpie" starred for the Seattle Indians, winning 20 games seven times. He won 35 games with three clubs (Braves, Athletics, Phillies) in the majors.

Ed Brandt (1928–1938): Fairmount Memorial Park, Spokane
A good hitting pitcher who threw a forkball, he won 18 games in both 1931 and 1933 for the Braves.

George Burns (1914–1929): Calvary Cemetery, Seattle
"Tioga George" had a career .307 batting average for five teams and won the 1926 American League MVP, batting .358 with a league-leading 216 hits and 64 doubles for the Cleveland Indians.

Harlond Clift (1934–1945): Terrace Heights Memorial Park, Yakima
Playing on the sad-sack St. Louis Browns, Clift toiled mostly in obscurity, even though he was the best hitting third baseman of his era and featured a glided glove.

Jack Fournier (1912–1918, 1920–1927): Fern Hill Cemetery, Aberdeen
A pure hitter with a stone glove, the first baseman hit .354 for the Brooklyn Robins in 1923 and led the NL in homers with 27 in 1924.

"Indian" Bob Johnson (1933–1945): Mountain View Memorial Park, Tacoma
Johnson, who was half Cherokee, hit for power and average and made seven All-Star teams, mostly with the Athletics. His brother played for the Red Sox.

Harry Howell (1898–1910): Greenwood Memorial Cemetery, Spokane
He threw a spitball that helped him average 15 wins over five seasons with the Browns.

Fred Hutchinson (1939–40, 1946–1953): Mount Olivet Pioneer Cemetery, Renton
Born in Seattle, the fiery Hutchinson starred as a pitcher for the Rainiers and Tigers and managed the Tigers and Reds as well, leading Cincinnati to a pennant in 1961.

Ray Oyler (1965–1970): Sunset Hills Memorial Park, Bellevue
Oyler's scant production at the plate as a member of the 1968 World Series champion Tigers endeared him to Pilots fans, who created a fan club in his honor when the shortstop was selected in the expansion draft.

Earl Torgeson (1947–1961): Grand Army of the Republic Cemetery, Snohomish
Inheriting the same nickname as Averill, the Snohomish native was a smooth fielding first basemen who starred as a rookie for the Braves, hitting .281 and clouting 16 homers. After injuring his shoulder in 1949, Torgeson bounced around playing key roles on the pennant-winning 1959 Chicago White Sox and 1961 New York Yankees.

87 Willie Horton and 300

It left in a hurry, a white blur traveling in a straight line that disappeared over the left-field fence before anyone had time to contemplate its meaning. To the man who gave up the laser shot it meant nothing more than a 3–2 deficit. To the man who hit it, however, it represented a milestone—and maybe a little more.

Willie Horton had been a star for the Detroit Tigers in the '60s and early '70s. But by 1977, Horton, now in his mid-30s, had been moved to designated hitter where he started a slight decline. The rebuilding Tigers had also found another DH more productive, Rusty Staub, so they traded Horton to Texas six days into the start of the '77 season. The trade wounded Horton, and he and the Rangers never meshed. He made three more major league stops before he became a free agent at the end of the 1978 season. Despite playing for four different ballclubs over the last two seasons, Horton's bat remained a threat. For that reason he hoped to land a multi–year contract. The Mariners, coming off a 104-loss season, desperately needed a hitter with thunder. And they had an opening at DH.

The Mariners signed the former All-Star to a two-year deal and put him in the lineup every day. He exceeded expectations. Horton hammered a club-record 29 home runs and collected a career-best 106 RBIs—hitting cleanup for a team that finished 12th in runs scored. Seattle fans were smitten, tagging him as the franchise's second "Ancient Mariner." (Diego Segui was first.) Unlike the mariner of Samuel Coleridge fame and to a lesser extent Segui, Horton was no albatross. His great season earned him Comeback Player of the Year honors in the American League. That marked the first time a Mariner had won a national award.

"We had a very exciting team when I was out there," Horton told *The Seattle Times* in 1995. Perhaps no moment was more exciting than the home run described earlier, Horton's 300th career dinger on June 6, 1979. It was a homer drenched in irony. The blast came off Horton's former team, the Tigers. It came against a future Tigers great, Jack Morris. It came after Horton had a home run changed to a single the day before when umpires ruled the ball Horton had tattooed into the Kingdome bleachers actually grazed a speaker. For a franchise just growing whiskers, the 300th bomb was heady stuff. It helped the Mariners stake their claim to Major League Baseball's rich history.

Horton became one of only 38 players in big league baseball at that time to reach the 300 plateau in home runs. "Yes, No. 300 is a big thrill," he said after the game. "And it's even bigger because we won [4–3]." The victory was aided in no small part by another fan favorite, Ruppert Jones, who threw a frozen rope to catcher Larry Cox in the ninth inning to cut down the Tiger attempting to score on a sacrifice fly.

A few nights later the Mariners held a Willie Horton Night to honor his home run milestone. "That meant so much to me," he said. "They gave me 300 silver dollars, and they're in my den now." The organization also peppered the stands with 300 Horton autographed baseballs.

Alas, Horton's comeback season was his last productive one. He retired a year later. Horton eventually settled back in Detroit and has been involved in the Tigers front office at various levels over the years. In 2000 Horton was memorialized, along with a select few other great Tigers, with a statue at Comerica Park. His No. 23 is retired as well.

88 Mariners Fan Fest

Held annually since 1999, this event, usually the last week of January, is a great opportunity to meet popular Mariners in person. Often the newest M's will be in attendance as well as marquee minor league prospects. Admission for adults is reasonable, and children under 14 are free.

Fans can:

- Get autographs signed from Mariners players and coaches.
- Participate in Dugout Dialogue with Mariners players, coaches, and front-office personnel, which is also streamed online.
- Run the bases.
- Tour the Mariners clubhouse.
- Ride the Safeco Field zip line.
- Throw a pitch in the bullpen to test the speed of their fastball.
- Play catch in the outfield.
- Hit against a simulated fastball of a Mariners pitcher in the visitor batting cage. (In 2014 the pitcher featured was Felix Hernandez.)
- Participate in a *Family Feud*-style baseball trivia contest.
- Test out the real equipment of the Mariners, including bats, batting helmets, gloves.
- Browse the history of the Northwest baseball exhibit.
- Meet the Mariner Moose.
- Visit the Safeco Field Roof control room.
- There are many activities for the little tykes as well, including a large inflatable slide, face painting, and a home run obstacle course.

89 Visit the Ichiro Museum

This is a "thing to do" for any Mariners fan. We would call it a "must-see," but obviously its Far East location makes it much more challenging to visit for Seattle residents.

For years Ichiro's father Nobuyuki Suzuki collected items that belonged to his son with the intention of opening a museum in his honor. In November of 2002, two seasons into Ichiro's Mariners career, his father opened the museum in Toyoyama, Japan, just outside Nagoya. It's housed in a four-story building and run by Nobuyuki and his wife, Yohsie. Admission is around $11. A sign in English explains the purpose of the museum: to "share our joy with all of you who also cheer for Ichiro."

Memorabilia includes items from Ichiro's childhood through his time with the Yankees. There is the obvious and the not so obvious and—like Ichiro—the weird, mysterious, and quirky.

Some highlights:

- Individual awards from his career with the Orix Blue Wave and Mariners (which includes his four Gold Gloves won as a Mariner)
- The bike Ichiro rode to high school
- Action figures and toys from his childhood
- Photographs with relatives, teammates, and celebrities, including one with President Obama
- The abacus Ichiro used for arithmetic
- The calligraphy set he used to write daily assignments and essays
- Ichiro's training sweat suit and undershirt he wore at Meiden High School

Outfielder Ichiro Suzuki, whose father opened up a Japanese museum in his honor, hits a solo home run in 2004 off Baltimore Orioles pitcher John Parrish.

90 Spring Training

The relaxed pace and intimacy of spring training lures thousands of Seattle baseball fans every March to warm and endlessly sunny Arizona, the site of the Peoria Sports Complex and the spring home of the Mariners.

Since the franchise's inception, the Mariners have trained in Arizona and been part of the spring Cactus League. Diablo Stadium in Tempe hosted the Mariners from 1977 until 1993. The stadium, which had sat empty and unused for years, required massive upgrades before the M's moved in that first spring. Many of the improvements remained unfinished well into the middle of the Cactus League schedule.

In 1994 the Mariners moved into their spring home, which they share with the San Diego Padres. The two clubs pioneered the shared spring training facility. Before this some clubs had played in the same park, but one tenant dominated. The Padres and Mariners are equal tenants in every respect. Separate parking lots, training facilities, and clubhouses create enough distance between the two franchises that the sharing arrangement is only marginally noticeable.

Gamedays are lively, and a jovial atmosphere pervades. Fans can purchase seats in the stadium or grab a first-come-first-serve spot on the grass, which provides unblocked access to sun. Most of the games sell out; so purchase tickets in advance.

Peoria is a northern suburb of Phoenix. Numerous strip malls and restaurants—many within walking distance—surround the park. At the stadium you can also buy food from one of the many food tents. There is even an all-you-can-eat buffet in the left-field section. You can book a hotel within walking distance of the park.

91 Diego Segui

He threw the first pitch in Mariners history. He also pitched three innings of relief in the Seattle Pilots' first game. As a trivia question, Diego Segui knocks it out of the ballpark—and literally beyond. He was the answer to one of the trivia questions given by the space shuttle crew in 1984, as part of exercises designed to keep the astronauts' minds sharp and break up the crushing boredom of their daily routine. No one guessed him as the correct answer. But for a while it appeared he might be the right answer for the Mariners.

The Cuban native, who had had a serpentine-like 14-year career in Major League Baseball as a reliever and spot starter with stops in Kansas City, Washington, Seattle, Oakland, St. Louis, and Boston, was purchased from the San Diego Padres by the Mariners on October 22, 1976. Casting a wide net while they searched for pitching depth, the Mariners figured they had nothing to lose by signing the 39-year-old veteran who had spent the previous season pitching in the Pacific Coast League for Hawaii. M's manager Darrell Johnson remembered Segui from his days as a coach for the Boston Red Sox, whom Segui helped lead to the 1975 American League pennant. Others in the Mariners' front office also recalled Segui's first stint in Seattle. He gave the Pilots one of his best seasons as a pro, steadying a shaky pitching staff and earning team MVP honors—despite pitching part of the year with a torn fingernail that made gripping the ball difficult.

As fit as teammates 10 years younger, Segui rediscovered during the spring his trademark pitch, the forkball, which seemed to carry more downward bite than ever before. He started racking up strikeouts and quickly climbed the Mariners' depth chart, which was admittedly thin. Then, a few days after striking out eight Angels in six innings of Seattle's 10–5 Grapefruit League win, Johnson informed Segui that he had made the team and would be the Opening Day starter.

The local papers called it "a truth-is-stranger-than-fiction twist." Segui called it something else. "I have a very strong feeling about it, something special." On the mound Segui was renowned for his quirks. He rubbed the ball excessively after every pitch and blew into his hands, which led to charges he threw a spitball. He circled the mound languidly, stopped to resettle the dirt with his foot in front of the rubber, and often paused between pitches. The routine drove batters crazy.

The Mariners hoped Segui would continue to drive American League hitters up the wall. Instead, they just dented the outfield fences with hard hit balls. On Opening Day Segui's forkball didn't fork much, and he got hammered. His first pitch found the strike zone, but on the delivery, Segui's hat twisted off and with it his control. He proceeded to walk the first batter. Then he changed hats, allowed a run, and struck out the side. Segui lasted only three and two-thirds innings, as the Angels roughed him up for six runs en route to a 7–0 victory. "I tried. I was behind the hitters too much, too many pitches," he sighed after the game.

Segui lost his next six games, and for the rest of the season, his role diminished, though he did strike out 10 Red Sox in a game, a team record that stood a half decade. Seattle released Segui after the season, figuring resources could be better spent than on a 39-year old coming off a 5.69 ERA and 0–7 record. That ended his 15-year major league career. In reflecting on Segui's woebegone season, Hy Zimmerman, a Mariners beat writer for *The Seattle Times*, wrote: "Diego…commanded respect from all Mariners. But now, he is gone. Yet, there is cause for neither pathos nor bathos, for neither the maudlin nor the mawkish. As stated, he is pushing 40. And he did have that last major league fling, even if his flinging went sour.

Here his pitching record will soon be forgotten. Remembered will be that gentle little smile, that sincerity of speech, that complete devotion to his team. It is a true plus that Diego passed this way."

92 Seattle's Baseball Heritage

Amateur and semi-pro baseball captivated the town's residents from the mid-1870s through the 1880s. Rollicking teams such as the Seattle Reds and Seattle Alkis battled nines from the Northwest and Western Canada for city and regional pride.

Professional baseball finally appeared in 1890 with Seattle, Tacoma, Spokane, and Portland comprising the Pacific Northwest League. The Seattles played near the foot of Madison Street, a difficult trek because the trolley ended a few miles short of the ballpark. The Northwest's first pro league lasted from 1890 to mid-1892.

Former professional baseball player Daniel Edward Dugdale, a big man with big ideas, arrived in Seattle en route to the Klondike Gold Rush in 1898. The Midwest native amassed wealth in real estate and launched several professional baseball teams. He built two professional ballparks, both more fan-accessible than Madison Park Grounds. Dugdale's Seattle squads, including the Clamdiggers, Chinooks, and Siwashes, competed in the Pacific Northwest and Northwestern League in 1898, 1901–1903, and 1907–1918 and won five pennants. This launched the popularity of professional baseball in Seattle and earned Dugdale plaudits as the father of Pacific Northwest professional baseball.

In 1903 the Seattle Siwashes appeared as a charter member of the Pacific Coast League, originally an "outlaw" league in direct

competition with the sanctioned Pacific Northwest League and
Dugdale's Seattle Chinooks. Playing a 230-game schedule, Seattle's
PCL team lasted until 1906 and featured stars such as Harry
"Rube" Vickers who won 39 games in 1906, a Pacific Coast League
record that still stands. George Van Haltren, a 17-year star in the
big leagues in the 1880s and 1890s, had 933 at-bats for the 1904
Seattle Siwashes. Though Seattle dropped out of the PCL after the
1906 season, the league has run continuously from 1903 to the
present day.

The Rainiers, known briefly as the Purple Sox, returned to
Seattle as a Pacific Coast League franchise in 1919. A fan contest
resulted in a franchise name change to Indians in 1920, and in 1924
they won Seattle's first PCL crown. Chehalis, Washington, native
Vean Gregg, a former major league star who led the American
League in ERA for Cleveland in 1911, won 25 games and Brick
Eldred, Jimmy Welsh, slugger Ray Rowher, and speedy Bill Lane
powered the offense. That same year Lou Gehrig and Babe Ruth
visited Seattle to perform in exhibition games.

The Depression weakened the Indians financially, though they
remained competitive and produced stars such as slugger Mike
Hunt and pitcher "Kewpie" Dick Barrett. In late 1937 local brewer
and civic leader Emil Sick bought the franchise, ushering in the
golden era of Seattle minor league baseball. In June of 1938, Sick's
Stadium debuted. It was considered one of the finest baseball parks
in the country. Under Sick's ownership the newly re-christened
Rainiers developed into a model minor league franchise. They
won five PCL pennants, including three straight from 1939–1941,
and invariably fielded competitive teams. The Rainiers frequently
led all of the minor leagues in attendance, often outdrawing more
populous PCL and other minor league cities and some major league
teams as well. The overflowing, enthusiastic crowds came out to
watch a parade of Rainier stars, including "the dean of Seattle
baseball" Edo Vanni, fan favorite outfielders Bill Lawrence and

Jo Jo White, comical Bill "The Rooster" Schuster, and perennial 20-game winners Barrett and Hal Turpin.

Many Rainiers later enjoyed fine careers in the major leagues, including Sammy White, Earl Torgeson, "Jungle Jim" Rivera, Vada Pinson, Maury Wills, and Seattle's favorite son, Fred Hutchinson. As a 19-year-old fresh out of nearby Franklin High School, Hutchinson won 25 games for the Rainiers in 1938. Snohomish native Earl Averill followed up his Hall of Fame major league career with a last year in pro ball with the Seattle Rainiers in 1941. "The Rainiers were the king of the hill in summertime," said John L. O'Brien, renowned longtime Washington State legislator.

Leo Lassen was the beloved radio voice of the Rainiers. The Dave Niehaus equivalent of this earlier generation of Seattle baseball fans announced games from 1931 to 1960. Lassen, a former sportswriter with a high-pitched voice, helped deepen interest in baseball across the region with his passionate and knowledgeable broadcasts, which filled the airwaves during the summer. He broadcast road games from Seattle but knew the tendencies and mannerisms of the players in the PCL so well that many assumed the broadcasts emanated from the road instead of his Seattle-based studio.

Sick's Rainiers competed in the PCL as an independent for most of their tenure, which helped strengthen the bonds between the city and the team. Major league expansion to the West in 1958 and Mr. Sick's selling the team in 1960 diminished that bond, and attendance and fan interest suffered. The Boston Red Sox assumed control of the Rainiers in 1961, and in 1965 the new-parent California Angels dropped the name Rainiers in favor of "Angels." In a final burst of glory, the Angels won Seattle's last PCL crown in 1966 under future Hall of Fame manager Bob Lemon. Rico Petrocelli, Jim Lonborg, and Wilbur Wood were among the future major league stars appearing as Rainiers in this era. John Olerud Sr. was a catcher for the 1966 Seattle Angels, foreshadowing his son's tenure as a Seattle Mariner, starting 34 years later.

Seattle's long run in the PCL came to an end after the Seattle Angels' 1968 season, which paved the way for the maiden voyage of Major League Baseball in Seattle: the one-and-done 1969 Seattle Pilots.

93 Ken Griffey Jr. Plaque in Baltimore

In the era when retro ballparks felt fresh and invigorating, and the All-Star Game Home Run Derby attracted the biggest sluggers and drew intense interest, Ken Griffey Jr. seized the moment to leave a lasting impression.

In his 1993 Home Run Derby duel with Texas Rangers bopper Juan Gonzalez at Camden Yards, the groundbreaking new park in Baltimore that attracted 47,000 fans for the contest, Griffey launched a home run that crashed against the iconic B&O Warehouse just beyond the right-field fence.

The ball traveled roughly 465 feet before bouncing off a Plexiglas window on the building, which is located on Eutaw Street. To this day, it is the only ball to ever hit the warehouse— during batting practice or a real game.

Griffey ended up losing the Home Run Derby 12–11 to Gonzalez. The Texas slugger hit a ball, one that traveled 473 feet to center field, even farther than Griffey's warehouse smash. But no one remembers that. What they remember is Griffey's majestic and so far unmatched blast to right field that collided with part of Baltimore's history. For that reason, there is commemorative plaque on the B&O Warehouse where Griffey's ball landed.

Sporting his cap backward as usual, Ken Griffey Jr. was always a slugger to watch in the Home Run Derby. (Getty Images)

94 The Mariner Moose

He's big. He's furry. He doesn't tell long yarns about life at sea. Indeed, he doesn't even talk. So how did a team named after seafarers end up choosing a large, four-legged creature who prefers forests over water?

The simple answer: a fan contest. When owner Jeff Smulyan decided the Mariners needed a mascot to spice things up at the Kingdome in 1990, he turned to the club's young fans to help him choose. More than 2,500 Pacific Northwest children under the age of 14 submitted entries. The winner came from Ammon Spiller of Ferndale, Washington. "I chose the Moose because they are funny, neat, and friendly," Spiller wrote. "The Moose would show that the Mariners enjoy playing and that they still have a few tricks up their sleeves. It shows they're having fun no matter what the situation."

In the 25 years since its debut, the Mariner Moose has posed for hundreds of thousands of photos with fans all over the region and provided endless entertainment at the ballpark through thick and thin, fulfilling the young writer's vision. The Moose also starred in numerous commercials, including a 1996 Nike ad in which he was Ken Griffey's running mate. All of this has made him one of the most recognizable mascots in sports. And hardly anyone these days wonders why the Mariners have a moose for a mascot.

Moreover, just as the contest winner had envisioned, the Mariner Moose always seems to have "a few tricks" up his sleeve. In 1995 at the Kingdome he orchestrated the largest Macarena dance in the world. That same year he attempted to break the indoor hang gliding record—even though he had a broken ankle sustained while rollerblading behind an ATV during the 1995 American League Division Series.

That year wasn't the only time the Moose and an ATV combined to stir up trouble. In 2007 the M's mascot lost control of the ATV he was motoring around in the outfield at Safeco Field and collided with Red Sox outfielder Coco Crisp, who luckily avoided injury. Alas, these aren't the only mishaps that have befallen the Moose and those around him over the years. After all, strange things are bound to happen when you put a full-antlered moose inside a ballpark teeming with people.

All kidding—and mild controversies aside—the Moose has become an essential part of the tableau of a day at Safeco Field. Kids and kids at heart can meet the Moose during games at prescribed times in his den. If the M's win, he waves the Mariners flag and does a victory lap. He also appears at more than 300 community events annually. If you want to bring a little Mariner-infused fun into your house or party, you can also hire the Mariner Moose for private events.

95 Minor League Affiliates

Below is the list of the minor league teams that have been a part of the Mariners franchise.

Triple A
Tacoma Rainiers (since 1995)
Calgary Cannons (1985–1994)
Salt Lake City Gulls (1982–1984)
Spokane Indians (1979–1981)
San Jose Missions (1978)

Some Mariners, including Julio Cruz, were loaned to the Hawaii Islanders during the 1977 season when the M's didn't have a Triple A affiliate.

Double A
Jackson Generals (since 2011)
West Tennessee Diamond Jaxx (2007–2010)
San Antonio Missions (2001–2006)
New Haven Ravens (1999–2000)
Orlando Rays (1998)
Memphis Chicks (1997)
Port City Roosters (1995–1996)
Jacksonville Suns (1991–1994)
Williamsport Bills (1989–1990)
Vermont Mariners (1988)
Chattanooga Lookouts (1983–1987)
Lynn Sailors (1980–1982)

High A
High Desert Mavericks (since 2007)
Inland Empire 66ers (2003–2006)
San Bernardino Stampede (2001–2002)
Lancaster JetHawks (1996–2000)
Riverside Pilots (1993–1995)
Split squads: San Bernardino Spirits and Peninsula Pilots (1990–1992)

Low A
Clinton LumberKings (since 2009)
Wisconsin Timber Rattlers (1995–2008)
Appleton Foxes (1993–1994)
Split squads: San Bernardino Spirits and Wausau Timbers (1988–1989)

Split squads: Wausau Timbers and Salinas Spurs (1984–1987)
Split squads: Wausau Timbers and Bakersfield Mariners
(1982–1983)
Wausau Timbers (1981)
San Jose Missions (1980)
Split squads: San Jose Missions and Alexandra Mariners (1979)
Stockton Ports (1978)

Short Season A
Everett AquaSox (since 1995)
Bellingham Mariners (1977–1994)

Rookie
Split squads: Pulaski Mariners and Peoria Mariners (since 2008)
Arizona League Mariners (1989–2007)
Butte Cooper Kings (1984)

The Short Season Single A Bellingham Mariners finished first in their league seven times as a Mariner affiliate, which is tops among all M's minor league teams. Bellingham also won four championships.

The Triple A Tacoma Rainiers play in Cheney Stadium, which was built in 1960 and is the oldest park in the Pacific Coast League. The light standard and blue reserved seats of Cheney are actually pieces of old Seals Stadium in San Francisco, which is where Joe DiMaggio once played and hit in a professional baseball record 61 straight games.

96 Ken Griffey Jr. Plaque at Everett Stadium

On June 16, 1987, at Everett Memorial Stadium, 17-year old Ken Griffey Jr. collected his first professional hit. Fittingly, the hit cleared the outfield fence for a home run, though it was an opposite-field shot. "It was not a jaw-dropping home run like he would hit later on," said Vince Bruun, who covered the game for *The Everett Herald*.

A capacity crowd of 3,122 packed the stadium, filling the stands and the grassy area down the right-field line. Most came to watch Griffey, playing for the visiting Bellingham Mariners against the AquaSox, a San Francisco Giants affiliate. As Griffey rounded the bases, the crowd gave him a standing ovation.

Today, there is a plaque on the sidewalk, at the corner of 38th and Lombard in Everett, Washington, where Griffey's ball landed.

97 Become an RBI Club Member

Mariners fans can join the Real Baseball Involvement Club (RBI) to gain a more intimate fan experience. The club holds monthly luncheons in downtown Seattle open to all members. Luncheons include guest speakers from the Mariners, ranging from players to front-office personnel, and other notable figures from across Major League Baseball.

Members get insights on the decisions made by the organization, hear stories from current and past great Mariners managers and players, and have an opportunity to get involved in the club's charitable work.

Contact the club directly to join. They do have certain requirements that most avid fans should be able to meet. Membership fees are under $200 a year.

98 Worst Trades

The bad trades outnumber the good ones—and by a margin so ridiculous you can't help but think two things. The first is that future excavators of Mariners baseball will identify this disparity as a partial explanation for why so many of the harvests went bad. The second is how uncharitable the Baseball Gods have been to the Mariners.

In the meantime, let's revisit the trades the M's wish they could have had back.

Each trade is evaluated on the basis of how many wins (based on Wins Above Replacement or WAR) the Mariners gave up and how many they received in return.* The higher the difference means the worse the trade. Trades driven by money, personality, and roster issues are all treated the same—because ultimately, regardless of the reason for the trade, the object of every transaction is to add more wins than you give up.

10. *December 1987* Mike Morgan to the Baltimore Orioles for Ken Dixon (-22.2)
9. *December 1996* Mike Hampton to the Houston Astros for Eric Anthony (-23.2)

8. *October 1981* Buddy Black to the Kansas City Royals for Manny Castillo (-23.8)

7. *February 2008* Adam Jones, Tony Butler, Kam Mickolio, George Sherrill, and Chris Tillman to the Orioles for Eric Bedard (-24.7 and counting)

6. *July 2006* Shin-Soo Choo and Shawn Nottingham to the Cleveland Indians for Ben Broussard (-28 and counting)

5. *August 1986* Dave Henderson and Spike Owen to the Boston Red Sox for Rey Quinones, Mike Brown, Mike Trujillo, and John Christensen (-30)

4. *December 1995* Tino Martinez, Jeff Nelson, and Jim Mecir to the New York Yankees for Sterling Hitchcock and Russ Davis (-34)

3. *December 1991* Bill Swift, Mike Jackson, and Dave Burba to the San Francisco Giants for Kevin Mitchell, Mike Remlinger, and $500,000. (-41.8)

2. *August 1996* David Ortiz to the Minnesota Twins for Dave Hollins (-44.8)

1. *July 1997* Jason Varitek and Derek Lowe to the Red Sox for Heathcliff Slocumb (-57.9)

* The Randy Johnson trade in 1998, as measured by net WAR, was a big loser, coming in over -60. But in this case, conceding to context doesn't seem unreasonable. The Mariners received a boatload of value in return for a guy with an expired shelf life in Seattle. That's how the deal escapes making this list.

99 Jesus and the Ice Cream Sandwich Debacle

Jesus Montero was once known as the best prospect in the New York Yankees organization and one of the best in baseball. Now he's known as a player whose career may be over after he threw an ice cream sandwich at a scout.

Before Montero's lactose-induced tirade ended his 2014 season in bizarre fashion, the Mariners acquired the talented catcher along with right-handed pitcher Hector Noesi for Michael Pineda and right-handed pitcher Jose Campos before the 2012 season. It was a steep price to pay. After all, Pineda was an All-Star as a rookie in 2011, when he recorded the second most strikeouts per nine innings in the American League. But the Mariners *had* pitching. Their ace, Felix Hernandez, was a two-time All-Star. What Seattle really needed was a way to boost its anemic offense, which generated a .233 batting average and scored just 556 runs, a mark that ranked worst in the majors. Montero seemed like a perfect candidate to do just that.

The deep-pocketed Yankees had outbid the Boston Red Sox, Cleveland Indians, and New York Mets for the 16-year-old catcher from Venezuela, and some within the Yankees organization likened his hitting ability to that of Robinson Cano, who would sign with the Mariners before the 2014 season. Montero could not only hit for average and power, but the 6'3" 220-pounder was also thought to possess a strong arm perfectly suited to throw out would-be base stealers.

And during his 18-game stint with the Yankees in 2011, he showed that he might live up to the potential, hitting .328 with four home runs. His first year with the Mariners showed promise as well. Though he was a designated hitter instead of a catcher for much of the 2012 season, he hit .260 with 15 home runs and 62 RBIs in 135 games.

The next season is when his promise began melting away like an ice cream cone during a late summer's day.

Just two weeks into the 2013 season, he lost his starting catching position and began rotating with Kelly Shoppach. Montero slumped, his batting average hovered around .200, and the Mariners shipped him to the minor leagues on May 23. Then later that month, he tore meniscus in his knee, requiring surgery. Montero returned to action in mid-July and played in 12 minor league contests before accepting a season-ending suspension because of his connection to the Biogenesis performance-enhancing drug scandal.

Perhaps you thought such an awful 2013 season—which included struggles at the plate, knee surgery, and a suspension—would've motivated him for a redemptive 2014 season. Instead Montero reported to the team about 40 pounds overweight, uttering the infamous comment: "After winter ball, all I did was eat." That understandably displeased Mariners general manager Jack Zduriencik. "He's got a ton to prove," he told *The Seattle Times*. "It's all on him."

With that pressure on him, Montero responded by hitting .235 in six games for the Mariners. After he strained an oblique muscle, the Mariners sent him to Single A for a rehab assignment. Because of the injury, he had not yet been put on the Everett AquaSox roster and was serving as a first-base coach to help out against the Boise Hawks. At the end of an inning during that late August game against the Hawks, Butch Baccala, a scout, yelled at the portly Montero to leave the field and then ordered an ice cream sandwich for him. Montero allegedly screamed profanities, while menacingly holding a bat, and then threw the sandwich at the scout before being restrained by Everett pitching coach Nasusel Cabrera. Montero was not ejected from the game, but he remained in the dugout until the contest completed. "We recognize that fans, including children, were impacted by this incident, and [inappropriate] language…was used," Zduriencik said in a statement. "We recognize the severity of this incident and want to assure the Hawks and their fans that it will be dealt with appropriately."

Baccala was let go by the Mariners, and Montero, now 25, was suspended for the rest of the season.

If there's consolation for Seattle fans, New York didn't exactly receive great production from Pineda either. Though he went 5–5 in 2014 with a 1.89 ERA, it was his first season of any significant impact for the Yankees. Pineda underwent surgery to repair a torn labrum in his right shoulder, and shoulder problems caused him to miss the entire 2012 and 2013 seasons.

100 Bill the Beerman

He was the Waldo of Seattle sports. In the heady days of the late '70s, when the Seahawks and Mariners joined the established SuperSonics of the NBA to give the city three professional sports teams, one image kept popping up at all three of the teams' games. And then it started appearing in Oregon and Boise, Idaho, and Indianapolis and minor league ballparks across the country.

The image, of a burly man sporting a fur trapper's beard with a voice that boomed like a real supersonic, is seared indelibly into the minds of anyone who attended Mariners games in the '70s and '80s. Bill Scott sold beer during the franchise's first few years. He also sold passion.

A Seattle native, Scott started working at the Kingdome as a vendor shortly after it opened in 1976. Originally, the job supplemented his income. Regularly voted by his Shoreline High School classmates as "Peppy Person of the Week," the garrulous Scott, who also delivered his high school commencement address, capitalized on his extroverted personality to sell beer—lots of it. "Give your tongue a sleigh ride," he barked over the cheering crowd. Later he added, "Freeze your teeth..." to the beginning. As he honed his pitch, he added a few more flourishes, such as:

"He who has something to sell,
And goes and whispers in a well,
Will never gather in the dollars,
As he climbs the stairs and hollers,
'Cold Beer.'"

Bill Scott eventually became "Bill the Beerman" when the parents of a child who wanted Scott's autograph shouted out to him, "Hey, Bill, Bill the Beerman."

"He had conditioned his voice to take that pounding," said his friend Ken Wilson in a 2007 interview with *The Seattle Times* about Scott's ability to be heard over the din of the Kingdome. "He could scream through a whole game and then sound just normal."

The beer pitchman plied his trade before major sporting events became polluted by artificial noise machines and scoreboard exhortations to "cheer." Scott took it upon himself to encourage loud support of the home team. It started while he sold beer through the seventh inning. Then he'd come back and rouse the fans with more cheers. Eventually, he devoted more and more of his time to leading the crowd in vocal support of its team. Finally, he gave up the vendor job to become what he called a "synergy facilitator." A professional cheerleader, if you will, though Scott bristled at the term. But he made it work.

Mariners games. Seahawks games. Sonics games. He showed up at them all to whip the crowd into a supportive and cheering frenzy. At various times the franchises paid him for the work. Then Scott pushed the boundaries of his support. Wilson took a job with the Portland Trail Blazers and paid Scott to serve as head cheerleader. He stayed with Portland until Paul Allen bought the Blazers. When not cheering/working in the Pacific Northwest, Scott traveled around plying his trade in minor league ballparks, college arenas, and even for the Indianapolis Colts. "It was his energy and his heart," Michael Bouton, who hired Scott to work for the minor league baseball Boise Hawks, told *The Seattle Times*. "He had those things as well as the passion to bring about the element of what people go to sport events for. It isn't just to be entertained, but it's also to be an active participant."

Scott, though, never moved out of Seattle. And in 1995 the Mariners offered him free tickets and other goodies (but no money) to lead cheers during the M's improbable late-season charge to the playoffs. Every game down the stretch, the "energy facilitator" lubed the crowd while standing on top of the dugout with bellows of "Let's Go M's," "Swing," or "Yeer Outta Heeere." The players regularly handed him glasses of water. Fans mobbed him between innings. And he scribbled his autograph on baseballs, tickets, and hats. Griffey would hit a home run, the Kingdome would lose it, and then all eyes returned to Scott for the next cheer. The city was drunk with Mariners mania—and Scott was the most intoxicated of all.

The Mariners didn't ask Scott back after that season, not in an official capacity. (They had the Mariner Moose after all.) But Scott remained active in Seattle sports and he is credited with helping to create the Seahawks 12th Man. In December of 2006, in fact, the Seahawks feted him by raising the 12th Man flag in his honor. He received the loudest cheer on a day the Seahawks lost to the 49ers.

Bill "The Beerman" died in 2007 after a five-year battle with cancer. "There were thousands of people who went to [Seattle sporting events] who felt they knew Bill personally," said his best friend Chuck Meyer, a Seattle attorney, to the *Seattle Post-Intelligencer.* "He talked to everyone, made them feel very important. Kids would go, 'Wow. My dad knows Bill the Beerman.'"

Acknowledgments

This book would not have been possible without the help of all those who have covered, with skill, compassion, and humor, much of this territory before me.

I'd like to especially thank the folks at Sportspress Northwest for their invaluable contributions, especially Dave Eskenazi and Steve Rudman.

I'd also like to thank the great team at Triumph Books for all of their contributions, with a special shout-out to Mitch Rogatz, Tom Bast, Noah Amstadter, and Jeff Fedotin.

I want to thank my wife Becky for her unwavering support, encouragement, and patience.

Finally, my daughter Hannah, who discovered baseball when she discovered Ichiro, gets a big hug and thanks for her patience as I retreated to my office for hours and hours at a time.

Sources

Books

Arnold, Kirby. *Tales from the Seattle Mariners Dugout*. Champaign, Illinois: Sports Publishing LLC. 2007.

Beckett Publications. *Ken Griffey, Jr.: In the words of Reggie Jackson, Dave Duncan, Rickey Henderson, Tony LaRussa, Ken Griffey, Sr., Tim McCarver, and others*. Dallas, Texas: Beckett Publications. 1999.

Donnelly, Chris. *Baseball's Greatest Series: Yankees, Mariners and the 1995 Matchup That Changed History*. New Brunswick, New Jersey: Rivergate Books: An imprint of Rutgers University Press. 2010.

Epting, Chris. *Roadside Baseball*. Santa Monica, California: Santa Monica Press LLC. 2009.

Gorman, Lou. *High and Inside: My Life in the Front Offices of Baseball*. Jefferson, North Carolina: McFarland & Company, Inc., Publishers. 2008.

Griffey, Ken Sr. and Pepe, Phil. *Big Red: Baseball, Fatherhood, and My Life in the Big Red Machine*. Chicago, Illinois: Triumph Books. 2014.

Griffey, Ken Jr and Vancil, Mark, editor. *Junior: Griffey on Griffey*. New York, New York: HarperCollins. 1997.

Isaacson, Melissa. *Sweet Lou: Lou Piniella: A Life in Baseball*. Chicago, Illinois: Triumph Books. 2009.

Moyer, Jamie and Platt, Larry. *Just Tell Me I Can't*. New York, New York: Grand Central Publishing. 2013.

Pahigian, Josh and O'Connell, Kevi,. *The Ultimate Baseball Road Trip*. Guilford, Connecticut: Lyons Press. 2012.

Seattle Post Intelligencer. *A Magic Season: The Year the Mariners Made Seattle a Baseball Town.* Seattle, Washington: PI Books. 1995.

Seattle Post Intelligencer. *Mariners 2001: A Joy Ride into the Record Books.* Seattle, Washington: PI Books, 2001.

Shatzkin, Mike and Charlton, Jim. *The Ballplayers: Baseball's Ultimate Biographical Reference.* New York, New York: Arbor House William Morrow. 1990.

Thiel, Art. *Out of Left Field: How the Mariners Made Baseball Fly in Seattle.* Seattle, Washington: Sasquatch Books. 2003.

Wells, John. *Shipwrecked: A People's History of the Seattle Mariners.* Kenmore, Washington: Epicenter Press. 2012.

Newspapers and Periodicals
The Seattle Times
Seattle Post-Intelligencer
Los Angeles Times
Orlando Sentinel
The Tacoma News Tribune
Sports Illustrated
Chicago Tribune
Chicago Sun-Times
Kitsap Sun
Everett Daily Herald
Mariners Magazine
The New York Times
Seattle Magazine
The Sporting News
Nostalgia Magazine: Puget Sound Edition
USA TODAY
St. Louis Post-Dispatch
The Boston Globe
Gainesville Sun

Peoria Journal Star
The Christian Science Monitor
Seattle Weekly
The Stranger
Cincinnati Enquirer
The Washington Post
The Olympian
Louisville Courant
Fort Lauderdale Sun-Sentinel
The Baltimore Sun
The Wall Street Journal
The Spokane Spokesman-Review
Associated Press

Digital Media
Espn.com
Grantland.com
Mariners.com
Brewers.com
Baseballprospectus.com
Ussmariner.com
Lookoutlanding.com
Mariners.scout.com
Hardballtimes.com
Historylink.org
Sportspressnw.com
Seattlesporsthell.com
Eriklundegaard.com
Nwsportsbeat.com
Seattlest.com
Baseball-Reference.com
Washington.edu
Sabr.org

1995mariners.com
Seattlepilots.com
Slate.com
Jasonsacks.tripod.com
Miscbaseball.wordpress.com
Todayifoundout.com
Thebiglead.com
Seattlesportsnet.com
Propellermag.com
M.pitchfork.com
Mascothalloffame.com
Komonews.com
Bleacherreport.com
Mynorthwest.com
Springtrainingonline.com
Stadiumjourney.com
Marinersrbiclub.com
Baseballtoddsdugout.com
Roarfrom34.blogspot.com
Lebanon.macaronkid.com
Mlkhk.com
Thepostgame.com
Baseball-fever.com
Tomreeder.wordpress.com
Alpepper.tripod.com
Nerdbaseball.com
Enjoytheenjoyment.com
Losangeles.angels.mlb.com
Boywonder.wordpress.com
Detroitathletic.com
Coveritlive.com
Goodmenproject.com
Cbssports.com

Proballnw.com
Nbcsports.com
Csnnw.com
Westportwa.com
Sodomojo.com
Rfpoftheday.wordpress.com
Yardbarker.com
Pinstripealley.com
Deadspin.com
Sports-yahoo.com
Beyondtheboxscore.com
Thisgreatgame.com
Jockbio.com
Toddradom.com
Baseballlibrary.com
Toronto.bluejays.mlb.com
Kingdometokingscourt.com
Oocities.org
Chicago.cubs.mlb.com
Ondeckcircle.wordpress.com
Lennyrandlesportstours.com
Seatownmariners.com
Whitesoxinteractive.com
Bizjournals.com
Andrewclem.com
Realclearsports.com
Factsanddetails.com
Pbs.org